BEHAVIOR MODIFICATION WITH EXCEPTIONAL CHILDREN

Principles and Practices

Richard J. Morris

The University of Arizona

Scott, Foresman and Company
Glenview, Illinois
London, England

To my loving wife, Vinnie, and our children, Stephanie, Michael, and Jacqueline

Scott, Foresman Series in Special Education
Richard J. Morris, Series Editor

Library of Congress Cataloging in Publication Data
Morris, Richard J.
    Behavior modification with exceptional children.
    (Scott, Foresman series in special education)
    Bibliography.
    Includes index.
    1. Behavior modification.   2. Mentally handicapped
children—Education.   I. Title.   II. Series.
BF637.B4M67   1985   155.4'528   84-27643
ISBN: 0-673-15844-6

123456-MAL-90 89 88 87 86 85

PREFACE

The clinical and research literature on behavior modification with exceptional children has grown at an exponential rate during the past fifteen years. What has emerged from the literature is the well-documented view that many behavioral procedures now have sufficient empirical support to merit their use in a wide variety of schools, clinics, and other settings. Teachers, school psychologists, clinicians, counselors, parents, aides, and others who work with children who are emotionally disturbed, autistic, learning disabled, or mentally retarded, or who have visual or hearing impairments, speech and language disorders, physical handicapping conditions, or other chronic health impairments can use these procedures effectively.

This book is written specifically for those students who plan to work or currently work with exceptional children—whether the children are mildly, moderately, or severely handicapped. Its primary purpose is to present a systematic and detailed guide to planning and implementing behavior modification procedures for exceptional children. The book will therefore be particularly useful to students preparing to enter the fields of special education and school psychology, as well as those entering the mental health and developmental disabilities fields and psychiatric nursing. In addition, those professionals involved in in-service training programs will find this book helpful, as will parents of exceptional children.

Much of the book is based on a series of research-oriented training programs that were carried out with special education teachers, parents, classroom aides, and habilitation workers who work with developmentally disabled, emotionally disturbed, learning disabled, and other exceptional children in either a school or institutional setting or in the child's natural home environment. The material is discussed in a nontechnical and readable fashion and contains the most recent information on the use of behavior modification with exceptional children. It is assumed that the reader has no previous knowledge of behavior modification or theories of learning. To supplement the text material, numerous examples of the use of behavior modification techniques in the classroom, clinic, and home environment are presented. Moreover, in order to maximize the reader's understanding and review of the material, chapter summaries are presented at the beginning and study questions are provided at the end of chapters.

Portions of *Behavior Modification with Exceptional Children: Principles and Practices* were prepared under a research grant (No. G008300350) to the author and Dr. Thomas R. Kratochwill from the U.S. Department of Education, Special Education Programs, for training parents of severely handicapped children in the use of behavior modification procedures. This book is also based on an earlier book by the author, *Behavior Modification with Children: A Systematic Guide* (Winthrop 1976).

ACKNOWLEDGMENTS

Many people contribute a significant amount of time to ready a book for publication. Special appreciation is given to Trudy Eckhoff for spending many hours deciphering my handwriting and typing the manuscript. Appreciation is also due Drs. Thomas R. Kratochwill and Rebecca A. McReynolds for critically reading the manuscript and providing helpful suggestions on various chapters, and to Drs. Rebecca A. McReynolds, John H. O'Neill, Kenneth R. Suckerman, and M. Catherine Wheeler for their assistance in developing a number of the prescriptive programs presented in Chapter 6. Many of these programs were first prepared during the conduct of research and a series of demonstration projects at the Syracuse Developmental Center, Syracuse, New York. The contributions of Ron Barber (Program Manager, State of Arizona Division of Developmental Disabilities—District II), Kenneth V. Karrels, and Dr. Ronald L. Hoschouer are also greatly appreciated. These individuals, as well as Dr. Bruce D. Sales, have been a very stimulating source for discussions regarding ethical issues and behavior modification. Thanks are also due to Drs. Bruce Baker, William Gardner, Harold Keller, Thomas Kratochwill, and Lee Meyerson for their helpful comments on early drafts of the manuscript.

I also wish to express my gratitude to Christopher Jennison of Scott, Foresman and Company, Craig Pugh, Associate Editor at Scott, Foresman, as well as the editorial staff working on this book.

Finally, several other people need special acknowledgment. First, Drs. Lee Meyerson and Nancy Kerr interested me initially in the area of behavior modification with exceptional children and also have sustained this interest for almost twenty years. They have been not only outstanding role models, but also valued friends. Second, my wife, Vinnie, has been a tremendous source of support for my work, as have my children, Stephanie, Michael, and Jacqueline, my brother Charles J. Morris, and my mother, Pearl W. Koenig.

CONTENTS

Chapter **3**
The Use of Reinforcement   *44*

Chapter **4**
Teaching Desirable Behaviors to Children   *66*

Chapter **7**
Problems and Difficulties in Conducting a Behavior Modification Program   *171*

Chapter **8**
Legal and Ethical Issues of Behavior Modification   *186*

Chapter **1**

HISTORY AND OVERVIEW OF BEHAVIOR MODIFICATION

This chapter begins with a brief history of treatment approaches with children. A discussion of the general assumptions that form the basis of behavior modification approaches follows. This is followed by a presentation of those behaviors that have been treated successfully with exceptional children using behavior modification procedures. The chapter closes with guidelines for the reader in the use of this book.

HISTORY OF TREATMENT APPROACHES WITH CHILDREN

Although we currently find a great deal of interest in the education and treatment of exceptional children, this is a relatively recent event in the history of providing educational and mental health services to exceptional children and youth. In fact, the literature on the formal treatment of most exceptional children can only be clearly traced to the early twentieth century (e.g., Achenbach 1974, 1982; Kanner 1948). One notable exception relates to the treatment and care of children who were diagnosed as mentally retarded.[1]

The early treatment of mentally retarded children can be traced to the work of Jean Itard and his attempts, beginning in 1799, to educate the Wild Boy of Aveyron (Itard 1962). According to Humphrey (1962),

> *"Itard . . . came to the conclusion that the boy's condition was curable. The apparent subnormality [of the boy] Itard attributed to the fact that the child had lacked that intercourse with other human beings and that general experience which is an essential part of the training of a normal civilized person" (p. vii).*

Itard placed the child under his care for five years at the Paris institution where he worked. Although the boy improved tremendously over this period of time, he did not achieve Itard's initial expectations and predictions; he never became a "normal" human being. Itard's work, however, influenced the writings, research, and treatment practices of others working in the field of mental retardation including the work of Edouard Séguin.

Itard's and Séguin's humane philosophy, in turn, led directly in the United States to the building of residential schools for mentally retarded persons—the first facility established in Watertown, Massachusetts, in 1848 as part of the Perkins Institution for the Blind (MacMillan 1982), and the second built in Syracuse, New York, in 1851 as an independent facility for mentally retarded persons. Séguin and others (e.g., Samuel Howe) intended for these facilities to be established on an experimental basis as educational institutions rather than as custodial asylums. The assumption was that after the mentally retarded children (called in those days idiots, imbeciles, morons, or, more generally, feebleminded) received training or educational intervention to help them function in society, they would then be returned to their natural homes in the community. The assumption, however, was not found to have empirical support (Baumeister 1970). Few children ever returned to their homes, and by the beginning of the twentieth century, the state "educational" school for the mentally retarded became the state "custodial" institution or school—an emphasis that was maintained until the 1970s (Baumeister 1970).

Other developments in the early twentieth century contributed substantially to our present-day concern with the treatment, education, and care of exceptional children. These developments were: (1) the mental hygiene movement, (2) the establishment of child guidance clinics, and (3) the introduction of dynamic psychiatry and subsequent child therapy approaches (Morris & Kratochwill 1983a). Clifford Beers, a law student at Yale University and former patient in a state mental hospital, is most often credited with changing the direction in America of the treatment of mentally ill persons. His book, *A Mind That Found Itself* (Beers 1908), described the mistreatment that he and others received while they were patients. The book gained considerable popularity and led, in turn, to Beers and others forming an organization, the National Committee for Mental Hygiene, to promote the establishment of better treatment methods for people having emotional problems, to inform the public of the conditions in state mental hospitals, and to sponsor research on the prevention and treatment of mental illness. This work led to the establishment of mental hygiene programs in the schools and the beginning of the child guidance movement (Kauffman 1981).

Although the child guidance movement had begun prior to Beers's work, the movement gained impetus following the publication of his book and the establishment in 1909 of the Juvenile Psychopathic Institute (now called the Institute for Juvenile Research) in Chicago. The institute worked directly with juvenile offenders, stressing an interdisciplinary approach to the understanding and treatment of children's behavior problems. Other child guidance clinics soon developed across the United States, and by the 1930s there were many such clinics, in virtually every state, whose staff worked with children having a variety of behavior problems (Kanner 1941). The presence of these clinics in communities across the country gave the public the impression that children having a variety of behavior problems could be helped.

Little interest, however, was shown by the staff in these clinics for working with children who were mentally retarded—especially, those who were severely and profoundly retarded (Kanner 1964). If these children were seen by a staff person, the work performed would typically center on the identification of an educational, vocational, or institutional setting for them or the assessment of their intellectual functioning (Kanner 1941, 1964). The expectation was that the educational, vocational, or institutional settings to which the mentally retarded children were referred would know what to do for them.

The introduction of Sigmund Freud's *psychoanalysis* in the early twentieth century, as well as subsequent child therapy approaches, also contributed substantially to our present-day emphasis on the education and treatment of exceptional children. Freud worked mainly with adults, and derived his psychoanalytic treatment method from his therapeutic work with them (e.g., Jones 1961). On occasion he did treat a child who was having problems. One of the first cases involving a child on which he consulted—Freud never treated the child directly—concerned a boy called "Little Hans" (Freud 1909). Hans was almost five years old and was very afraid of horses. His fear that one would bite him caused him to be reluctant to leave the house.

Although Hans's problem was treated successfully, it was not until fifteen to twenty years later that Freudian psychoanalytic child therapy, combined with the play activities of children, was more widely used (e.g., A. Freud 1981). Since therapists could not rely on the verbal communication skills of children, they introduced the use of children's play to help both the therapist and the patient understand and work through the child's problem.

Psychoanalytic play therapy was influential in the development of most of the later forms of child therapy. Two therapy approaches developed, however, which were quite different from psychoanalytic forms of therapy. The first treatment method emphasized the importance of establishing a meaningful relationship between the child and the therapist and de-emphasized the Freudian approach of attributing unconscious meaning to the child's verbalizations and play activities. Therapy involved providing children with a warm, permissive, and accepting environment in which there were few limitations placed on them, one where they could be themselves and reach their fullest potential of psychological growth and mental health. This general approach is often associated with Frederick Allen (e.g., Allen 1942) and Virginia Axline (e.g., Axline 1947). They each developed a slightly different therapy approach, although both agreed that the child as a person should be the focus of therapy.

The second nonpsychoanalytic approach to develop, and the one which is the subject of this book, dates back almost as far as the Freudian approach. It emerged largely from the experimental psychology laboratory rather than from direct interaction with patients (as was the case with both the Freudian and relationship forms of therapy). This therapy approach became known as *behavior modification*. Behavior modification is based on theories concerning how people and animals learn to do various things, or *how people and animals learn to behave*.

Generally speaking, there are four general theoretical positions concerning learning and conditioning that form the basis of contemporary behavior modification approaches.

One of the first learning theory positions was that of Pavlov (1927, 1928), called *classical conditioning*. According to this view, certain physical stimuli in one's environment such as food, light and noise, elicit specific reflex or unlearned responses—such as salivation in the case of food placed in a person's mouth, or an eyeblink in the case of a puff of air blown in one's eye. The stimulus part of this reflex pattern is called an *unconditioned stimulus* (abbreviated UCS) whereas the response component of this reflex is called an *unconditioned response* (abbreviated UCR). Pavlov further observed that at times a neutral stimulus that was paired in time with a particular UCS could produce a response like that of the UCR in a UCS-UCR reflex pattern, even though (1) the neutral stimulus was not a natural part of the particular UCS-UCR reflex pattern and (2) the UCS did not occur when the neutral stimulus was presented. The neutral stimulus in this case was called a *conditioned stimulus* (abbreviated CS) because it was associated in time with the UCS, and the reponse that was similar to the UCR was called a *conditioned response* (abbreviated CR) since the organism produced this response because of the previous pairing in time of the CS and UCS. This learning paradigm can be diagramed in the following manner:

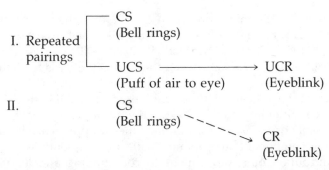

Thus, through this conditioning paradigm, an organism can be taught to produce a response (CR) to a stimulus (CS) that is not the stimulus (UCS) that automatically produces or elicits the response (UCR).

Perhaps the most famous study in behavior modification that demonstrated the application of classical conditioning to children was performed by Watson and Rayner (1920) with an eleven-month-old child called Little Albert. These investigators reported that through classical conditioning they could teach Little Albert to become afraid of a live white rat, and that this conditioned fear could be generalized to a fear of other animals and furry objects (e.g., a white rabbit, dog, and piece of cotton). Initially, it was reported that the rat (CS) did not elicit any fear or startle reaction (UCR) from the child, but after its presence was paired several times with a loud noise (UCS), it produced fear responses (CR) from Albert (Morris & Kratochwill 1983b).

Another learning theory position is Skinner's (1938, 1953) *operant conditioning* in which it is assumed that a major component of human learning involves the performance of responses that are controlled primarily by their consequences. Thus, a person's responses or behaviors are assumed to operate on his or her environment and therefore produce certain consequences (Skinner 1953). These consequences will then result in either an increase or decrease in the frequency of occurrence of the responses. Although Skinner (1938) acknowledged the existence of reflexes and classical conditioning, he maintained that most learning in organisms occurred through operant conditioning. This approach operates primarily on only those behaviors or activities that can be observed directly by the behavior modifier, and is oriented toward modifying the relationships that exist between particular observable behaviors and their consequences.

An extension of the operant conditioning position to applied settings has been called *applied behavior analysis* (Baer, Wolf, & Risley 1968). In particular, this approach utilizes operant procedures to modify behavior of social and personal importance. A great deal of literature has been published over the years on applied behavior analysis and the use of operant conditioning procedures with exceptional children (e.g. Graziano 1975; Harris 1977; Kazdin 1980; Mash & Terdal 1981a; Matson & Mulick 1983; Morris & Kratochwill 1983c; Ollendick & Cerny 1981; Ross 1980), and it is this approach that forms the basis for much of the present book.

A third theoretical position combines elements of both classical and operant conditioning, and is associated with Mowrer's (1939, 1960) *two-factor learning* or *S-R mediational learning* theory approach. This approach has many components in common with operant conditioning such as the contribution of reinforcement to conditioning and learning. The major difference between this position and operant conditioning is the emphasis on underlying drives such as anxiety that are presumed to motivate a person's observable behavior, and the view that behavior is both classically and operantly conditioned. For example, a child's avoidance of a feared stimulus, activity, or event is assumed to be motivated by anxiety which, in turn, was classical conditioned in the child through the pairing of a neutral CS and an aversive UCS (e.g., Morris & Kratochwill 1983b). Thus, the anxiety mediates the operant response of avoidance behavior.

Two popular behavior modification procedures have their roots in two-factor learning theory. The first method, discussed in Chapter 6, has to do with bladder control (enuresis) and bowel control (encopresis). In each case, we teach the child to associate a neutral stimulus (CS; toilet) with the unconditioned reflex pattern of defecation or urination— for example, pressure on the bladder (UCS) elicits urination (UCR). The child is then reinforced for his or her successes in eliminating in the toilet. Procedures and equipment for controlling these behaviors are also presented in Appendix F.

The second procedure derived from two-factor learning is called systematic desensitization (Wolpe 1958; Wolpe & Lazarus 1966). This procedure is used mainly to reduce the frequency and intensity of fear reactions in people by substituting an activity (in the actual or imagined presence of the feared stimulus) which is antagonistic to the fear response (Morris & Kratochwill 1983b). A variation of this procedure, contact desensitization, has been used with children having various exceptional needs and is discussed in Chapters 5 and 6.

The fourth theoretical position is the *social learning* theory approach of Bandura (e.g., Bandura 1969, 1977b; Bandura & Walters 1963). This view involves the development of behavior through vicarious learning. Here the person acquires a response by directly observing a model perform the behavior and acquiring a symbolic representation of the modeled event. As Bandura (1977b) states, "Social learning theory . . . assumes that modeling influences operate principally through their informative function, and that observers acquire mainly symbolic representations of modeled events rather than specific stimulus-response connections" (p. 16). Modeling, according to Bandura, is governed by four subprocesses: observer attentional processes, observer retention processes, observer motoric reproduction processes, and reinforcement and motivational processes to regulate the observer's performance of the modeled behavior. Bandura (1977a) has also emphasized the notion of "reciprocal determinism," where a person's behavior involves a reciprocal interaction between their behavior, cognitive processes, and environmental influences. In addition, he has noted that behavioral procedures may serve the function of creating and strengthening "personal efficacy." A distinction is made here between outcome expectations that relate to whether a behavior will result in a certain consequence and efficacy expectations that relate to one's personal conviction that he or she can perform a particular behavior. Modeling approaches to behavior change are discussed in Chapter 4, and a procedure for teaching exceptional children to imitate is discussed in Chapter 6.

These different theories of learning have been tested and refined in scientific laboratories over the past several decades. Three general assumptions repeatedly supported by this research are that people and animals behave in predictable ways, there are principles that explain the manner in which people and animals learn to do things, and procedures based on theories of learning can be developed to change the behavior of organisms. On the basis of these assumptions, psychologists began applying what they learned to their understanding of the development and treatment of behavior and learning problems in children and adults.

The procedures derived from these theories of learning were largely confined for decades to, for example, child psychology laboratory settings at universities and to research settings within residential treatment facilities, special education classrooms, and home environments. The findings from the research conducted showed overwhelmingly that many of the behavior and learning problems and behavior deficits that exceptional children demonstrate can be modified using behavior modification procedures.

It was not until the early to mid-1960s that behavior modification procedures began to be used with any regularity outside of the laboratory or applied research setting—with most of the early work being carried-out in institutional settings with severely and profoundly mentally retarded, autistic, and psychotic children. In the early to mid-1970s these procedures began to be used on a more frequent basis in special education settings with a wider variety of exceptional children—such as those children having learning disability, mild or moderate mental retardation, emotional disturbance, visual or hearing disabilities, cerebral palsy or other physical handicapping conditions, speech difficulties and/or multiple handicapping conditions.

Although other intervention approaches (e.g., Freudian psychoanalytic theory and the phenomenological/humanistic approach of Carl Rogers and Virginia Axline) have a much longer history of direct use in child therapy and in the classroom setting with special needs children, few professionals would now question the tremendous impact that behavior modification procedures have had in changing children's behaviors in a wide variety of settings. In fact, many states now require special education teachers to have a college course on behavior modification or classroom management procedures before granting certification in a particular area or areas. Similarly, many school psychology and other related graduate programs now require their students to enroll in a course in behavior modification to meet the requirements of the program.

GENERAL ASSUMPTIONS OF BEHAVIOR MODIFICATION

Before discussing specific behavior modification procedures, we shall review some of the general working assumptions of behavior modification (from Kazdin 1980; Morris 1976; Morris & Kratochwill 1983b; Rimm & Masters 1979).

Behavior is learned.   Although most scholars in behavior modification accept the fact that forms of exceptionality (for example, certain types of mental retardation) are biologically or genetically caused, this does not necessarily mean that all behaviors and behavior and learning problems observed in exceptional children are also biologically or genetically caused (see, for example, Matson & Mulick 1983). Similarly, just because we do not know the cause of a particular behavior or learning problem, or series of behaviors in an exceptional child, we do not have to assume that the cause is biological or genetic. The assumption that behavior modifiers make is that *a particular behavior or learning problem in a child has been learned*, unless there is evidence to suggest the contrary. Thus, tantrums, noncompliance, eating and dressing problems, throwing objects, isolate play, fears, noncompletion of educational tasks, name calling and so forth are assumed to be learned by the child within the classroom, home, recreational, or other setting.

Behavior problems are learned separately.   Many children have more than one behavior or learning problem—especially children receiving special education services. For example, a seven-year-old emotionally disturbed child may not complete his workbook assignments several times each week, have a fear of dogs, occasionally urinate in his pants during the day, and call other kids "bad names." The assumptions that behavior modifiers or behavior change agents would make are that

(1) each of these behavior problems was *learned* by the student, and (2) each behavior problem was *learned separately* from the other problems and developed independently. For example, there is no reason for the behaviors shown by the seven-year-old child above to develop or occur together—any one or two of them could be present without the other or others. Unless there is *obvious evidence* to suggest that some of the behaviors were caused by a biological or genetic condition, behaviorally oriented persons assume these behaviors were learned, and learned separately.

Behavior and learning problems can be modified using behavior modification procedures. A substantial amount of behavior modification research has been performed over the past thirty years on a variety of childhood behavior and learning problems (see, for example, D'Alonzo 1983; Kauffman 1981; Matson & Mulick 1983; Morris & Kratochwill 1983b, Repp 1983; Ross 1980; Smith 1981). This research suggests that behavior modification procedures can be used effectively to change behaviors in children. This is not to suggest that such procedures represent "the answer" to the treatment or intervention of behavior and learning problems in exceptional children, but *the research does suggest that behavior modification procedures have wide application, and merit consideration in the treatment of various childhood behavior and learning problems.* Some research even suggests that these procedures can be used effectively in the modification of some behavior and learning problems that have an obvious physical or biological cause. For example, some researchers (e.g., Meyerson, Kerr & Michael 1967) have been able to teach walking to children who have cerebral palsy or another physical problem that disrupts their coordination and the muscular development in their legs. Other researchers (see, for example, Whitman, Scibak & Reid 1983) have been able to develop various social behaviors (for example, eye contact, imitative behavior, speech, and toilet habits) and control disruptive behaviors (for example, hitting others, making loud sounds and self-hitting) in brain damaged children. This suggests that even if a child has obvious brain damage, some behavior and learning problems can still be treated using behavior modification procedures.

The behavior or learning problems that a child shows in a particular situation indicate only how he or she typically behaves in that specific situation. It is an obvious fact that children behave differently under different circumstances. A child may be a difficult management problem at home but a "perfect angel" at school; a boy may throw a tantrum to get what he wants from his mother but never do so in front of his father; a girl may never feed herself when her mother is present, but feed herself in front of a baby-sitter; and a girl may raise her hand in one class and wait for the teacher to call on her, but talk out of turn in another class and infrequently raise her hand or wait for the teacher to recognize her. In each instance the behavior problem to be modified occurs only in a particular situation. *It is therefore assumed, unless there is contradictory evidence, that a child's particular behavior or learning problem is specific to the conditions under which it occurs and does not generalize to other situations.*

This is an important assumption because it forces the behavior modifier to look for possible reasons that a child, for example, learned to behave disruptively in one classroom setting and behave appropriately in another classroom. Thus, this assumption helps the behavior modifier localize the possible reasons for the student learning to behave in a disruptive way.

Emphasis is placed on changing the child's behavior or learning problem in the here and now.   Unlike certain forms of child therapy and classroom intervention approaches (e.g., the psychoanalytic position) *behavior modification focuses on what is presently contributing to the child's behavior, and on what can presently be done to change the behavior.* The emphasis is not on determining what developments in the child's early history caused his or her present difficulty. *Emphasis is on the present* and on determining how the behavior can be changed in the situation or situations in which it occurs.

For example, if a ten-year-old boy is very aggressive at school—hitting his classmates when he becomes angry with them, destroying their personal property, and verbally threatening to get even with them for what he feels they have done to him—the emphasis of the classroom intervention would not be on determining what occurred in the child's earlier years to "make him so angry at school." Instead, treatment would be directed toward determining what factors in the child's present life situation are triggering these problem behaviors, and what can be changed in his environment to modify the way he behaves. The teacher would not ask such "why" questions as "Why do you feel so angry with your classmates?" and, "Why do you feel your classmates are against you?" Nor would the teacher try to help the child identify events in his past that are presently making him so aggressive. Rather, "what" questions would be asked about the child and the classroom situation—for example, "What is occurring in the classroom right before Peter starts hitting a classmate?" or "What occurs in the classroom right after Peter starts hitting a classmate?" or "What can be changed in the situation to reduce the possibility of Peter hitting a classmate?" After these types of questions are answered—given the assumptions that have been made so far—a behavior modification procedure can be initiated.

The goals of behavior modification are specific. Since the orientation of behavior modification is toward identifying what can be changed in the child's environment to modify his or her particular behavior, it follows that the goals of the procedure or procedures are specific; that is, the goal of each procedure is to change a particular behavior of the child, rather than to achieve a more general goal of "helping the child get better" or "helping the child reach his highest level of personal adjustment." *A particular procedure is chosen to use in the modification of a particular behavior or learning problem. The goal of behavior modification, therefore, is only the modification of that specific problem.*

Behavior or learning problems are caused by the environment; unconscious factors play no essential role. Advocates of behavior modification do not accept the belief that there are unconscious causes or factors that contribute to a child's particular behavior or learning problem. The emphasis of an intervention procedure is on identifying those factors in the child's immediate environment that can increase or reduce the number of times that the child performs the behavior.

Insight is not necessary for changing a child's behavior. Since proponents of a behavioral orientation do not accept the belief that an underlying or unconscious psychological conflict is responsible for a child's behavior, it follows that they do not believe that a child must be aware of the unconscious or other underlying reasons for his or her behavior before any positive behavior change can take place.

Symptom substitution does not occur. Some teachers and child therapists believe that when the underlying problem is ignored and only the superficial problem (e.g., hitting or tantrums) is treated or worked on, the child will continue to develop new problem behaviors or learning difficulties until the "deeper" or unconscious issue is resolved. Although the question has not been totally resolved, the available research literature overwhelmingly indicates that new symptoms will not develop in a child when (1) the appropriate behavior modification procedure has been used and (2) there has been an accurate identification and modification of those factors that contribute to the child's behavior or learning problem. If new symptoms do develop in the child or the old symptom or symptoms return, it is probably because the same or similar precipitating factors that were in the original situation are present again (cf. Ullmann & Krasner 1969).

These, then, are the general assumptions that underlie behavior modification procedures with children. They represent a somewhat ideal position, however. In actual practice, not all proponents of behavior modification agree with each of these assumptions. Their disagreements with particular assumptions, however, do not prevent them from using these tested procedures.

CHILDREN'S BEHAVIORS CHANGED USING BEHAVIOR MODIFICATION PROCEDURES

A list of some of the behaviors that have been changed using behavior modification procedures appears in Table 1.1. While this is not an exhaustive list of all of the behaviors that have been modified, it is a representative summary of those behaviors treated in an institutional setting, home environment, or special education or regular classroom setting. Three categories of behaviors are listed in the table: behaviors strengthened, developed, and reduced.

1. *Behaviors Strengthened* are those behaviors that a child does only some of the time. The behavior modifier has to strengthen these behaviors (cause them to occur more frequently).

2. *Behaviors Developed* are those behaviors which a child does not perform. Here, the behavior modifier or change agent typically develops these behaviors in the child and then strengthens them until they reach an acceptable level.

3. *Behaviors Reduced* are those behaviors judged to be inappropriate for the particular situation in which they occur. The behavior modifier or change agent chooses a particular procedure with the goal of reducing the problem behavior until it reaches an acceptable level. In some cases the goal is to reduce the behavior to a lower level of occurrence and/or teach the child to perform the behavior only in a particular situation.

Although this list does not cover all behavior and learning problems that have been treated with behavior modification procedures, it does suggest that a substantial number of behaviors have been changed using these techniques.

In this book we will concern ourselves with a variety of behavior modification procedures, describing them in a nontechnical manner, in the hope that the reader will be able to apply these procedures to the various behaviors targeted for change in the exceptional children with whom he or she works.

HOW TO USE THIS BOOK

This book is intended for use in work with a variety of exceptional children in various settings—whether the children are mentally retarded, autistic, learning disabled, emotionally disturbed, sensory im-

TABLE 1.1
Selected Children's Behaviors Treated Using Behavior Modification Procedures

Behaviors Strengthened	Behaviors Developed	Behaviors Reduced
Assertiveness	Arm/leg movement	Bowel movement in pants
Attending to educational tasks/teacher	Color discrimination	Classroom disruption
Completion of educational tasks	Cooperative play	Climbing
Eating solid foods	Copying/tracing pictures	Constipation
Gross/fine motor skills	Echoing sounds	Crawling
Instruction/command following	Eye contact	Destroying objects
Math skills	Imitation (motoric and verbal)	Fears/phobias
Memory for spoken words	Independent dressing/undressing	Fecal smearing
Performing educational tasks	Independent walking	Fire setting
Personal hygiene skills	Letter discrimination	Gestures with fingers
Playing with toys	Making change	Hair pulling
Question answering/asking	Manual communication/use of signs	Headbanging
Reading	Name discrimination	Hitting others
Sitting	Naming objects	Hyperactivity
Social interaction	Pedestrian skills	Loud vocal utterances
Speech articulation	Reading	Mutism/selective mutism
Spontaneous speech	Self-feeding	Overeating
Talking to others	Shoe tying	Pinching, biting, kicking others
Toileting	Size discrimination	Refusing to eat
Use of eating utensils	Smiling	Rocking
Use of orthopedic devices for walking	Speech	Self-hitting/scratching
Use of particular arm/leg	Toilet training	Self-stimulation
Vocational/Prevocational skills	Tooth brushing	Stealing/grabbing food
Walking unaided	Tricycle/Bike riding	Stuttering/stammering
Writing skills	Using telephone	Tantrums, crying
	Washing face/hands	Throwing objects
	Word discrimination	Thumbsucking
		Tics
		Urinating in bed at night/urinating in day in pants
		Vomiting
		Yelling, screaming, hand-slapping

Adapted from Morris (1976, 1978) and Morris and McReynolds (in press).

paired, physically handicapped, multiply handicapped, gifted and/or brain damaged. Since basic behavior modification procedures are presented, the book should first be used as a resource book to introduce the reader to behavior modification procedures for changing children's behavior and learning problems. Second, the book should be used as a reference volume, not only for reviewing the use of particular procedures, but also as a guide in helping the reader decide which method or methods should be used for treating a particular child's behavior.

The book should therefore be read first in its entirety (especially Chapters 1 through 5), and the reader should answer the study questions at the end of each chapter as well as review the chapter summary *both before and after* reading a particular chapter. The study questions are intended to help the reader review the material presented in each chapter.

Chapter 6 should be reviewed in detail. In this chapter, the emphasis is on gaining an understanding of how and which behavior modification procedures should be used for changing specific behavior problems. Behavioral prescriptions are presented for changing particular childhood behaviors. These prescriptions are presented in a systematic format, and should be used *only* after the reader has gained an understanding of the application of behavior modification procedures (Chapters 1 through 5), the problems and difficulties associated with starting a behavior modification program (Chapter 7), and the ethical and legal issues associated with conducting behavior modification (Chapter 8). The procedures are not difficult to use and do not require an extensive knowledge of psychology, but it is important to have a good working knowledge of these procedures before beginning a treatment program with a particular child.

STUDY QUESTIONS

1. Who was Jean Itard? (Review pp. 1–2 to check your answer.)

2. What are the three major developments that contributed to our present-day concern with the education and treatment of children? (Review pp. 2–4 to check your answer.)

3. What are the three major forms of child therapy that have been used by therapists over the past fifty to sixty years? How do the three therapy approaches differ from each other? (Review pp. 3–8 to check your answer.)

4. What are the four learning theory positions that have formed the basis of behavior modification procedures? (Review pp. 4–7 to check your answer.)

5. Two important assumptions in behavior modification are that specific be-
    havior problems are learned (unless there is obvious evidence to the con-
    trary) and that such behaviors indicate only how the child behaves in a
    particular situation. Think about a particular exceptional child who has one
    or more behavior problems and try to determine how he or she might have
    learned to behave in this way. Are there some situations in which he or she
    sometimes shows this behavior, or never shows this behavior? If there are,
    why do you think that he or she has learned to show the behavior in some
    situations and not in others?

6. Review the list of children's behaviors that have been treated using behavior
    modification procedures. Are there some behavior or learning problems
    exhibited by exceptional children with whom you work (or plan to work)
    that have been treated successfully using behavior modification? On a
    separate sheet of paper, write these problems down, and later in the book
    use this list to help you develop behavior modification treatment programs
    for these children.

7. What is the difference between strengthening a behavior and developing a
    behavior in a child? (Review p. 12 to check your answer.)

NOTES

1. Two other exceptions relate to the provision of services to the deaf and blind. A
    residential program for deaf people was established in 1817 in Hartford, Connecticut,
    named the American Asylum for the Education and Instruction of the Deaf, now
    called the American School for the Deaf. Another institution was established in
    Watertown, Massachusetts, in 1829 for blind persons, called the New England Asylum
    for the Blind, later named the Perkins Institution for the Blind (Kirk & Gallagher 1979).

Chapter **2**

BEHAVIOR ASSESSMENT: IDENTIFYING AND RECORDING BEHAVIOR

This chapter first discusses the identification of a child's behavior or learning problem, and notes the importance of being very specific in stating what behavior needs to be changed. A discussion then follows on how to observe and count the behavior to be changed, as well as how to keep a chart on the child's progress. The chapter ends with a brief statement on making initial observations of the child's learning or behavior problem and deciding which behavior should be changed first.

IDENTIFYING THE BEHAVIOR TARGETED FOR CHANGE

Before a behavior modification program is started, one must first state what behavior is to be changed. This sounds like a simple task, and it is—once you learn the correct way to identify the behavior targeted for change (often called the *target behavior*). In identifying a target behavior we are, of course, assuming that this behavior is learned and that it occurs because there are events in the child's immediate environment that encourage or set the occasion for the behavior to take place. This assumption follows directly from those assumptions discussed in Chapter 1.

To help identify and understand what target behaviors are, the reader should refer again to Table 1.1 (p. 13). This table lists a number of behaviors that have been changed using behavior modification procedures. Notice that many of the behaviors are stated rather specifically as target behaviors, so that all of the people who work with a particular child will know exactly what behavior is being changed or was changed. Contrast these target behaviors with the following list of target behaviors, which are not specific:

Johnny/Jennifer should:

- learn to have respect
- not be aggressive
- communicate better
- get along with other children
- be good
- not be so dependent
- learn to have self-confidence
- be kind
- not be destructive
- be more independent
- have more self-respect
- finish his/her school work
- listen in school
- pay attention when someone calls him or her
- learn to do things by self
- be more polite
- learn sanitary procedures
- learn daily hygiene
- learn to develop his or her physical potential
- learn self-assertiveness
- learn table manners
- have a higher self-esteem
- learn safety rules
- learn recreation rules
- learn to be polite
- behave in school

In reading through this list, it is difficult to understand exactly what is being or was changed in the child. For example, in the case of the proposed target behavior "Johnny should not be aggressive," we do not know if the teacher was interested in teaching Johnny not to hit others, not to kick others, not to push others, not to bite others, not to scream and yell at others, not to throw things, not to take toys from others, or not to pull the others' hair. Similarly, it is difficult to know exactly what was going to be changed in the proposed target behavior "Jennifer should learn daily hygiene." Should the child learn to wash her hands, wash her face, brush her teeth, clean her fingernails, comb her hair, and so forth? We do not know for sure.

If the behavior modifier is not certain which behaviors need to be modified in a child, behavior checklists like the ones presented in Appendix B should be used. These checklists list a number of social, emotional, academic, and self-care behaviors that are commonly taught to children to help them progress socially, academically, and developmentally (see, for example, Hammill & Bartel 1982; Kauffman 1981; Smith 1981; Snell 1978; Whitman et al. 1983). By rating a child on one or each of these checklists, the behavior modifier will be able to determine some of the child's behaviors that need to be modified. The teacher or other professional could also use such checklists or rating scales as the *Adaptive Behavior Scale* of the American Association on Mental Deficiency (Lambert, Windmiller, Cole, & Figueroa 1981), the Vineland Social Maturity Scale (Sparrow, Balla & Cicchetti 1983), the Woodcock-Johnson Psycho-Educational Battery (Woodcock 1977), or the Portage Guide to Early Education (Shearer 1972). Information gained from each of these scales would permit the behavior modifier to focus on specific behaviors for change. This information would also assist a teacher, school psychologist, and others in formulating a child's Individual Education Program (IEP).

In behavior modification programs, we must state specifically what target behavior is to be changed. Once this is accomplished, neither the behavior modifier nor others who observe the child will be confused about knowing when the target behavior has or has not occurred. Instead of stating, for example, that you want Johnny to learn to stop being aggressive, you must state precisely what you want him to learn. Do you want him to stop hitting others, stop kicking others, stop throwing things at others, or what? Similarly, instead of saying, as in the next case study example, that Salena should stop her "annoying and immature" behaviors at school, these global descriptions of her should be broken down into more specific and observable target behaviors.[1]

> Salena is a twelve-year-old girl in a classroom for learning disabled students. She was referred to the school psychologist by her teacher who stated that she exhibited a number of annoying and immature behaviors at school. The psychologist first discussed with Salena's teacher what the teacher

meant by "annoying and immature behaviors." It was determined that these behaviors included poking other students with her pencil, throwing paper airplanes, not completing her assigned tasks, and crying when told to come in from the playground. Next, Salena's teacher was assisted by the psychologist in specifying exactly those behaviors she wanted Salena to perform. The target behaviors that she decided to work on with Salena in the classroom included completing her assigned tasks, not touching other students, not throwing paper airplanes, and coming into the classroom from the playground without crying.

In the next example, Mary's parents wanted her to develop "self-sufficiency," but again this very general or global descriptive term had to be broken down into more specific and observable behaviors.

Mary is an eight-year-old moderately retarded girl who attends public school daily and is in a self-contained classroom. Although she has progressed quite well in school and is now beginning to read and write on her own, Mary's parents are very concerned about her "lack of self-sufficiency." Each parent tried separately for many months to help her become more "self-sufficient," but they failed and decided to consult with her teacher about this problem. The teacher first had to convince Mary's parents not to talk in global or general terms about Mary, but to state very specifically what they wanted her to learn. Each parent had a different (although overlapping) idea about what he or she meant by Mary's "lack of self-sufficiency." After a number of tries at stating the target behaviors in specific terms, both parents agreed that they wanted Mary to learn to (1) button her blouse and coat, (2) tie her shoes, and (3) walk to and from the school bus stop by herself.

To Salena's teacher "annoying and immature behaviors" did not necessarily mean the same as it did to the school psychologist. Similarly, "the lack of self-sufficiency" did not necessarily imply the same meaning for Mary's teacher as it did for Mary's parents. But, as soon as the target behaviors were specifically stated in each example, everyone understood which behaviors were going to be modified.

To make sure that a target behavior is specifically and objectively stated—as opposed to describing the child's behavior(s) in global or general terms—the behavior targeted for change should be able to pass the IBSO test (or, the *Is*-the-*B*ehavior-*S*pecific-and-*O*bjective test).

IBSO TEST QUESTIONS

1. *Can you count the number of times that the behavior occurs in, for example, a fifteen minute period, a one hour period, or one day? Or, can you count the number of minutes that it takes for the child to perform the behavior? That is, can you tell someone that the behavior occurred X number of times or X number of minutes in a particular period of time?*

Your answer should be *yes*. For example, can you make statements like the following: Stephanie completed four math assignments in a two-hour period; Michael slapped his face with his hand 127 times in the classroom today; or Jacqueline took three minutes to tie both of her shoes following an instruction from her teacher.

2. *Will a stranger know exactly what to look for when you tell him or her the target behavior you are planning to modify? That is, can you actually see the child performing the behavior when it occurs?*

Your answer should be *yes*. For example, can you make a statement like the following: The target behaviors for Tyler are (1) he will hang up his coat each morning within one minute of entering the doorway to the classroom, and (2) he will sit in his chair with his feet touching the floor and his face and chest region facing the chalkboard within 30 seconds of him taking his hands off his coat.

3. *Can you break down the target behavior into smaller behavioral components, each of which is more specific and observable than the original target behavior?*

Your answer should be *no*. For example, if you choose to modify a child's handwashing behavior, you should not be able to break down this target behavior into smaller behavioral components (e.g., turning on the water with hands, wetting hands, rubbing hands with soap, and so forth) with each of the behavioral components being more easily observable than the original target behavior of washing hands. Thus we should be able to observe the behavior of washing hands as easily as we can observe the component behaviors.

If the target behavior that the teacher or other behavior modifier chooses to modify fails any question on the IBSO test, then he or she should refine this behavior until it passes the test.

IDENTIFYING UNDESIRABLE TARGET BEHAVIORS

As a practice lesson to help the reader identify target behaviors, choose a child whom you feel shows undesirable behavior(s). Using the format in Table 2.1, list the specific undesirable target behaviors that need to be changed. Apply the IBSO test to each behavior on your list. Next show the list to a friend and ask him or her if he or she knows exactly which behaviors are being proposed for change in the child. If the behaviors pass the IBSO test and the friend feels that he or she could correctly identify each behavior without any ambiguity, then one can be confident that the target behavior has been objectively specified.

Next to each behavior in Table 2.1 state whether the behavior should be (1) eliminated completely, (2) reduced in the number of times

TABLE 2.1
List for Identifying Undesirable Target Behaviors

Situation Cues	Behavior	Behavior should be: Eliminated Reduced Restricted (*choose one*)	Consequences
	1.		
	2.		
	3.		
	4.		
	5.		
	6.		

it occurs, or (3) restricted to certain appropriate situations (that is, the child should be taught that such behavior is only appropriate in particular settings or situations).

Behavior modification assumes that a problem behavior is learned and, therefore, occurs because (1) certain events called *situation cues* have stimulated the occurrence of the behavior and (2) other events called *consequences* have encouraged the repeatable demonstration of this behavior (Baer, Wolf, & Risley 1968; Kanfer & Phillips 1970; Ollendick & Cerny 1981). This has become known as the ABC approach to behavior modification (*A*ntecedents, *B*ehavior, and *C*onsequences). That is, certain antecedent events, or situation cues, set the occasion for a particular behavior to occur, and the performance of the behavior produces or leads to certain consequences. The ABC approach can be diagramed in the following manner:

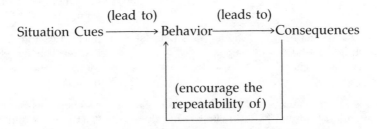

Situation cues can consist of three categories: (1) *setting events* in the environment, such as persons, activities, events, or objects in the environment, and/or the manner in which the environment is organized or structured; (2) *internal events* within the child, such as hormonal imbalance, neurological dysfunction, cognitions (e.g., random thoughts, attributions, and expectancies); and (3) *combination of setting and internal events*, such as a neurological dysfunction setting the occasion for a child having a seizure and persons in the classroom in the immediate past providing the child with frequent attention (direct conversation, touching, eye contact), while the seizure is taking place. Of these three possible situational cues, the one that is the least difficult to identify is the setting events category; the most difficult to identify is the internal events category (Bijou & Baer 1979; Nelson & Hayes 1981).

Consequences are those activities, objects, or events that immediately follow or are contingent on the occurrence of a particular behavior (Bijou & Baer 1979). Consequences are typically external to the child but may be internal, such as cognitions, hormonal changes, electrical changes in neurons (Kanfer & Saslow 1969).

The reader should review the list in Table 2.1 and write down the situation cues and consequences of each behavior. Some examples of situation cues and consequences for certain target behaviors are the following:

Cue	Behavior	Consequence
"Billy, it's time to go to bed."	Crying and screaming loudly	Mother/habilitation worker says Billy can stay up longer and watch television.
"Beth, get dressed for school."	Beth takes at least one-half hour to dress.	Mother says, "Why can't you dress faster. You are always so slow," and helps her finish dressing.
John is receiving no attention from his peers on the bus.	John leaves his seat and runs down the aisle of the bus.	The bus driver yells at John, "Sit down," and the children on the bus laugh and look at John.
Betsy tells Miguel not to touch her or she will "tell the teacher."	Miguel pulls Betsy's hair.	Betsy cries and tells teacher; teacher tells Miguel, "Stay away from Betsy."
Maria is not receiving any attention from her peers or teacher.	Maria leaves her seat and climbs onto the window ledge in the classroom.	Teacher yells to her, "Get down," and students laugh and look at her.
No one is playing with or talking to Aaron on the playground.	Aaron walks up to Michael and hits him.	Michael cries and tells playground monitor; the monitor removes Aaron from the playground and sits down and talks to him about his behavior.

Cue	Behavior	Consequence
Marcus grabs Roberto's colored pencils from him in class.	Roberto bites Marcus' arm.	Marcus cries and the teacher tells him that he should not take other people's property (the teacher says nothing to Roberto about biting).
Father reads at the dinner table and rarely looks at Abraham.	Abraham throws food at his sister. She screams.	Father puts down his paper and yells at Abraham for misbehaving. Father does not return to reading paper.
Chris sees a dog.	Chris cries and runs to her mother.	Mother comforts her by holding her and says "Don't be afraid. Everything is okay."
Amanda is chosen by her teacher to read out loud in her reading group.	Amanda mispronounces the first five words in the reading passage.	Teacher interrupts Amanda and says "I will read the sentences for you and you listen." Amanda does not have to read the sentences out loud in the reading group.

A record sheet appears in Appendix C that can be used to assist the behavior modifier in identifying various situational cues and consequences for a particular target behavior(s).

Sometimes behavior modifiers cannot easily identify both the situation cues and the consequences of a certain behavior or learning problem. When this occurs, the behavior modifier should make a concerted effort to observe the child for a few days in the particular setting in which the behavior or learning problem occurs, trying to answer the following questions:

1. What happens immediately before the target behavior occurs? Does someone say something to the child that triggers the target behavior? Does someone come near, hit, or look at the child? Is the child working on a particular educational or other task and beginning to fail or show disinterest?

2. What happens immediately after the target behavior occurs? Does the child receive exactly what he or she requested? Does someone comfort him or her or say something? Does someone move away from him or her? Does the target behavior result in exactly what the

child wanted to occur? If so, what was it that he or she wanted to occur?

If it is still difficult to identify the situation cues and consequences of the target behavior, the behavior modifier should then think about those situations or settings in which the target behavior does not occur. Specifically, the behavior modifier should ask himself or herself the following questions:

1. What is going on in this (these) situation(s) which does not take place in the situation where the child shows the target behavior?

2. What possible situation cues are absent in this setting, but present in the target behavior setting?

3. What potential consequences for the target behavior are available to the child in the target behavior setting that are not available in this setting?

4. What are the major differences between this setting and the target behavior setting? Are some of these differences potential reasons that the target behavior does not occur in this setting?

Some undesirable behaviors (e.g., nonimitative behavior, lack of speech, not being toilet-trained, not reading at a "normal" rate, not copying accurately from what is on the chalkboard, not eating with a spoon) that a child demonstrates may not have obvious situation cues or consequences that encourage the repeatability of the behavior. Such behaviors may be due to learning deficits in the child (i.e., the child has not learned these behaviors), and require that we redefine these undesirable behaviors in terms of desirable behaviors and then use behavior modification procedures to teach the child these desirable behaviors (Bijou & Baer 1979). For example, instead of eliminating the behavior of a child's eating food with his hands, the behavior modifier redefines this undesirable behavior and state that he or she wants to teach the child to use a fork to eat his food. Or, instead of wanting to eliminate a child's inaccurate copying of words and numbers from the chalkboard, the teacher would redefine the undesirable behavior and state that he or she wants to teach the child to copy accurately each word or number that he or she requests other students to copy from the chalkboard.

Other undesirable behaviors may not have obvious situational cues or consequences because the cues and consequences are *both* internal for the child. For example, it is possible that the antecedent events and consequences for a child's self-stimulation (such as rocking, strange or contorted finger or hand movements, looking up at fluorescent lights followed by rapid eye blink movements, and so forth) are both due to internal factors. Speculation concerning whether internal events are setting the occasion for and maintaining a behavior should take place, however, only after an extensive analysis has been completed of the observable *A* and *C* factors that may be contributing to the occurrence of the behavior. When such speculation does occur, the ABC analysis should be discontinued since the probability of someone being able to modify these internal events is not very high.

There may also be some undesirable behaviors (e.g., writing with a pen on walls, clothing, furniture, and/or paper; removing clothes) that a child shows that you do not want to reduce or eliminate; rather, you want to teach the child the appropriate settings in which he or she should demonstrate these behaviors. These undesirable behaviors may initially occur in many settings, and the child must be taught that they should occur only in certain settings. In such cases, as we will discuss later, the child has to be taught that the behavior can occur *only when certain situation cues are present*, or only under certain conditions (Sulzer-Azaroff & Mayer 1977).

IDENTIFYING DESIRABLE TARGET BEHAVIORS

Just as undesirable behaviors should be specifically stated, so too must desirable target behaviors. These behaviors can either be strengthened (increased) or developed (established) in a child. By stating that a behavior should be strengthened, we mean that it is not occurring as often as we wish and we want to increase the number of times it occurs. Some examples follow of identifying desirable behaviors to strengthen.

> *Roberto is a sixteen-year-old emotionally handicapped student who often leaves school early without permission, approximately three times per week. The target behavior that his teacher chose to strengthen was staying in school the whole day until the 2:00 pm release bell rings.*

> *Billy is a four-year-old autistic child who eats occasionally with a fork or spoon and the rest of the time with his hands. The target behavior that his teacher chose to strengthen was Billy's use of a spoon or fork at lunchtime.*

> *Betty Ann is a twenty-year-old mildly retarded student who only knows how to ride the city bus from her home to school and back. She will graduate from school soon and will be placed at a community job station several miles from her home and in a different direction from her school. Since she learns rather quickly and is very responsible, her parents have agreed to permit her teacher to teach her to ride the bus from home to the job station and back.*

When we want to develop a desirable behavior in a child, this means that the child is not presently performing the target behavior and must be taught how to do it. In the next example, you can see a distinct difference between developing and strengthening a desirable behavior.

Raymond is a three-and-a-half-year-old moderately retarded child who does not eat with a spoon or fork. He occasionally eats with his hands, but he often demands that his mother or babysitter feed him. Since the parents felt that there was no obvious reason he could not feed himself (and this was confirmed by the child's pediatrician), they chose as their target behavior developing independent eating in Raymond—first developing spoon eating and then developing eating with a fork.

Willy is a seven-year-old learning disabled child who also has a seizure disorder—the seizures are being controlled by medication. Willy cannot discriminate accurately between such letters as d and b, k and l, q and p, g and p, and q and g. He also "forgets" ten of the sounds associated with the letters or letter clusters in the alphabet. His teacher first chose as her target behavior teaching him to correctly discriminate 100% of the time, over 15 consecutive trials, between the letters d and b. After reaching criterion, she decided to teach him to correctly discriminate between k and l, then q and p, and so on. Concurrent with this training she decided to teach him to 100% accuracy over 15 consecutive trials the sounds associated with each of the ten letters or letter clusters that he did not know.

There are some desirable behaviors that do not have to be strengthened or developed in a child. The child performs these behaviors adequately, but only in a few settings. Here the child must be taught to *expand* the number of settings or situation cues in which the behavior occurs (Bijou & Baer 1979). For example, some children follow commands, but only from one teacher; they "do not listen" to anyone else. Other chidren will use the toilet in their homes or at school to have a bowel movement or urinate, but will not use a "strange" toilet, preferring to soil their pants. Still others will sit in their seats at school when the teacher is present, but not when a substitute or guest is present. In each of these cases, the child has to be taught to expand the number of situations in which he or she will perform the desirable behavior.

Alicia is four-and-a-half years old. She attends a normal preschool program and except for slowness in learning the alphabet and discriminating between colors, shapes, and sizes, she shows no signs of learning disability, mental retardation, or possible brain damage. The parents report few "out of the ordinary" behavior problems and feel that she is emotionally well balanced. However, they do report one major problem with her. Alicia refuses to move from her crib to her "big bed" to sleep at night. She sleeps comfortably and undisturbed in the crib, but cries and has tantrums as soon as she is told that she must sleep in her "big bed." The parents chose sleeping in the "big bed" as the target behavior to expand.

In the next example, a high school student needs to expand his level of school work productivity into his math class.

Brock is a fifteen-year-old mildly retarded student in a departmental high school program. He attends and completes his work in all his classes, except math class. When it is time for math class, he enters the classroom and sits down, but does not do his work or copy problems from the board. Instead, he often talks to his neighboring classmates, takes their papers, shuffles his feet around on the floor, or will get up and leave class and wander the hallways. This is the only class in which he performs these activities. His teacher, who is also his social studies teacher, chose to work on expanding his level of classroom productivity from the social studies class to the math class. The three target behaviors that she first chose to expand were sitting in class and not talking to neighbors, sitting in class and not taking other students' papers, and sitting in class until the period bell rings.

Once again, the reader should think of a child whose behavior needs to be changed. This time, using Table 2.2, list those desirable target behaviors which you feel the child should demonstrate. Make sure that they are specifically stated and that each target behavior passes the IBSO test. Next to each behavior, indicate whether you want to strengthen, develop, or expand the target behavior.

OBSERVING AND COUNTING THE TARGET BEHAVIOR

Once the target behavior has been identified and a decision has been made whether to eliminate, reduce, restrict, strengthen, develop, or expand it, the next step is to observe and count the behavior. Neither

TABLE 2.2
List for Identifying Desirable Target Behaviors

Behavior	Behavior should be: Strengthened Developed Expanded (*choose one*)
1.	
2.	
3.	
4.	
5.	
6.	

observing the behavior nor counting it is very difficult. But, in order to make sure that these activities do not occupy most of the behavior modifier's time, it is necessary to develop an observation plan concerning when to observe the occurrence or nonoccurrence of the target behavior (Kazdin 1980, 1981).

Some target behaviors will determine how often the behavior modifier can observe the behavior; other behaviors will determine in what way to observe the behavior; and still others will determine both how often and in what way to observe the behavior (Kazdin 1981). For example, if the target behavior is the elimination of food grabbing at the lunch table, the behavior modifier would observe the child each time he or she eats at the table. If the target behavior is the development of imitative behavior or recognition of letters, the behavior modifier would plan out daily observation sessions in which he or she would teach the child to imitate or recognize letters. And, if the target behavior is the strengthening of sitting in one's seat in the classroom, the teacher or other behavior modifier would observe the child at selected times throughout the day.

Two types of observational sheets are often used in behavior modification programs (e.g., Miller 1980; Rojahn & Schroeder 1983). The first one is a time-sampling procedure, an example of which appears in Table 2.3. This procedure is used when (1) the behavior modifier is interested in knowing how often during the day (or part of the day) the target behavior occurs and (2) the plan is to strengthen, eliminate, or greatly reduce the occurrence of this behavior. When the particular observation time occurs, the behavior modifier observes the child for about 3 to 5 seconds and determines if the child is or is not performing the target behavior. If he or she is performing the behavior, a plus sign (+) is placed at that time period; if the student is not performing the behavior, a minus sign (−) is placed at the period. The number of time periods that one chooses is determined by how often the target behavior occurs and the constraints on the teacher's or other behavior modifier's time. In addition, the observation periods need not occur at regular intervals: that is, irregular observation periods can be used at some times every 15 minutes, at other times every 5 minutes, 10 minutes, or 30 minutes. This irregular procedure, however, cannot be used in all cases.

In Tables 2.4 and 2.5 we present two additional examples of the use of this observational approach. Table 2.4 shows a sheet for observing a child's in-seat behavior or seat-related academic tasks on a regular basis. Table 2.5 shows an irregular time sheet for observing how often the same type of behavior occurs in class.

The second major method of observing a target behavior is during scheduled periods when the child is in close or one-to-one contact with the behavior modifier (for example, during a reading group, speech

TABLE 2.3
Sample Observation Sheet for Determining the Number of Times in a Day that a Child Has Dry Pants

---

+ = Yes, the behavior is present   Child's name: _____

− = No, the behavior is not present   Date: _____

OBSERVATION SHEET

7:00 A.M.	11:45	4:30
7:15	12:00 P.M.	4:45
7:30	12:15	5:00
7:45	12:30	5:15
8:00	12:45	5:30
8:15	1:00	5:45
8:30	1:15	6:00
8:45	1:30	6:15
9:00	1:45	6:30
9:15	2:00	6:45
9:30	2:15	7:00
9:45	2:30	7:15
10:00	2:45	7:30
10:15	3:00	7:45
10:30	3:15	8:00
10:45	3:30	8:15
11:00	3:45	8:30
11:15	4:00	8:45
11:30	4:15	9:00

---

therapy session, self-help training session, and so on). Here, one or two periods per day or three to five periods per week are scheduled with the student to observe how often the behavior occurs or does not occur. These periods usually last between 10 and 45 minutes, depending on the target behavior and the tolerance level of the child and/or teacher or other behavior modifier.

Implicit in the observation of a child's target behavior is counting how often it occurs. In behavior modification we do not simply get a general impression of how often the event occurs; we actually count the number of times it occurs. This permits us to gain an objective understanding of how good, bad, or severe the child's behavior is, and, alternatively, what progress has taken place since we began the particular intervention procedure.

In the case of the time-sampling procedure, we indicate at each time period whether the behavior did (+) or did not (−) occur and then

TABLE 2.4
Sample Form for the Time-Sampling Observational Approach on a Regular Basis

---

+ = Yes, the behavior occurred   Child's name: _____

− = No, the behavior did not occur   Week of: _____

OBSERVATION SHEET

Day of the week	min.	Hour in the Day				
		9:00	10:00	11:00	1:00	2:00
Monday	15					
	30					
	45					
	60					
Tuesday	15					
	30					
	45					
	60					
Wednesday	15					
	30					
	45					
	60					
Thursday	15					
	30					
	45					
	60					
Friday	15					
	30					
	45					
	60					

---

count the number of times the behavior occurred on that particular day. For those target behaviors that are being taught or changed during scheduled periods, we use a different counting approach. Specifically, we use a simple tally sheet like the one shown in Table 2.6. We indicate with a tally mark each time the target behavior occurs and indicate with a zero each time the behavior does not occur. We then count the number of times that the behavior occurred in that particular situation.

Sometimes we measure with a stopwatch instead of a tally sheet, counting the number of minutes or seconds it takes the child to perform the target behavior. The use of a stopwatch is described in the next case study involving a young boy who was slow in dressing himself.

TABLE 2.5
Sample Form for the Time-Sampling Observational Approach on an Irregular Basis

---

+ = Yes, the behavior occurred   Child's name: _____

− = No, the behavior did not occur   Date: _____

DAILY OBSERVATION SHEET

8:30	9:50	1:45
8:40	10:05	1:50
8:45	10:35	2:00
9:00	10:40	2:30
9:15	10:55	2:45
9:20	1:00	3:00
9:25	1:05	
9:40	1:15	

Manuel is a six-and-a-half-year-old child who is very slow in dressing himself. He knows how to dress himself and does not make mistakes in dressing himself. However, he takes between twenty and thirty minutes to get dressed. Manuel's mother chose as the target behavior teaching him to dress faster. She counted the number of minutes each day it took him to get dressed by himself, starting the stopwatch immediately after he finished breakfast and she told him to "go upstairs and get dressed for school."

The counting of the number of minutes or seconds to perform a behavior may also be used, for example, for the following: amount of time it takes a student to complete an academic task like a page of math problems, answering study questions, completing a workbook assignment; time it takes to follow a set of verbal instructions that the teacher knows the student can complete; and the time it takes for a student to sit in his or her seat upon entering the classroom.

CHARTING THE CHILD'S PROGRESS

Besides observing and counting the target behavior in behavior modification procedures, we must also keep a chart of the exceptional child's progress (e.g., Mash & Terdal 1981; Miller 1980). This chart enables us to know a great deal about the relative effectiveness of the intervention procedure in regard to the child. For example:

1. Charting helps us readily determine the progress of a child's or student's treatment in an unbiased and objective fashion.

2. Charting allows us to determine how regular the child's progress is, i.e., to determine whether progress is steady or fluctuates.

TABLE 2.6
Typical Tally Sheet Used in Behavior Modification

I = Behavior occurred	Child's name: _Sharon_
O = Behavior did not occur	Date: _11/17_
	Time Session Started: _10:00_
	Time Session Ended: _10:10_

SESSION TALLY SHEET

I I O I I I I I O I I O O O O I I I I
I I I I O I O O O I I I I I O I I I I I I I I
O O O I I I I I I I O O O I O O O I O O O I
I I I I I O I I I I I I I I I I O I I I I I I
I I I I I O O I I O I I I I I I

Total Number of Target Behaviors: _80_
Length of Session: _10 min._

3. Charting provides information to those who will work with the child in the future about which behavior modification procedures worked successfully and which did not.

4. Charting enhances the teacher's or other behavior modifier's accountability.

The typical chart used in behavior modification programming is presented in Figure 2.1. A chart, or graph, as used in behavior modification consists of two major lines: the Days, Sessions, Hours, Weeks, or Months line and the Number of Times, Percent of Times, Number of Minutes, or Number of Steps line.

The former is fairly straightforward—it lists the number of consecutive days, sessions, hours, or weeks in which treatment occurs. Most of the time, the behavior modifier will be recording the target behavior either per day or per session. Occasionally, however, a student's behavior occurs very often during the school day. In this case, the behavior modifier may want to consider recording how often it occurs per hour and using a new chart each day. On the other hand, sometimes a child's target behavior does not occur very often. In this case, the behavior modifier would probably want to record how often it occurs per week.

The Number of Times line *records how often the target behavior occurs in*

FIGURE 2.1
Standard chart used in behavior modification work

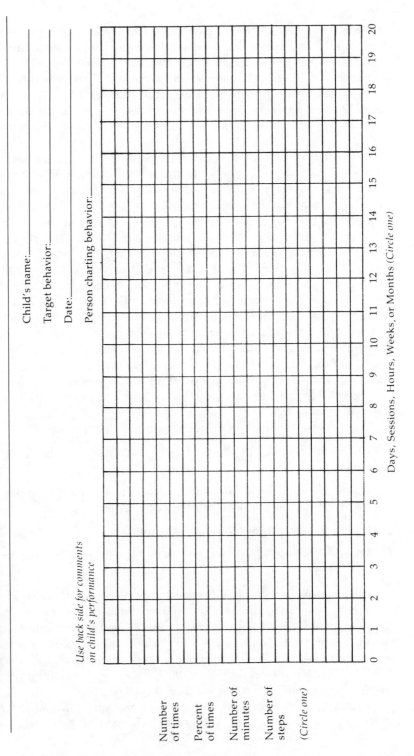

a particular day, session, hour, week, or month. For example, if we were recording the number of times a child threw food at the lunch table, we would *first* count how often he threw food and, *second*, record for Day 1 the number of times the target behavior occurred. Thus, if he threw food ten times we would record for Day 1 the number 10. This is accomplished by finding the number on the Number of Times line in Figure 2.1 and placing a dot where the ten line *crosses* the Day 1 line. This is shown in Figure 2.2.

We can also chart the percent of times a child performs a particular behavior. Charting percent is just as simple as charting number of times. Percent charting is especially useful when we are interested in knowing *how many times the child was correct out of a specific number of tries.* For example, Figure 2.3 charts the progress of a child (Jimmy) who was being taught to imitate what his teacher was doing. Jimmy's teacher would perform a particular behavior and then encourage Jimmy to imitate that behavior. The teacher was interested in determining Jimmy's *percentage correct* during each session. Since the teacher did not always perform the same number of behaviors to be imitated each session, it would not be fair to Jimmy only to record the number of times he was correct at each session. If the teacher performs 20 behaviors in the fifth session and 15 behaviors in the sixth session and Jimmy imitated 10 in the fifth session *and* 10 in the sixth session, we would never know that his behavior had improved unless we recorded his percentage correct. His percentage correct in the fifth session was 50% and in the sixth session was 67%.

How do we calculate percentage correct? It is not difficult:

1. Count the number of times that the child showed the target behavior.

2. Count the number of times that the child was requested to perform (or attempted to perform) the target behavior.

3. Divide the total from No. 2 into the total from No. 1.

4. Multiply the result from No. 3 by 100. This will give you the percentage correct.

An example of the use of these steps is presented in Table 2.7.

Finally, we can also chart the number of minutes or the number of steps completed. The Minutes chart is used when we are interested in knowing how long it takes a child to perform the target behavior. The Steps chart is especially useful when we are using a program such as those in Chapter 6. Here, *we record the last step that the child successfully completed* at the end of each session or each day.

Charting may seem complicated and time consuming at first, but *charting a child's progress actually takes very little time and provides the teacher*

FIGURE 2.2
Example of how a chart is used to record the number of times a child throws food at the lunch table

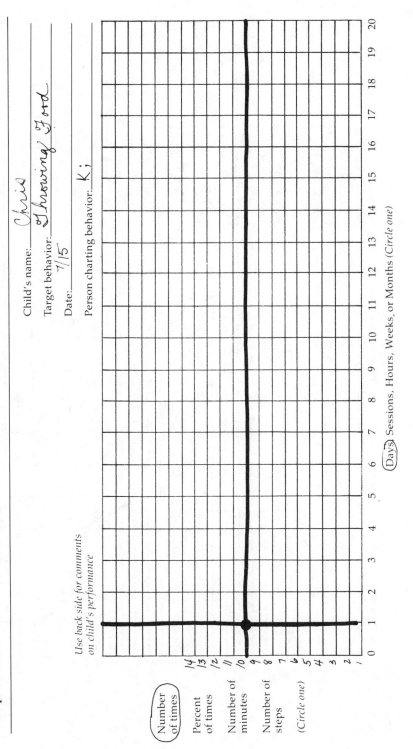

FIGURE 2.3
Chart of Jimmy's progress in terms of the percent of times he was successful in imitating his teacher

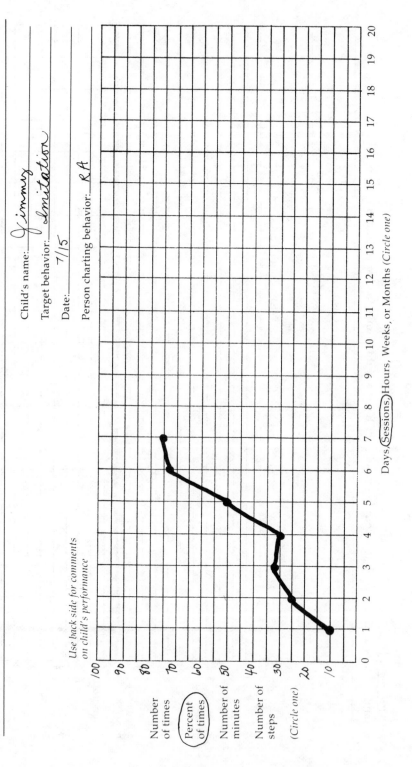

TABLE 2.7
Example of the Calculation of Percent Correct

Bobby imitates his therapist 50 times out of the 65 times that he is asked to imitate. What was Bobby's percentage of correct imitations?

1. Bobby imitated 50 times
2. Bobby was asked to imitate 65 times
3. Divide 65 into 50; 50/65 = .769
4. Multiply .769 by 100. .769 × 100 = 76.9

Bobby scored 76.9% correct imitations.

or other behavior modifier with a clear, objective pictorial representation of how well the child is doing.

After the behavior modifier decides whether he or she is going to record the number of times, percent of times, number of minutes, or number of steps, the behavior modifier should be sure to *circle the measure* that he or she is going to use. Similarly, after the behavior modifier decides whether he or she is going to count the target behavior each day, session, hour, week, or month, the behavior modifier should be sure to *circle how often* he or she is going to measure the behavior.

The next two cases illustrate some additional ways in which target behaviors are charted.

Desmond is a seven-year-old moderately retarded child who is very slow in responding to his mother's commands. His mother never "pushed" him because she felt he could not move faster because he was retarded. She consulted with Desmond's teacher about his slowness and the teacher said that she had never noticed this problem. The mother then spoke to the school psychologist who suggested that she choose one particular command that she can ask at three different times during the day. She was then told to buy a stopwatch and to count how long it takes him to follow the command each time (that is, each session). She was to give the command only once each session.

Listed in Figure 2.4 is Desmond's chart for the first five days (or 15 sessions).

Susan is a five-year-old hyperactive child who "can never sit still." Her mother told the psychologist that Susan's "nervousness" is particularly bad when she sits down to eat. In order for both the mother and the psychologist to determine how often Susan gets up from her seat, the mother was told to count for the next five days the number of times per day that Susan leaves the table during breakfast, lunch and dinner.

Figure 2.5 shows how often Susan left the table.

FIGURE 2.4
Chart of the number of minutes it took Desmond to follow a command over a 15-session period

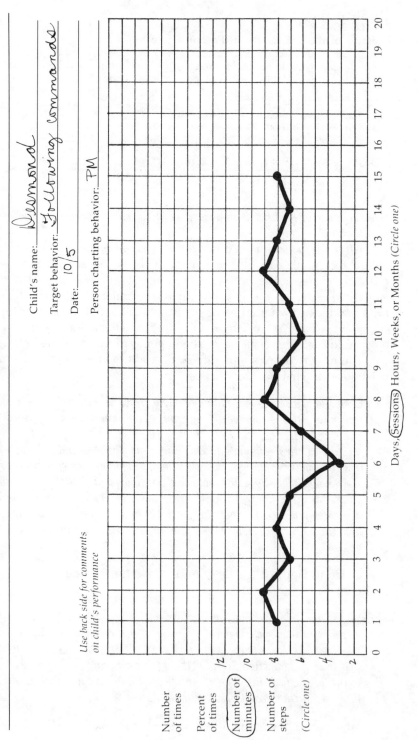

FIGURE 2.5
Chart showing number of times per day that Susan left her seat during breakfast, lunch, and dinner

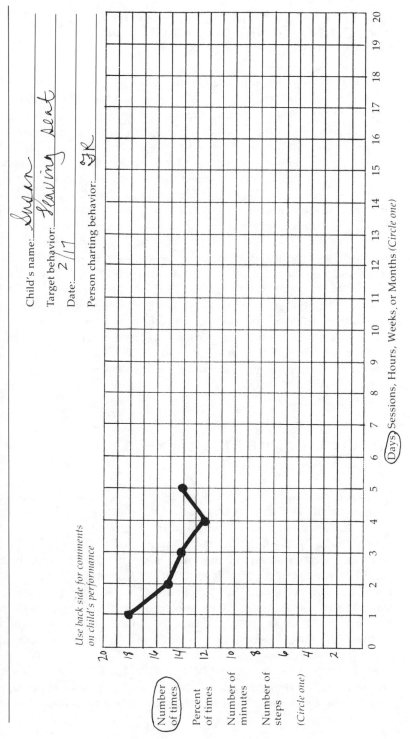

GETTING AN INITIAL IMPRESSION OF HOW OFTEN THE CHILD'S BEHAVIOR OCCURS— BASELINE PERIOD

Now that the reader has learned about how to identify a target behavior as well as how to count and chart it, the next step we will discuss is actually observing and charting the target behavior. This initial observation period occurs directly before the behavior modifier plans to start the behavior modification treatment procedure and is called the *baseline period*. We establish a baseline in order to know what the initial level of the exceptional child's target behavior is before we start the behavioral intervention program. This allows us to compare the exceptional child's progress during the intervention period to his or her behavioral level before the training program began so that we know whether the program is having any effect on the child's target behavior. Baseline information is especially important because sometimes we think a child is progressing with the use of the intervention procedure when, in fact, his or her behavior during intervention is not appreciably different from baseline. If no progress occurs after a while, it is time to take a critical look at the particular intervention procedure that the behavior modifier is using to make sure it is being applied correctly and consistently, and/ or determine if it is time to switch to another behavior modification procedure. The baseline period should at least last five days, or between 5 and 15 sessions. Figures 2.4 and 2.5 represent baseline periods for Desmond and Susan.

WHICH TARGET BEHAVIOR SHOULD BE CHANGED FIRST?

It is not uncommon for a particular child to have more than one target behavior that needs to be changed (e.g., Mash & Terdal 1980). The question then arises: which one first? To begin, the behavior modifier should list all of the target behaviors that need changing. The one the behavior modifier should change first is the one that he or she thinks would be the *easiest to strengthen*, reduce or develop in the child.[2] This will give the behavior modifier exposure to working with behavior and learning problems and also give him or her early feedback concerning how behavior modification treatment proceeds. It's better to know for yourself that the procedures work before beginning to tackle more difficult target behaviors.

After the behavior modifier becomes familiar with the use of various behavior modification procedures, he or she can begin working on more than one target behavior in the child. The behavior modifier should not try, however, to treat too many target behaviors at the same time. It is much easier to follow the progress of a few behaviors, and to remember what one should do whenever the behaviors do or do not occur, than to treat many target behaviors at a time and possibly forget what is supposed to be done.

RECORD KEEPING, CHARTING, AND OBSERVING

Although the behavioral assessment methodology discussed in this chapter has been used in a variety of settings with many different populations (see, for example Hersen & Bellack 1981; Haynes 1978; Mash & Terdall 1976, 1981a), it is expected that it will not be able to be used by every teacher or other behavior modifier because of various constraints placed on their respective time and resources. These observational procedures, however, can be adapted to the environmental situation of the particular behavior modifier. For example, if a teacher cannot observe a student as frequently as is presented in Table 2.5, but can afford to observe a child for 5 to 8 minutes, three or four times per day, then he or she could adapt Table 2.4 accordingly.

The behavior modifier should also consider asking a colleague to independently observe the targeted child on as many occasions as possible, and to record the target behavior when it is observed (Kazdin 1980; Mash & Terdal 1981b; Rojahn & Schroeder 1983). By comparing findings, these independent observations would provide the behavior modifier with information regarding the reliability of his or her observations. As a general guideline, every effort should be made to have at least 30% of the observation periods observed by an independent rater. This situation would also provide an independent verification of the specific and objective nature of the target behavior(s) decided upon following the application of the IBSO test to the behavior(s).

The behavior modifier may also wish to set a criterion on a child's chart that indicates what level needs to be reached by the exceptional child for the program to be designated a success, and so that the behavior modifier knows when the program can begin to be gradually withdrawn (e.g., Ollendick & Cerny 1981). For example, in teaching eye contact to a child we recommend in Chapter 6 that a criterion be set of 90% or more correct responses per scheduled period for three consecutive scheduled periods. The criterion that is to be established should be based upon the available research literature on the topic, the behavior modifier's familiarity with the child and his or her speed of change, and the intensity or severity of the target behavior. The criterion should also be established prior to the initiation of the behavioral program.

STUDY QUESTIONS

1. Which of the following target behaviors is/are not well defined? Circle the incorrect one(s).
   a. aggressiveness
   b. tying shoes at home before leaving the house
   c. spitting in the classroom
   d. eating appropriately
   (Answer: a, d. Review pp. 17–20 to check your answer.)

2. Why should a target behavior be stated very specifically? (Review pp. 17–19 to check your answer.)

3. What are the three steps in the IBSO test? (Review pp. 19–20 to check your answer.)

4. What is a *situation cue*? (Review pp. 21–23 to check your answer.)

5. Choose a child whose behavior you would like to change.
   a. What is the target behavior to be changed?
   b. Apply the IBSO test to the target behavior.
   c. List the *situation cues* which you believe lead to the target behavior.
   d. List the *consequences* which you believe follow the target behavior.
   (If necessary, review pp. 19–23.)

6. What do the following phrases mean?
   a. Strengthening the target behavior
   b. Expanding the target behavior
   c. Restricting the target behavior
   (Review pp. 25–27 to check your answers.)

7. What is an observational plan? How is it used? (Review pp. 27–31 to check your answers.)

8. Why should a child's progress be charted? (Review pp. 31–32 to check your answer.)

9. Charles is an eleven-year-old severely retarded child who is being taught to imitate simple movements of his therapist.
   a. In the first baseline session, Charles scored 3 correct imitations out of 45 demonstrated by his therapist. What is Charles's percentage correct?
   (Answer: 6.6%. Review pp. 34–37 to check your calculations.)
   b. Over the 10 treatment sessions, Charles scored the following percentages correct: 0, 0, 6.6, 6.6, 13.3, 6.6, 13.3, 20, 20, 40. On the chart in Appendix D record these numbers.

(Compare your chart to the one on p. 73. If necessary, review pp. 31–35).

10. Why is it important to have a baseline period? (Review p. 40 to check your answer.)

NOTES

1. Throughout this book the case studies and case examples have been modified appreciably to protect the anonymity of the children, parents, teachers, and/or therapists involved.
2. The behavior modifier, however, should also consider the severity of the target behaviors on the list and how annoying the behaviors are to others in the child's environment. The behavior modifier may not be able to wait on these other behaviors in order to gain experience on intervening with the easiest behavior.

Chapter 3

THE USE OF REINFORCEMENT

The use of reinforcement in behavior modification with children is discussed in this chapter. The nature of reinforcement is presented first and examples of various types of reinforcers are provided. A discussion then follows of the different ways in which reinforcement is given—for example, on a continuous versus an intermittent basis. Next, those factors which influence the effectiveness of reinforcement are considered. The chapter ends with a section on the use of tokens as reinforcers, and with a brief presentation of a few common misconceptions regarding the use of reinforcement.

WHAT IS REINFORCEMENT?

Reinforcement is typically defined as an event that immediately follows a target behavior and that results in an increase in the frequency of occurrence of that behavior (e.g., Skinner 1938, 1953). Thus, reinforcement is something that *follows* a particular target behavior and *strengthens* (or, results in an increase in) the number of times that behavior occurs.

Because reinforcement is defined for our purposes in terms of its effects on the child, something that might be reinforcing (or rewarding) to one child may not be reinforcing to another child. Some children prefer to eat candy, popcorn, peanuts, or Cracker Jack. Others dislike all of these things, but love play activities and/or video games, or prefer just a smile and a hug from the teacher or behavior modifier. It is therefore very important for the behavior modifier to determine what is reinforcing for each child with whom he or she works.

There are many ways of determining what is reinforcing to a child. First, one could observe the child during mealtime, snacktime, and play activity periods to see what he or she likes and dislikes; some children prefer candies over liquids, others do not like either, but like teacher attention, and still others prefer to play video or other electronic games over anything else. Others have more unusual preferences—for example, one sixteen-year-old educable mentally retarded girl preferred having someone "give me five" (handslap), a ten-year-old autistic boy preferred emptying the wastepaper baskets in class and receiving brown paper lunch bags, and a nine-year-old hyperactive girl preferred spending five minutes with the school nurse. The child could also be asked what he or she likes the most and what he or she would prefer to receive as a reinforcement. Or, the behavior modifier could use *a reinforcement menu* (e.g., Addison & Homme 1966). This menu lists by picture and/or name those objects, activities, or events the behavior modifier knows the child likes. The child is then asked before each scheduled training or intervention period or at the beginning of the school day which item or items on the menu he or she would like to work for during the particular period of time. The behavior modifier would then use these chosen reinforcers. As an alternative, the child could be given a preference test before the start of the school day or a scheduled training period. For this test, the behavior modifier needs to have available three to six different types of objects and events that the child likes. The child would then be systematically exposed to each item (for example, giving him or her a few small stickers, tickling him or her, or letting the child play briefly an electronic game, and so forth) and determine which one(s) he or she prefers for that time period. This preference test is especially useful for those exceptional children who are nonverbal.

The following is a list of various types of reinforcers which many exceptional children enjoy:

1. *Objects*—toys, pencil and paper, clay, comic book, whistle, bubble blower, balsa wood airplane, stickers

2. *Activities*—swinging, going on merry-go-round, running, dot-to-dot sheets of paper, playing catch, playing video or other electronic games, flying a kite

3. *Social praise*—"Very good," "That's right," "Fine," "I'm so proud of you," "You're terrific"

4. *Nonverbal messages*—smiling, tickling, hugging, kissing, rubbing back

5. *Edibles*—small amounts of candy, ice cream or gelatin

6. *Liquids*—small amount of Kool-Aid, juice, soda, lemonade, or chocolate milk

In Appendix E we present a more extensive list of possible reinforcers. If these reinforcers are to be given to a child when he or she performs a correct behavior, they must be distributed in small amounts or quantities or for short time periods—otherwise, it is possible that the child will tire quickly of or satiate on the reinforcer (Snell & Smith 1978). Also, it is recommended that whenever possible the behavior modifier should

1. Use a reinforcer that is appropriate for the child's age

2. Try never to use edible or liquid reinforcers, unless reinforcers from the other four reinforcement categories listed above are found to be ineffective in changing the child's behavior.

Also, reinforcers are preferable that can be easily distributed and require relatively small amounts of time for the child to use (Bijou & Baer 1979; Ollendick & Cerny 1981; Ross 1981).

Think of a particular child to work with. Using the previous list as well as the list in Appendix E, write down three reinforcers that are potentially reinforcing to the child for each of the six reinforcement categories listed below:

- Objects
- Activities
- Social praise
- Nonverbal messages
- Edibles
- Liquids

For some exceptional children, social praise is not a very effective reinforcer, whereas toys, games, and/or playing electronic games are quite effective. Even though praise is not a very good reinforcer, the behavior modifier should plan to pair it whenever possible with the giving of the more effective reinforcer. A child might be told, for example, after he or she has performed a correct behavior, "Very good," or "Good boy," or "Good girl" and then given their preferred reinforcer. When praise is given, it should also be behaviorally descriptive—that is, the praise should be associated with exactly what the child did that was correct. For example, the behavior modifier could say:

"Great, you put all of the————away. That's just fine."

"I am so happy that you sat down when the bell rang".

"I really like it when you complete your math work on time".

The only instances where social praise should not be given are when its use, for example, produces aggressive behavior, tantrums, conduct problems, crying, and/or withdrawal on the part of the exceptional child. Such behaviors suggest that social praise is aversive and/or tension provoking for the child and, thus, its continued use would be counterproductive to the child's target behavior being modified.

Generally speaking, however, no matter what reinforcer is used with children, always praise them and let them know that they are doing a fine job. The amount of happiness and joy that the behavior modifier expresses should be slightly exaggerated in the beginning of the behavioral program by varying one's voice intonation. Like many children, exceptional children respond well to an adult's joy, enthusiasm, and concern over what they have done. Then, as the child begins to perform the particular behavior more regularly, the behavior modifier should gradually taper off his or her enthusiasm until it reaches a more moderate level. Here is an example of the use of slightly exaggerated joy and happiness to help an autistic child learn a simple matching task:

> *Wil is a four-year-old nonverbal autistic child. He feeds himself, is toilet trained, and makes some discriminating sounds. The task of the teacher was to help Wil learn to point to a particular animal in a picture of five animals after seeing a toy figure of that animal. In one session, Wil was shown a horse and was then asked to "point to the horse in the picture." After a few unsuccessful tries, Wil pointed to the correct figure. The teacher jumped up, shouted "Hurray!" praised Wil, danced around in a circle with him, patted him on the back, smiled joyously, and gave him a big loving hug. Wil, who did not like candy or juice but liked to be hugged and have his back scratched, smiled and giggled and then sat back down with the teacher for another trial.*
>
> *The next time, a toy tiger was shown to Wil, and after studying the picture for a brief moment he first pointed to the wrong picture and appeared to wait for the excitement to occur again. When it did not, he then pointed to the correct picture. The excitement followed again.*
>
> *As the training sessions progressed, Wil became more skilled in identifying correct pictures and the teacher began gradually to decrease the activities which followed each correct response. The dancing around finally stopped as did the shouting of "Hurray!" but the teacher continued patting Wil on the back and giving him social praise.*

Occasionally a teacher, aide, parent, or clinician forgets to reinforce an exceptional child for a correct behavior or does not remember what he or she is supposed to do when a child performs a correct behavior. One way of preventing this is to become very familiar with a child's program plan, but the following way is even better: make up signs describing what is supposed to occur when the correct behavior occurs, and hang them in various places so that they are easy to see. For example,

PRAISE LEROY WHEN HE EATS WITH A SPOON

TELL KARLA HOW HAPPY YOU ARE TO SEE HER PLAYING
WITH OTHER CHILDREN

PRAISE TONY WHENEVER YOU NOTICE HIM NOT PULLING
SOMEONE'S HAIR

SCHEDULES OF REINFORCEMENT

Up to this point, we have been talking about using a reinforcer each time the child performs a correct behavior. There are instances, however, in which this continuous use of reinforcers is not preferable. In some cases the child may tire of receiving reinforcers and therefore perform the desirable behavior less often. Or the behavior modifier may not have the time to reinforce the child each time the correct behavior occurs.

But even if it is possible to reinforce an exceptional child for each correct behavior, the literature indicates that this procedure may not be the most desirable (e.g., Bijou & Baer 1979; Ross 1981; Snell & Smith 1978). In most cases in which reinforcement has been given continuously, (i.e., following the occurrence of each target behavior), the behavior rapidly decreases if the reinforcers are removed. This will not occur if, after the child is on his or her way to learning the target behavior, the behavior modifier begins rewarding him or her on an *intermittent* or *partial* basis instead of on a continuous basis. Continuous reinforcement therefore refers to the delivery of a reinforcer after each time the child performs the target behavior; intermittent reinforcement refers to the periodic delivery of a reinforcer after the child performs the correct target behavior.

The two most widely used schedules of reinforcement with exceptional children within a classroom setting are the fixed ratio and variable ratio schedules (e.g., Snell & Smith 1978).

Fixed Ratio Reinforcement Schedule

In this schedule, the child receives reinforcement only after he or she has performed a fixed number of the target behaviors. The particular ratio—that is, the number of correct behaviors per one reinforcer—is determined by the behavior modifier and is based on what he or she feels is an appropriate ratio level for the child. Thus, a fixed ratio of four (abbreviated FR 4) means that the child will be reinforced after he or she has performed four target behaviors. A FR 6 means the child will be reinforced after performing six target behaviors. An example of the use of a fixed ratio schedule is the following:

> Mrs. Martin was interested in teaching a mildly retarded child, Earline, how to discriminate between colors. She sat Earline in front of a series of rubber rings and two shoe boxes. Some of the rings were painted red and some were yellow; similarly, one of the boxes was red and the other was yellow. Mrs. Martin then told Earline to place the red rings in the red box and the yellow rings in the yellow box. Earline began sorting the rings.
>
> After the baseline sessions, Mrs. Martin introduced reinforcers for correct responding. Each time Earline was successful, she received a lot of praise from her teacher as well as a piece of candy. Within ten minutes of the first training session, Earline sorted all of the rings and was 40% success-ful. By the end of the third training session, she was about 80% successful. Mrs. Martin then decided that during the fourth session she would discon-tinue reinforcing Earline on a continuous basis and instead reinforce her on a FR 2.
>
> Earline scored about 80% again in the fourth session. The schedule was then changed to a FR 3 in the next session and this time Earline scored almost 90% correct—obviously pleased with her successes and not affected by the schedule changes.

Variable Ratio Reinforcement Schedule

This schedule is like the FR schedule except for one major difference: the child does not always receive the reinforcer after the same (fixed) num-ber of correct responses. A variable ratio schedule of three (abbreviated VR 3), for example, means that the child will be reinforced on the average after every three correct responses. Thus, in one instance, he or she might receive a reinforcer after he or she makes one response, at another time after two responses, at another time after three responses, another time after four responses, and another time after five—but on the average he or she is being reinforced after every three responses. The particular arrangement of how many correct responses should be performed before each reinforcer occurs is randomly predetermined by the behavior modifier. Thus, in the VR 3 example, the arrangement of giving reinforcers could have been after 1, 3, 2, 4, 5 responses, after 3, 2, 4, 5, 1 responses, and so forth. An example of the use of a variable schedule follows:

> Cori is a learning disabled eight-year-old who has a reading sight vocabu-lary of approximately fifty words. When Cori was first learning to read these words, her teacher praised her after every word she read correctly. When Cori was 85% successful with reading her sight words, her teacher began varying her praise for correct responses according to a VR 3 sched-

ule. First, Cori was reinforced after 2 correct responses, then 4 correct responses, then 3 correct responses, then 1 correct response, then 5 correct responses.

Two reinforcement schedules that are not very frequently used in behavior modification work with exceptional children in the classroom setting are the fixed interval and variable interval schedules (Snell & Smith 1978).

Fixed Interval Reinforcement Schedule

In this schedule, the child receives a reinforcer after a fixed interval of time has passed, but only upon performing the target behavior when the fixed interval has been completed. For example, a fixed interval of one minute (abbreviated FI 1′) means that a one-minute period must elapse before the child may have the opportunity to receive the reward; however, the child cannot receive the reinforcer until he or she performs the target behavior at the moment the fixed interval occurs or after the interval period has passed. Behaviors that are performed prior to the end of the interval period are not reinforced.

Variable Interval Reinforcement Schedule

This schedule is like the FI schedule except the child does not always receive the reinforcer after the same fixed interval. Instead, the child is reinforced on a variable time schedule that is randomly determined by the behavior modifier. For example, if we set up a variable interval schedule of two minutes (abbreviated VI 2′) this would mean that, on the average, the child is being reinforced after two minutes have elapsed. A child on this schedule, for instance, might be reinforced after 15 seconds, 45 seconds, 1 minute, 3 minutes, or 5 minutes—but on the average every 2 minutes. This form of interval schedule produces a steadier level of responding than does a FI schedule, and, as with the VR schedule, the particular times after which the child is reinforced are randomly established.

Other Reinforcement Schedules Used with Exceptional Children

In addition to the major schedules of reinforcement presented above, there are three secondary schedules of reinforcement that are often used with special needs children (see, for example, Bijou & Baer 1979; Snell & Smith 1978). Each can be used on a continuous or intermittent basis in a wide variety of settings.

Differential reinforcement of a low rate of behavior (DRL). This refers to reinforcing a child for responding at a lower rate than the child was doing during the baseline period. This schedule can be used in two ways. First, the child receives reinforcement each time the child performs a target behavior, providing that a fixed time interval has passed since the last target behavior was performed. Second, the student receives reinforcement providing he or she has performed *fewer* target behaviors during a specific time interval than the student performed during baseline. For example, a DRL of one response in 30 seconds (abbreviated DRL 1:30") means that a 30-second period must elapse between a child's responses before the child can receive reinforcement. When the 30-second period is passed, then the first target behavior performed at or after this time period will be reinforced.

> Beth is a nine-year-old learning disabled child who has been placed in a self-contained class for learning disabled children. Her teacher reports difficulty teaching Beth to "slow down" and think about the math problems that she is working on. It seems that whenever Beth is given a worksheet of math problems, she always finishes the worksheet within 12 minutes, scoring less than 20% correct. Since her teacher reports that Beth "does not seem to think" and "just puts down any answer as quickly as she can," she decided to start a DRL 45" schedule of reinforcement, reinforcing Beth on a continuous basis for pausing at least 45 seconds between writing down the answers to her math problems.

Differential reinforcement of a high rate of behavior (DRH). The differential reinforcement of a high rate of behavior refers to reinforcing a child for responding at a higher rate than the child had been doing during the baseline period. Here, the child receives reinforcement each time he or she performs a high rate of behavior within a certain period of time. For example, a DRH of five responses within a 15-second period (abbreviated DRH 5:15") means that the child must perform five behaviors within a 15-second period in order to be reinforced—the reinforcement occurring following the performance of the fifth target behavior, providing this behavior occurred before or at the end of the 15-second time period.

> Alex is a seven-year-old child who is a very slow reader, reading approximately six words every 30 seconds. His pronounciation of the words is correct, but it takes him a while to sound out each word in his book. His teacher decided to use a continuous DRH schedule of reinforcement to increase his reading rate. She started at a DRH 8:30" and then proceeded to DRH 10:30", DRH 15:30", and so on until he could read at a rate that was similar to his peers in his reading group.

Differential reinforcement of other behaviors (DRO).   This refers to reinforcing a child for the performance of behaviors other than the target behavior. In other words, the child receives reinforcement at various times if he or she is engaging in activities other than the target behavior. Since reinforcement is provided when the target behavior is missing or is omitted, this procedure has also been called *omission training*. For example, a DRO 30″ means that the child will be reinforced every 30 seconds, provided that he or she is not performing the target behavior.

> *Martita is a ten-year-old emotionally handicapped student who is main-streamed into a regular classroom two hours per day. She talks a great deal in class. Her frequency of talking in class has increased to the point where she interrupts other students who are working and generally annoys her neighbors. Her teacher placed her on a continuous DRO 5′ schedule of reinforcement, where she received reinforcement at each 5-minute period provided that she was not talking, humming, or making any other audible noises with her vocal cords.*

There is no particular rule regarding when you should switch a child from a continuous to a fixed or variable schedule of reinforcement. The general rule of thumb is that once a child's behavior has stabilized and it seems that the child has been responding at an acceptable level, switch him or her to a fixed schedule and later to a variable schedule (e.g., Bijou & Baer 1979; Rimm & Masters 1979; Snell & Smith 1978). The child's reactions to the switch will tell the behavior modifier whether the change in the schedule occurred too soon or too abruptly. One way of avoiding any negative reactions to schedule changes is to make the changes in small gradual steps over a relatively long period of time. It is important to switch a child eventually to a variable schedule, since this is the type of reinforcement schedule that most often characterizes his or her interactions with parents, teachers, and others in the natural environment (e.g., Snell & Smith 1978).

When the behavior modifier uses, for example, ratio schedules, he or she should make sure that the schedule is not too thin—that is, he or she is not requesting the child to do too much work in order to receive a reinforcer. The child will eventually stop responding correctly if the child feels that the amount of effort expended is not equal to the payoff. Also, it is important that the child be able to successfully perform the behaviors that the behavior modifier is reinforcing, i.e., the behavior modifier's expectations regarding what he or she feels the child *should do* and what the child *can do* should be similar.

Finally, *intervention or training periods should not begin with the use of an intermittent schedule of reinforcement.* The behavioral program should begin with continuous reinforcement and then switched later to a fixed schedule (most often a ratio schedule) and finally to a variable (ratio) schedule (e.g., Kazdin 1980; Smith 1981).

WHAT INFLUENCES THE EFFECTIVENESS OF A REINFORCER?

Now that we have described what reinforcement is as well as the various schedules of reinforcement, we will discuss briefly what influences a reinforcer's effectiveness.

Immediacy of the reinforcer.   One of the most important factors affecting a reinforcer is how immediately it is given after the correct behavior occurs. Researchers have found that as the interval between performing the correct response and receiving the reinforcement increases, the relative effectiveness of the reward decreases (see, for example, Kazdin 1980; Ross 1981; Skinner 1953). This finding has led to the following general rule: *A reinforcer should be given to the child immediately after he or she performs the desired target behavior. Don't delay.*

Combining praise with the reinforcer.   Whenever possible, the behavior modifier should praise the child as the reinforcement is given (Bijou & Baer 1979; Miller 1980; Smith 1981). *Never give a reinforcer without praise,* unless it is obvious that the exceptional child does not like to be commended. Also, it is often a good idea for the behavior modifier to reflect his or her natural pleasure with the child's behavior—for example, smiling, showing joy and enthusiasm, and rubbing or patting the child on the back. Don't hold back the joy; don't hold back the happiness. Even when a child is on an intermittent schedule of reinforcement, it is a good idea initially to give praise whenever the child performs the behavior but does not receive tangible reinforcers (e.g., Smith 1981).

Schedule of reinforcement.   As we mentioned earlier, schedules of reinforcement actually influence the effectiveness of a particular reinforcer (Skinner 1938, 1953). The ideal scheduling of reinforcement begins with a continuous reinforcement schedule (Kazdin 1980; Ross 1981). Then, after the target behavior appears to be moderately well established, the behavior modifier should try out a low level, fixed ratio schedule (e.g., a FR 2 or FR 3). If the child seems unaffected by this change and continues to respond at the same or a higher rate, the behavior modifier should try a slightly higher fixed ratio schedule (perhaps a FR 5 or FR 7).

If the behavior modifier still meets with success, then he or she should try a variable ratio schedule (perhaps a VR 2), then gradually move to a higher schedule as the child's behavior stabilizes. Variable schedules are the best for maintaining the child's motivation and interest in performing the target behavior. We can readily appreciate this last point if we think about the "one-armed bandit" slot machines in Las Vegas or Atlantic City. The programming of these machines is based on the concept of a VR schedule of reinforcement. Thousands of people play the slot machines every day for many hours to get just one jackpot (reinforcer). The VR schedule these people are on maintains their motivation and interest in playing the machines (performing the target behavior).

A VR schedule also encourages generalization of a behavior, since the child learns that sometimes he or she will not receive reinforcement for performing the target behavior while other times he or she will get reinforced (e.g., Ollendick & Cerny 1981; Skinner 1953). For example, if we are teaching an exceptional child to play and interact with other children, we would plan (after the behavior is established) to withdraw gradually from the situation and only appear every so often to reinforce him or her for interactive play. The child would then be more likely to begin to perform the behavior not just for the tangible reinforcement from us, but also for the attention and involvement he or she receives from others and the increased self-esteem he or she begins to feel.

Type of reinforcer.   Although it may seem obvious that the type of reinforcement one gives a child will have an effect on his or her behavior (see, for example, Kazdin 1980), many people forget this fact. Some behavior modifiers, for example, continue to use the same reinforcer day after day, session after session. Just as most people like variation in the type of food they eat each day, most children prefer variety in the types of reinforcers they receive. The best rule is to *use a reinforcement menu or reinforcement preference test before starting each training period.* Let the child determine which reinforcer or reinforcers he or she prefers for that particular day or scheduled period.

If the child seems bored during training or does not seem to be behaving with any amount of vigor, switch to another reinforcer. Even if boredom or disinterest is not evident, it is often a good idea occasionally to alternate reinforcers within a particular training period or school day.

Quality and quantity of reinforcer.   Sometimes a behavior modifier forgets that peanuts, popcorn, juice, and so forth when left out more than a day or so can become stale and possibly spoil. *Be sure that fresh reinforcers are used throughout training.* If it does not taste fresh, then it should not be used with the child. A fresh supply should be used. The behavior modifier should try the reinforcer before the training period or school day begins.

How much a child is given each time he or she performs the target behavior is also important. Although a child may prefer a large bag of popcorn each time he or she performs a correct behavior, the child would soon become "stuffed" and uninterested in doing more. If edible or liquid reinforcers are to be used, it is best to give them in small amounts (e.g., Kimble 1961; Kazdin 1980). Similarly, if activity and physical contact reinforcers are used, they should be given for a correspondingly short period of time.

For example, food should be given in small bits. Popcorn and peanuts are a good size for behavior modification work. A few pieces of these foods should be given for each correct response. One level teaspoonful of a reinforcer is also a good size, e.g., a teaspoonful of ice cream, pudding, or gelatin. If liquids are to be used as a reinforcer, the behavior modifier should not give the child more than a few sips for each correct behavior. The dispensing of liquid reinforcement is discussed in Appendix F.

If, on the other hand, the behavior modifier plans to use an activity or playing electronic or video games as a reinforcer, he or she should make sure that the activity or play period does not exceed one to three minutes—unless, of course, he or she is planning to use something like recess or a trip to the zoo as reinforcement for good behavior that has taken place over a relatively long period of time.

Who gives the reinforcer? To maximize the effectiveness of a reinforcer, the behavior modifier should make sure that the child receives reinforcement from someone whom the child likes and to whom the child is attracted. In other words, reinforcement should be given initially by someone who is a meaningful figure in the child's life. After the behavior has become moderately well established, other people can be brought in to distribute the reinforcers so that generalization of the behavior to others can take place (e.g., Ollendick & Cerny 1981). If a behavior modifier plans to work with a child whom he or she has never met, it is best to first play with the child for a few hours over a period of days. In this way the two of them can get to know one another, and the behavior modifier can become more familiar with the child's likes and dislikes. The research literature in behavior modification provides numerous examples of the importance of establishing a good relationship with a person in order to enhance their behavior change as a result of using behavior modification procedures (see, for example, Goldfried & Davison 1976; Goldstein 1980, in press; Klein, Dittman, Parloff, & Gill 1969; Morris & Magrath 1983; Wilson & Evans 1977). As a general rule, therefore, *reinforcement should be given within a framework of a positive relationship with the exceptional child.*

Consistency in giving out reinforcement. The behavior modifier should make sure, whenever possible, that reinforcers are distributed in the same manner throughout the behavior modification program (e.g., Bijou & Baer 1979). This should be the case, even if the schedule of reinforcement changes. Specifically, the way in which a reinforcer is given to a child should not vary even though the reinforcement schedule changes, or the specific person who provides the reinforcement changes. In addition, the behavior modifier should make sure that the particular schedule of reinforcement that is being used is followed as consistently as possible. Oftentimes a behavior modification program will not be effective because of the inconsistency on the part of the behavior modifier(s) in either the schedule of reinforcement used or in how the reinforcers are being given out. In this regard it is important that all people involved in the reinforcement program apply the program in a very consistent manner.

TOKEN ECONOMY SYSTEM

It is unrealistic to expect a behavior modifier always to reinforce a child with such things as activities, games, popcorn, toys, juice, and so forth. Moreover, some behavior modifiers do not like to give out such reinforcers. What would be better and perhaps more efficient would be a *symbolic reinforcement system,* whereby the child could receive a reinforcement symbol for performing the target behavior and then continue what he or she was doing without spending time consuming the reinforcement. Such a system does exist. It is similar to our own dollar economy system, in which people receive symbolic paper (dollar bills or legal tender) for performing various behaviors (working at a job) and then exchange their paper reinforcement symbols for *actual* reinforcers (e.g., food, clothing, furniture, vacation trips, automobiles).

The name given to this type of system in behavior modification is *token economy system* (see, for example, Ayllon & Azrin 1968; Kazdin 1977, 1980; Ollendick & Cerny 1981; Repp 1983; Ross 1981; Smith 1981). It is called an economy system because it is based on a normal monetary system. However, instead of receiving dollars for performing a target behavior, the children receive tokens.

What Is a Token?

Tokens come in all types and sizes. The following are examples of token reinforcement symbols which have been used: gold stars, poker chips, metal washers, check marks or tally marks made on a sheet of paper, small pieces of colored paper, pennies, "happy face" stickers, stamps, points, and plastic buttons. The common factor underlying all these tokens is that each is given in the same way as any other form of reinforcement and all can be exchanged at a later time for an "actual" reinforcer (e.g., Kazdin 1977).

Although tokens come in different sizes and types, there are certain characteristics which all tokens and token systems have (Kazdin 1980; Ollendick & Cerny 1981; Repp 1983):

1. A token should be something that the child can see, touch, and count.

2. The child must be able to store the tokens, or be able to go to a specific place to see how many he or she has earned.

3. The child must be able to exchange the tokens for actual reinforcers.

4. A child should not be able to obtain a token from sources other than the behavior modifier or the assistants.

5. The child must know that a token can be exchanged for various reinforcers that he or she likes, and the child must be able to know in advance how many tokens are needed to "purchase" particular reinforcers.

6. With the exception of check marks or tally marks, the token should not be so small nor so large that it prevents the child from handling it.

The tokens which children accumulate during the behavior modification program are stored in various ways. In some instances, the children keep their tokens in walletlike cases; in other instances, when check marks are used, the children carry a report card on which the behavior modifier records each token they receive or they can be recorded on the chalkboard in class or on a card taped to the child's desk. In still other instances, tokens are stored for the children in a specific area to which they can go to look at or count the tokens they have received. For example, a child may have his or her tokens recorded on a poster that is taped to a wall in one section of the classroom or in his or her bedroom at home. For those behavior modifiers who choose stars, check marks, or tally marks, it is often helpful to let the child place or record his or her own token on the chart. Tokens can also be stored on metal rings kept on the child's belt. There is really no "best" system for either dispensing or storing tokens. It is best to try out different approaches to see which system best suits both behavior modifier and child.

How Is a Token System Established?

Guidelines for establishing a token economy system have been discussed extensively in the behavior modification literature (see, for example, Ayllon & Azrin 1968; Kazdin 1977). A summary of these guidelines is presented in this section.

   The first step is to identify what target behavior(s) the behavior modifier would like to change. Next, a decision needs to be made regarding the *medium of exchange* —that is, what particular item will be used as the token. Then reinforcers need to be chosen that can be exchanged for the tokens. The reinforcers should include whatever items the behavior modifier believes the child would choose given an unlimited selection. Some examples of reinforcers used in token systems are:

- Digital watch with electronic game (available for varying length of time)
- Candy bar (small/large)
- Chewing gum (stick/package)
- Assorted pieces of individually wrapped chocolates
- Bubble gum
- Taking a picture with an instant camera
- Comic book; picture book
- Bicycle ride (varying length of time)
- Watching television/watching a movie on video tape machine (varying length of time)
- Listening to favorite record(s) (varying length of time)
- Private use of battery-operated radio or tape machine with earphones (varying length of time)
- Private play time with behavior modifier or other significant person (varying length of time)
- Assorted jewelry
- Assorted toiletries
- Trips to zoo, museum, or park
- Different sized dolls and/or fictional plastic characters (like Walt Disney or *Star Wars* characters)
- Toys
- Games; video games; electronic games (varying length of time)
- Pennies
- "Happy face" stickers; other stickers
- Scratch and sniff stickers

- Sticker collection books

- Friendship beads/pins

- Tokens that can be used at a video games arcade

- Lunch at a restaurant with teacher or other behavior modifier

- Gift certificate at a toy store (varying amounts—for example, $.75, $1.00, $2.00, $3.00, $5.00)

- Gift certificate at a fast-food restaurant (various types of items—for example, french fries, hamburger, soda, two items, three items, etc.)

Reinforcers can also be chosen from lists like the one presented in Appendix E. In addition, the child can be asked which "things" he or she would like to have included as possible rewards.

After the target behavior(s) and the reinforcers are chosen, the next step is to price the reinforcers. Pricing is very subjective, although there are a few general guidelines which should govern how each item is priced. First, the greater the supply of an item, and the less its cost to the behavior modifier, the lower should be the price. However, supply is also affected by demand. If demand for a particular item is high (even if the supply is great), we may want to consider raising its price. Secondly, those items which require more of the behavior modifier's time (e.g., going for a walk, having lunch, playing a game or activity with the child) should have a higher price than those items requiring less time of the behavior modifier. However, if demand for these latter items is low (and the behavior modifier feels they are important for the child to have), then their price should be lowered.

Similarly, those items which are fewer in number (in terms of actual relative availability in stores) should also be priced higher. Finally, if the child continues to purchase one or two items and the behavior modifier feels that the child should choose other items, then a revaluation of the items should take place in which the high-demand items are increased in price and the low-demand items are decreased in price or are maintained at the same price.

Once the prices are set, it is often a good idea to watch closely in the beginning how the spending proceeds. Then, if changes are necessary, they can be made without much difficulty or delay. *A token reinforcement system should not be too lean or too fat.* The child should have an opportunity to buy something very small with one or just a few tokens, something great with many tokens, or something "nice" (but not great!) for an in-between number of tokens. We want the child to experience positive events or activities happening to him or her so the child will learn that more of these events/activities/objects will be available when the child earns more tokens. We therefore always want the child to be in a position to experience success—to earn enough tokens to purchase something—and to reduce the likelihood that the child will not earn any tokens on a given day or scheduled period and, thus, be discouraged.

In dispensing the tokens, the behavior modifier should give them in the same way he or she would give any other reinforcer. That is, the child should be praised for good behavior and then given the token (for example, the token should either be given to the child, placed in the child's "wallet," or recorded on a card so the child can see it). *It is important to give a token with the same amount of enthusiasm as you would give any other reinforcement.*

Initially, the child should be guided through the exchange system. For example, immediately after the child makes the first few correct responses and is given tokens, the child should be brought to the exchange area and assisted in buying particular items. This introductory phase should be continued for one to five days or scheduled periods, or until the child learns what he or she is supposed to do. After this phase, the exchange should be "opened" at the end of each scheduled period, class, training session, or school day. In some cases, it might be best for the exchange to be opened only once or twice per week, while in other cases the exchange might best be opened at the end of every hour of the school day or training session. The general rule is to try different time periods for the exchange to be open during the first three weeks that the token system is in effect—then decide which "exchange open" time schedule is best. Remember that children's spending patterns—like those of adults—vary. Some children prefer to save their tokens for "bigger" or more expensive items while others prefer to spend their tokens on many smaller items. The frequency with which the exchange is open should be responsive to the individual spending patterns of the children. Whatever the number of times that the exchange is opened each week, the behavior modifier should make sure that the child has enough time to buy things. The child should not be hurried, but dawdling should not be encouraged either.

Establishing a token economy system is not an easy task. It is time-consuming to develop, plan, and implement, and one needs to monitor it closely. In fact, the first three weeks of a token economy program should be viewed as "experimental" by the behavior modifier. At the end of this time period all aspects of the program should be critically reviewed. For example, should there be deletions, additions, or substitutions in the list of target behaviors chosen to change, or in the list of reinforcers being used? Should the token values assigned to each behavior and reinforcer be changed? Does the child appear interested and involved in the program? Are there changes in the program that the child or staff members would like to make?

Table 3.1 shows an example of a classroom token economy program for a ten-year-old emotionally handicapped boy who is mainstreamed

TABLE 3.1
Example of a classroom-based token economy program

Activities/Behaviors	Point Payments	Reinforcers	Point Costs
1. Hands in homework assignment to teacher each day	25 pts.	1. Use the classroom computer (15 minutes)	25 pts.
2. Each time electronic timer sounds, Bobby is not talking to neighbor, with feet on floor, and chest facing chalkboard	10 pts.	2. Have lunch with teacher in the cafeteria	250 pts.
		3. Tell a joke to the class	200 pts.
3. Receiving a C grade on a test	30 pts.	4. Listening to music on tape recorder (15 minutes)	25 pts.
4. Receiving a B grade on a test	45 pts.	5. Extra recess time (15 minutes)	40 pts.
5. Receiving an A grade on a test	60 pts.	6. Go to library (15 minutes)	30 pts.
6. Not hitting someone in classroom during school day	30 pts.	7. Helping children in first grade (30 minutes)	250 pts.
7. Raising hand in classroom before asking/answering a question and waiting until teacher says my name	15 pts.	8. Attendance taker in morning	150 pts.
		9. Free time in the gymnasium (20 minutes)	75 pts.
8. Not pushing someone in classroom during school day	30 pts.	10. Free time in the music room (20 minutes)	60 pts.
9. Each time electronic timer sounds, Bobby is sitting in seat, not talking to anyone, with feet on the floor, and is doing his assigned schoolwork	10 pts.		
10. Does not throw an object into the air in the classroom during the school day	30 pts.		

for the whole school day, except for 40 minutes at the end of each day when he attends a resource room program (to review his class assignments for that day). Specifically, he hits and pushes classmates, talks to neighbors, and throws objects into the air in class.

Table 3.2 shows a home-based token economy program for a seven-year-old gifted student who is also emotionally handicapped. Specifically, he is noncompliant, frequently late for school, and infrequently does his household chores.

As in Tables 3.1 and 3.2, a sheet of paper on the child's desk or a poster placed on the wall should describe for the child the payments associated with each activity or behavior as well as the costs for each reinforcer. A weekly or daily summary sheet like the one presented in Appendix C should then be used to keep track of the payments, costs, and total number of tokens leftover at the end of the training session, class period, or school day.

Is a Token System the Best Approach?

A token economy system is the preferred reinforcement system when one has to work with a group of children, whether in a classroom situation, in a home, or in a residential setting. It is also a good system to use when there are many target behaviors that the behavior modifier wants a particular child to learn, and when he or she does not want to carry around an entire selection of reinforcers for the child. *Token economy programs, however, are not for every child* (Kazdin 1977; Ollendick & Cerny 1981). Some children cannot adapt to the exchange system or learn to tolerate the delay in receiving reinforcement. Others may be too severely handicapped to learn the various aspects of a token system. But the only way to find out if a child will adapt to this system is to try it out. If it does not work, then a tangible reinforcement system can be used and try the token economy system again at a later time.

MISCONCEPTIONS ABOUT REINFORCEMENT

One of the most common statements that many teachers and other behavior modifiers make regarding the use of reinforcement is that reinforcing a child is nothing but bribery (e.g., Kazdin 1980). This is just not true. "Bribery" is used to encourage or provide incentive to someone to perform an activity that is defined as illegal or deviant by society. Reinforcement, on the other hand, is used to help a child perform an activity which is not viewed as either illegal or deviant by society. In fact, the behavior we are typically trying to teach the child is, in most instances, one which society values highly and encourages. Second, bribery typically occurs *before* the desirable behavior takes place (e.g., giving a policeofficer money so that he or she will not write out your speeding ticket), whereas reinforcement occurs *after* the desirable behavior takes place.

Often, one also hears the statement Why should I reinforce or

TABLE 3.2
Example of a home-based token economy program

Activities/Behaviors	Point Payments	Reinforcers	Point Costs
1. Clean room each night to mom's approval	10 pts.	1. Read in bed for ½ hr.	10 pts.
2. Clean cat's litter box each day	20 pts.	2. Going to a museum or art gallery with mom	250 pts.
3. Teeth brushed after breakfast (school days only) by 7:50 am	10 pts.	3. Go to a place of choice with Mom	250 pts.
4. Up and dressed in morning (school days only) by 7:20 am	25 pts.	4. Go to a restaurant	250 pts.
		5. Not set table one night	10 pts.
5. Make bed by 7:30 am (school days only)	25 pts.	6. Go to bed at 8:30 pm (otherwise 8:00 pm)	40 pts.
6. Do homework (based on home-work assignment sheet from school)	35 pts.	7. Use bike in after noon (1 hour)	30 pts.
		8. Watch television in afternoon only for 1 hour (must finish homework first)	30 pts.
7. Set table for dinner by 5:30 pm (each day)	5 pts.	9. Use computer (1 hour)	10 pts.
8. At school bus stop by 8:30 am	5 pts.	10. Play video games on television (1 hour)	30 pts.
9. Say "I am sorry" following a temper tantrum	5 pts.		

reward a child for something that the child is supposed to do (or, is his or her duty to do)? (e.g., Krumboltz & Krumboltz 1972). Without forging into a philosophical discussion regarding what one is *supposed* to do or what is one's *duty*, let us just say that we all are reinforced for doing things: we are reinforced with a salary for working, we are reinforced with a smile, a kiss, or a thank you for helping other people or for being nice to others, and we are reinforced by our supervisors or boss at work for doing a good job. There is no reason we should not treat a child in the same way. Just as reinforcement maintains much of our adult behavior, so should reinforcers be used to strengthen or develop an exceptional child's behavior.

The proper use of reinforcers is a very effective component of teaching exceptional children desirable behaviors. But reinforcers have limits. No matter how attractive a reinforcer is to a child, it will not be useful unless the child is developmentally, emotionally, and physically ready to perform a particular target behavior.

STUDY QUESTIONS

1. What is a reinforcer? What is a reinforcement menu? (Review p. 45 to check your answer.)

2. List the six types of reinforcers.
    a.
    b.
    c.
    d.
    e.
    f.
    (Review pp. 45–46 to check your answer.)

3. What should always be paired with the giving of a reinforcer? (Review pp. 46–47 to check your answer.)

4. How does a continuous reinforcement schedule differ from a variable reinforcement schedule? (Review p. 48 to check your answer.)

5. How does a FR 3 schedule of reward differ from a VR 3 schedule? (Review pp. 48–50 to check your answer.)

6. Define the following:
    a.   DRL
    b.   DRH
    c.   DRO
    (Review pp. 50–52 to check your answer.)

7. List six factors that influence the effectiveness of a reinforcer.
    a.
    b.
    c.
    d.
    e.
    f.
    (Review pp. 53–56 to check your answer.)

8. How does a token economy system work? (Review pp. 56–62 to check your answer.)

9. List five characteristics that all tokens should have.

    a.

    b.

    c.

    d.

    e.

    (Review p. 57 to check your answer.)

10. How are the prices in a token economy system established? (Review p. 59 to check your answer.)

11. How does bribery differ from the application of rewards? (Review p. 62 to check your answer.)

Chapter **4**

TEACHING DESIRABLE BEHAVIORS TO CHILDREN

Various procedures for teaching desirable behaviors are discussed in this chapter. An outline for developing a behavior program plan for an exceptional child is first presented. This is followed by a discussion of how to strengthen a desirable behavior and a presentation of some case examples involving the use of this strategy. Next, the development of a new behavior in a child is discussed, with case examples. The use of behavioral chaining, contingency contracting, group reinforcement, modeling, relaxation training, and self-control procedures is also reviewed.

DEVELOPING A BEHAVIOR PROGRAM PLAN

We learned in Chapter 1 that behavior and learning problems are assumed to be learned, and that these occur when certain situation cues are present and when particular consequences follow the behavior or learning problems. We also learned that a child's behavior is very much influenced by what happens to him or her immediately after he or she performs the target behavior. Thus, if a child's target behavior leads to satisfying (or reinforcing) consequences, we usually find that this behavior will be repeated whenever the same situation cues are present. This principle can be diagrammed in the following way:

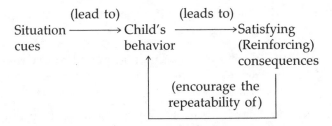

The first step in beginning a behavior modification procedure involves the formulation of a behavior program plan. At first this may seem complicated, but it really is not. Listed in the following outline are the primary questions that should be answered in the formulation of a behavior program plan involving teaching desirable behaviors. The purpose of the plan is to help the behavior modifier delineate exactly what to be doing before a behavioral intervention procedure begins, so that the behavior modifier is completely prepared to work with the exceptional child.

Outline for Developing a Behavior Program Plan

1. What is the desirable target behavior?

2. What method of observation will be used?

3. What will be recorded on the behavior chart?
   a. Circle one:
   Number of times the behavior occurred
   Percent of times the behavior occurred
   Number of minutes the behavior occurred
   Number of steps completed in the prescriptive program
   b. Circle one:
   Days (target behavior recorded daily during days child is in resource room or on program days)
   Sessions (target behavior recorded in individual training sessions or class periods)
   Hours (target behavior recorded during specific times or blocks of hours during the day)
   Weeks (target behavior recorded weekly)
   Months (target behavior recorded monthly)

4. How long will the baseline phase be?

5. What will be the criterion for success?

6. What *specifically* will be done when the target child makes a correct response?

7. What *specifically* will be done when the target child makes an incorrect response?

8. After the criterion for success has been reached by the child, how will the behavior program be faded-out?

9. Will there be a follow-up observation period to determine if the child has maintained the criterion for successful behavior change? If so, when *specifically* will the follow-up period take place?

10. Does the child need to learn to transfer the target behavior to other settings? If so, what *specifically* will be done to accomplish this transfer or generalization of the behavior? When will this be done?

11. Any additional comments about the behavior program?

Questions 4 through 9 define what the behavior program plan will be. The behavior modifier should be able to answer each of these questions after he or she has read through this chapter. Question 5, as was mentioned in Chapter 2, is a somewhat subjective question. Its answer is determined by what is expected of the child by society and by the behavior modifier's expectations and desires concerning the exceptional child.

Question 8 relates to how one terminates a program. For example, does the behavior program just stop when the child or student reaches criterion or does one gradually fade-out various components of the program? The general rule regarding teaching desirable behaviors to exceptional children is to gradually fade-out the reinforcement program as the child approaches or when the child reaches criterion (e.g., Bijou & Baer 1979; Ollendick & Cerny 1981). This is most often accomplished by switching the child from a continuous reinforcement schedule to a fixed schedule and then to a variable schedule of reinforcement; or, it can be accomplished by increasing gradually the average value of the variable reinforcement schedule that the child is currently on. The key term in terminating a behavior program directed at teaching a desirable behavior is *gradual fade-out*. The behavior modifier should be aware that he or she is not just mechanically distributing reinforcers to a child or student who is on a behavior modification program. A positive relationship has also developed over the length of the program, and an abrupt (versus gradual) withdrawal of the program could potentially have negative side effects to the point where, in some instances, the child could become disruptive in order to receive the behavior modifier's attention.

Question 9 relates to what has become known as *response maintenance* or follow-up assessment (Kazdin 1980). When we speak about the "success" of a behavior modification program, we really can talk about "success" at a number of points in time—after the child reaches the criterion for success, two weeks after the behavior modification program has been faded-out, six weeks after that point, three months later, six months later, one year later, and so on. Success, therefore, is a relative term that *must* be defined clearly by the behavior modifier before the behavior program begins. In order to resolve whether there should be a follow-up period, the behavior modifier should gather together in a meeting area all of the staff involved in implementing the behavior program to discuss this matter—and, where appropriate, invite the child and his or her parents to be present and to participate in the discussion. The goal of this discussion is to reach an agreement regarding (1) whether there should be a follow-up observation period, (2) how many follow-up periods there should be, (3) when exactly the follow-up periods should be held, and (4) who will do the follow-up observations.

Question 10 in the above outline relates to the area of transfer of training and generalization of the target behavior. This topic is most important in regard to exceptional children since we are often in situations where we want the target behaviors that we teach them to generalize to other environments and settings. Generalization and transfer of training is discussed later in this book (see Chapter 7).

Once a behavior program has been formulated, the behavior modifier is ready to begin intervention.

STRENGTHENING A DESIRABLE BEHAVIOR

Much of the behavior modification work that is conducted with exceptional children involves the use of reinforcement to strengthen various target behaviors. Presented in this section are a few case examples describing how reinforcers are used to strengthen particular behaviors. In the first case, different schedules of reinforcement are used to increase the number of class assignments completed each day in school.

> *Angela is a fourteen-year-old emotionally handicapped girl who has an average IQ. Her major difficulties in school are her noncompliance and the fact that she rarely hands in her class assignments. The goal that the teacher decided upon was to increase to 80% the percentage of class assignments that she completed (and handed in) each day in school for 10 consecutive days. Her teacher took a baseline for one week to determine the number of assignments Angela completed on a daily basis. Out of six assignments per day, baseline showed that she completed from 0% to 33% of her assignments during the week. The teacher observed that Angela either sat in class quietly, slept, or became tense and agitated and then cried.*
>
> *When she became agitated, Angela was usually sent to the nurse's office—an event that her teacher began to feel was reinforcing to Angela. Her teacher then decided to use spending time with the nurse as a reinforcer for Angela completing and handing in her class assignments. Specifically, each time Angela completed an assignment she was permitted to have a cup of soda with the nurse in her office (continuous reinforcement). As can be seen in Figure 4.1, Angela completed 100% of her assignments on the first*

FIGURE 4.1
Chart showing Angela's progress using different schedules of reinforcement

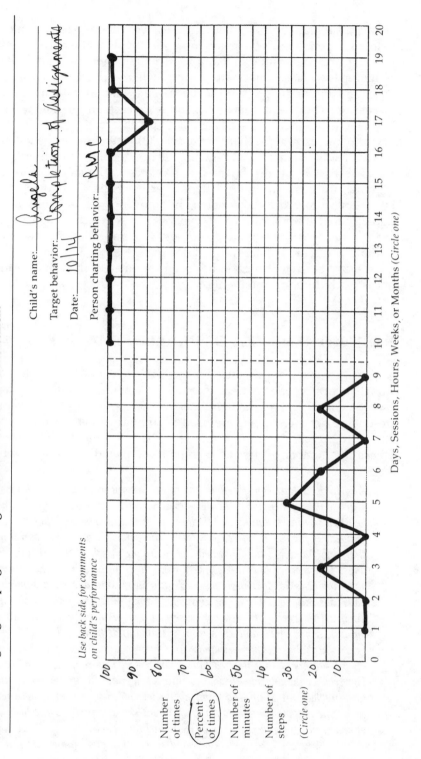

day of the behavior program and met the criterion for success by the tenth day of the program.

Angela was doing so well on her program that, by the fifth day, she was switched to a fixed ratio schedule of two assignments per reinforcer and then to three assignments per reinforcer; Angela agreed with these changes. As a possible side benefit of the program, the teacher also observed that by the tenth day of the behavior program Angela was no longer tense, agitated or crying in class.

In the next case example different schedules of reinforcement are also used to strengthen a child's behavior. Specifically, the behavior targeted for change was Carmen raising her hand to talk in the classroom. The teacher first used a continuous schedule of reinforcement and then proceeded to a fixed ratio followed by a variable ratio schedule of reinforcement.

Carmen is a ten-year-old mildly mentally retarded girl. The goal that the teacher established was to increase the percentage of times Carmen raised her hand to talk during the free group discussion time period, and to decrease the percentage of time she talked without raising her hand and being called on. The criterion for success was 100% raising hand to talk (and 0% talking without raising hand).

Baseline data were gathered for one week, with Carmen's teacher and the aide independently observing the two target behaviors. They found from these baseline observations that Carmen raised her hand to talk during free discussion period less than 10% of the time and talked out without raising her hand approximately 90% of the time. The teacher also discovered that she provided Carmen with eye contact and verbal attention (e.g., "Carmen, wait your turn"; "Carmen, raise your hand first") each time she talked out of turn and did not provide her with any praise for raising her hand.

Carmen's teacher decided to praise her each time she raised her hand to talk during the discussion period (continuous reinforcement), and to ignore her talking out of turn—saying nothing to her and not looking at her and continue talking to and listening to those children who raised their hand. This intervention resulted in an increase in the percentage of Carmen's hand raising within the first week, and a noticeable decrease in her percentage of talking-out behavior. By the middle of the second week of the behavior program, Carmen's percentages had reached about 65% raising hand and 35% talking out. Her teacher then switched Carmen to a FR 2 schedule of reinforcement for the next week, and a FR 3 schedule the following week. By the end of the third week Carmen reached the success criterion for both target behaviors, and the teacher switched her to a VR 2 reinforcement schedule—deciding to maintain her on this schedule for three more weeks. At the end of this period, her percentage of raising her hand to talk (and waiting to be called on) had stayed at 100%, and she no longer talked out without raising her hand.

Next, we see how *prompting* is used along with reinforcement to help strengthen a desirable behavior. Prompting is a *response aid* and consists of the gradual assisting of a child in the performance of the desired target behavior until he or she learns what is expected of him or her. When the child reaches this point of understanding, the prompting is then slowly withdrawn and the child is encouraged to perform the behavior on his or her own.

> *Jerry is a seven-year-old severely handicapped child who is nonverbal, minimally imitative, and not toilet trained. The target behavior that his teacher chose to teach Jerry was imitative behavior. Using the program presented in Chapter 6, the teacher ran five baseline sessions with Jerry. Before she performed each behavior, she said, "Jerry, do this." She ran three trials per session, and each session lasted about ten minutes.*
>
> *Since Jerry's baseline imitative level was low, his teacher decided to prompt each of the behaviors to be imitated so Jerry could learn what was expected of him. For example, after Ms. Thomas raised her arms out to the sides and requested Jerry to do the same, she saw that Jerry did not imitate her. She then placed her hands under his arms and gently lifted them out to his sides. After prompting each response, Ms. Thomas said, "Good boy," and reinforced him for performing the behavior. None of the prompted behaviors, however, were recorded as a success.*
>
> *After eight sessions of prompting almost every response, Jerry began to show signs of learning what to do. Consequently, his teacher began to withdraw her prompts, and Jerry began imitating Ms. Thomas's movements in response to the command "Jerry, do this." He was soon imitating at a much higher rate than during baseline. By the twentieth session, as can be seen in Figure 4.2, Jerry was correctly responding 60% of the time. By the thirty-fifth session (not shown), he was responding correctly 90% of the time.*

As the reader will note from these three examples, the use of reinforcement is a powerful way to strengthen a target behavior. But sometimes, as in this final example, reinforcement can be used inappropriately.

> *Julio is an eight-year-old learning disabled student who has an average IQ. He is mainstreamed most of the school day, except for the reading period when he goes to the resource teacher. He gets along well with his classmates, but has a great deal of difficulty sitting in his seat for any length of time. A psychological evaluation revealed that he is not hyperactive, but has a "high energy level."*
>
> *The teacher observed during the baseline period that he left his seat without permission on the average of 30 times per day. Previous attempts to handle this problem involved keeping him inside during recess, scolding him, and taking away morning free period. None of these methods worked.*

FIGURE 4.2
Chart showing Jerry's progress in learning to imitate simple behaviors

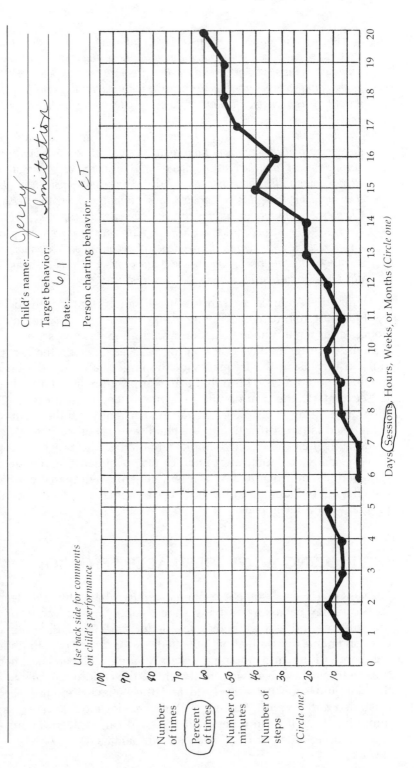

During a math project, she discovered that Julio liked scratch and sniff stickers, so she began reinforcing him with praise and a sticker each time he sat down in his seat. She carried out this program for a week as consistently as she could. She observed, however, that within a few days the frequency of his out-of-seat behavior had increased sharply to approximately 45 times per day.

In reviewing the program, the school psychologist and the teacher discovered that the only way Julio could receive a sticker was by first being out of his seat and then sitting down—the behavior being reinforced was sitting down in his chair, not staying seated or being seated. Julio's teacher then used an irregular or variable time sampling observation chart (see Chapter 2), and reinforced him at each designated time period that he was observed to be sitting in his seat. This resulted over a three-week period in an appreciable reduction in the frequency of his out-of-seat behavior, and by six weeks the number of times he was out of his seat was "not noticeably different" from that of the other students in class.

From this example, we can see that it is important that the behavior modifier not reinforce the wrong behavior. If the behavior modifier notices after ten to fifteen behavior modification training sessions, class periods, or program days that no progress was made on the part of the child in increasing the frequency of the target behavior, the behavior modifier should review his or her behavior program in detail—checking to see that (1) the appropriate behavior is being reinforced, (2) the program is being applied correctly and consistently, (3) the reinforcer(s) being used is (are) attractive to the child, and (4) other factors are not working against the effective implementation of the program. If progress still does not occur after another ten to fifteen training sessions, class periods, or program days of attempting to strengthen the behavior, then the intervention program should be terminated and a new behavior program plan developed.

DEVELOPING A NEW DESIRABLE BEHAVIOR

For various reasons, some exceptional children have difficulty learning such complex behaviors as tying shoes, eating with a spoon or fork, dressing or undressing themselves, letter and word discrimination, color and name discrimination, how to throw or catch a ball, toothbrushing, handwriting, and zipping a jacket. Although the behavior modifier tries to teach these behaviors to the child, the child often fails to learn the skill and soon both the child and the behavior modifier become frustrated and give up. Sometimes the behavior modifier even says to himself or herself or to others that the child cannot learn because the child is too retarded or disturbed or brain damaged.

Although it may be true that some exceptional children cannot learn some behaviors because the behaviors are too complex for their mastery level, it is also often the case that such children cannot learn complex behaviors because they are taught all parts of the behavior at once rather than being taught parts of the behavior separately. In most cases, in order to develop a new behavior in a child it is necessary to divide the behavior into its component parts and teach each part consecutively until the child learns the whole complex behavior (Kazdin 1980; Ollendick & Cerny 1981; Repp 1983; Smith 1981). This procedure is especially important to follow when the behavior modifier plans to teach a child various self-help, social, and academic skills

How to Teach a New Behavior

If the reader reviews Table 1.1 (Chapter 1), it will be noticed that many behaviors (some quite complex) have been developed in exceptional children. Although the particular target behaviors differ, the same teaching principle underlies the learning process. This principle, often called *successive approximation* or *shaping* (Skinner 1938, 1953), states that the child should be taught a complex activity in successive steps—with each step gradually leading to an approximation of the desired target behavior.

For example, with a severely handicapped child, instead of teaching the child the whole behavior of putting on a pair of pants, we would break up this complex behavior into its component parts. The parts would then be arranged in gradual successive steps, leading to the final step of pulling up one's pants. Here are the preliminary steps involved in learning to put on one's pants (a more extensive prescription for shaping this behavior is presented in Chapter 6):

1. Pull pants up from just below waist. (Use loose-fitting pants which have an elasticized waistband, no buttons, and no zipper.)

2. Pull pants up from hip region.

3. Pull pants up from knees.

4. Have child sit down with pants up to knees. Then have him or her stand up and pull pants up from knees.

5. Have child sit down with pants just over feet (by the ankles). Have child pull pants to knees, and then stand up and pull pants all the way up.

6. Have child sit down with pants just over toes. Have child pull pants to knees, and then stand up and pull pants all the way up.

7. Have child sit down. Place one of child's feet into one of the pant

legs until his or her toes show. Then have child place his or her other foot through the other pant leg and pull the pants to his or her knees. Then have him or her stand up and pull the pants all the way up.

8. Have child sit down. Place pants in front of child with the opening of one pant leg just touching the toes of one foot. Have him or her pull the pant leg up until the toes show. Then have him or her place the second foot in the other pants leg. Then have him or her pull the pants up to his or her knees, and have him or her stand up and pull the pants all the way up.

9. Place pants in front of child. Have him or her place one foot through one pant leg until his or her toes show, then place the other foot through the other pant leg, pull them up to his or her knees, and stand up and pull them all the way up.

As one can see, the nine steps are listed in order from the last step in the procedure, which the child performs first, to the first step, which the child performs last. Thus, in developing most new desirable behaviors in children, we start with teaching the last step and then work backward through the step-wise program. We do this because we want the child to have maximum opportunity to practice those steps which always lead to the completion of the target behavior (e.g., Skinner 1953). In this way, the child will experience the successful completion of a task and the reinforcement that also occurs as a result of such task completion.

The next case involves the shaping of a sign in a nonverbal, moderately mentally retarded child.

> Rachel is an eight-year-old, moderately mentally retarded, nonverbal girl. The goal of the program was to teach her to communicate using signs (manual communicaton). Specifically, Rachel's teacher wanted to teach her to sign "eat." She decided to work on teaching Rachel to sign "eat" during lunch time. Her first step was to take a baseline—during lunch time, she counted the number of times Rachel signed correctly or approximated the sign for "eat" when the teacher told her, "Rachel, sign eat," and then modeled the sign. The observations showed that Rachel was unable to sign correctly or even to approximate the sign for "eat."
>
> Rachel's teacher developed a behavior program for her to sign "eat" by means of a shaping procedure. For each trial, the teacher first modeled and gave the verbal cue, "Rachel, sign eat." The teacher then physically prompted Rachel's hand to her mouth as an approximation to the correct sign. The teacher then rewarded Rachel with a bite of her lunch and lots of praise. This step continued until the teacher observed that Rachel was making some attempt to place her hand to her mouth independently. At this point, the teacher began fading-out her physical prompts, but continued to

model the sign, and requiring that Rachel make some effort to approximate the sign "eat" by herself in order to receive her reward.

When Rachel was consistently approximating the sign, her teacher began to physically prompt her hand and fingers into the correct configuration for the sign "eat." As soon as Rachel independently made an effort to correctly approximate the sign, the teacher again began fading-out her physical prompts, but continued to model the sign, and required Rachel to correctly sign on her own in order to be reinforced. That is, the teacher was rewarding closer and closer approximations to the sign "eat." After several months of training, Rachel's teacher decided to evaluate her progress, so she again counted the number of times that Rachel correctly signed "eat" with no physical prompts at lunch time. These data showed that Rachel was able to independently and correctly sign "eat" at least 95% of the time.

There are six very important points to remember in developing or shaping a new behavior (Becker 1971; Krumboltz & Krumboltz 1972; Neisworth & Smith 1973; Watson 1973):

Reinforce the child for each success. Reinforce the child with praise and a small amount of his or her preferred reinforcer each time he or she successfully completes a step. We want to maximize the child's opportunity for success and the receiving of reinforcers and minimize his or her failures. We want the child to learn in a positive way and thereby help him or her build up his or her self-confidence and self-esteem. Be careful, however, not to reinforce the child for finishing the same step over and over. The child must also learn that he or she has to continue to make progress—even if it is slow—if the child is to receive reinforcement.

Teach the basic aspect of the target behavior first. The most basic aspect of the target behavior should be taught first. That is, we are interested in teaching at first only the very basic components of the target behavior. Refinements in the behavior should be taught only after all components are learned. The successive approximation program (abbreviated SAP) we have listed for putting on pants, for example, specifically states that the use of buttons, zippers, and similar devices should be avoided.

Break up the difficult steps into components. If the child has difficulty mastering a particular step, break up the step into smaller components so that the child can still experience success. Let us suppose that a child exposed to the SAP procedure we have listed above could not pull up his or her pants from just below the waist. What could we do to make the learning experience a positive one for him or her? We could break up the step into smaller components. For example, we could place our hands over the child's hands and prompt him or her to pull up his or her pants. In this way, he or she participates in the learning process and his or her behavior also leads to success and reinforcement. We could then repeat this step until the child learns what to do, and then gradually withdraw our assistance—making sure the child still experiences success.

Tell the child which behavior to perform.   Tell the child what he or she is to do before he or she actually performs the behavior. We eventually want the child to learn to perform the complete target behavior without always having to reinforce him or her for doing it. To accomplish this, it is necessary for the child to learn to respond to instructions. The easiest way for the child to learn this is to pair instructions with his or her performance of the various steps. Thus, in the SAP for putting on pants, we would first tell the child, "[Name], pull up (put on) your pants," and then encourage him or her to perform the particular step. These and all other instructions given to a student or child should always be vocalized in a similar manner.

Never switch from a continuous to intermittent reinforcement schedule.   Never switch a child who is learning a new desirable behavior from a continuous to an intermittent reinforcement schedule. The performance of steps in a SAP should always be reinforced on a continuous reinforcement basis.

Teach the SAP one-on-one.   The child should always be taught a SAP on an individual (one-on-one) basis in individual training sessions of three to seven times per week or more.

The number of steps in a SAP is largely determined by the child's own capabilities and the behavior modifier's subjective evaluation of how many steps there should be in the program. The general rule is to let the child's behavior guide the behavior modifier in determining how many steps there should be in a SAP and when additional steps should be added. In Chapter 6, we present a number of established successive approximation programs for developing various self-help, social, and academic skills in exceptional children.

What to Chart

When we are developing or shaping a new target behavior in a child, it is obviously difficult to chart the number of times the child performs the target behavior. Similarly, we can not record the percentage of correct behaviors. In both cases, the child's charted progress would be zero for a long time and not reflect his or her actual progress.

Instead, there are at least three possible alternatives for charting a child's progress. First, we could chart the number of steps the child has successfully completed on the SAP that was established. To do this, we number the steps in the SAP and then record at the end of each training session the last SAP step that the child completed successfully. If steps are added to the program after training begins, the chart as well as the SAP would be renumbered accordingly. Second, we could record the percentage of steps the child successfully completed on the SAP. Third, in the case where the behavior modifier has set a criterion level of a specific number of correct trials that must be achieved before proceeding to the next SAP step, the behavior modifier could chart percentage of trials completed for each step—having a separate graph for each step.

The chart in Figure 4.3 shows a child's progress through a modified version of the SAP presented in the previous section for putting on pants. In this graph, the number of steps completed on the SAP was recorded.

BEHAVIORAL CHAINING

After we have developed a number of behaviors in a child (for example, putting on pants, undershirt, and socks, and tying shoes), the next step is to teach the child to practice each of these behaviors in sequential order, leading to the final reinforced behavior (for example, dressing oneself). The procedure by which we teach a child to perform a sequence of behaviors is called *behavioral chaining*.

Behavioral chaining works like a SAP. For example, first we order the behaviors in that sequence which we deem appropriate, as diagramed here for dressing oneself:

Behavior A ⟶Behavior B ⟶Behavior C ⟶
(Put on underpants) (Put on undershirt) (Put on socks)

Behavior D⟶Behavior E⟶Behavior F ⟶
(Put on pants) (Put on shirt) (Put on shoes)

Behavior G
(Tie shoes)

Next, we go through the whole sequence with the child, prefacing the sequence with a statement like "Johnny, I now want you to get dressed." Then, when necessary, we physically prompt the child in going through the sequence until he reaches the last behavior (Behavior G in our example). At this point he is encouraged to perform this behavior by himself. We then reinforce the child for performing the last behavior. In addition, use praise, saying, "Good boy. Now you are completely dressed."

We then proceed to work backward down the sequence. In the next

FIGURE 4.3
Chart showing Brian's progress in learning to put on his pants by himself

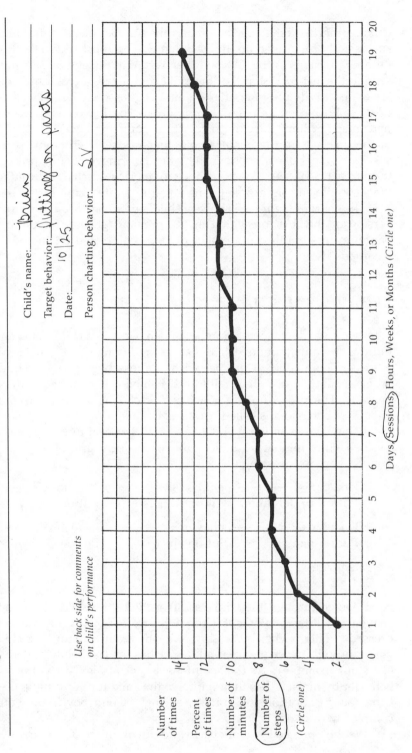

Child's name: _Brian_

Target behavior: _putting on pants_

Date: _10/25_

Person charting behavior: _SV_

Use back side for comments
on child's performance

Number
of times

Percent
of times

Number of
minutes

(Number of
steps) *(Circle one)*

Days, (Sessions) Hours, Weeks, or Months *(Circle one)*

several sessions, we would help the child through the same sequence of behaviors, initially saying again, "Johnny, I now want you to get dressed." Our assistance would continue until he reached the next-to-the-last behavior (Behavior F). Then he would be encouraged to complete the next two behaviors (Behaviors F and G) in the sequence, and reinforced as soon as he completed the last behavior. Again, we would also praise him and say, "Good boy. Now you are completely dressed." This procedure of working backward along the chain would continue until the child was back to the first behavior (Behavior A) in the sequence and was able to dress himself completely in response to the instruction "Johnny, I now want you to get dressed." Reinforcement would come only after he completed the last behavior in the chain, at which time we would say, "Good boy. Now you are completely dressed."

The procedure we have outlined has sometimes been called *reverse chaining* since the sequence is taught in reverse. There is also a *forward chaining* procedure. Here, the child is taught the chain from the beginning to the end. For example, in teaching speech to a child one might follow this sequence:

Behavior A ⟶ Behavior B ⟶ Behavior C ⟶ Behavior D
(Eye contact   (Imitation of   (Imitation of   (Verbal
training)   verbal sounds   words associ-   identification
                      and words)   ated with pic- of pictures)
                                           tures)

As an alternative, we could add a fifth component to the above chain. Specifically, between Behaviors A and B, we could add Behavior B', motoric imitation training (Harris 1977) following the behavioral prescription presented in Chapter 6.

There is yet a third way that chaining can be used, in which the reinforcing activity is an integral part of the chain, which is illustrated in the next case example.

Marty is a four-and-a-half-year-old moderately handicapped child who is nonverbal, moderately imitative, and toilet trained. Although he feeds himself, Marty is very finicky about what he will eat. His favorite foods are cereal, chocolate pudding, and ice cream. Although he will eat more nutritious foods such as eggs, hamburgers, and juice occasionally, in most instances he will refuse to eat them.

In an attempt to help Marty eat a more balanced diet each day, the following types of chained sequences were arranged for his meals. For breakfast he would have to have one helping of scrambled eggs before he could have the cereal of his choice. Diagramed, this chain is:

Behavior A ⟶ Behavior B
(Eat eggs)   (Eat cereal)

For lunch, he could not have one of his favorite sandwiches or any ice cream unless he first drank his juice:

Behavior A ———→Behavior B————————→Behavior C
(Drink juice)   (Eat peanut butter   (Eat ice cream)
                  and jelly sandwich)

Similarly, for dinner he could not have his pudding until he ate his helping of meat:

Behavior A ———→Behavior B
(Eat meat)   (Eat pudding)

From this example, we see that a low frequency behavior (or less preferred activity) in the chain is being strengthened by having the higher frequency behavior (or more preferred activity) immediately follow or be contingent on the completion of the previous behavior. This notion is based on the Premack principle (Premack 1965) where a high frequency behavior that the child engages in is used as a reinforcer for the performance of a low frequency behavior—for example, using five minutes of freehand drawing in a seven-year-old learning disabled child as a reinforcer for 15 minutes of reading.

This use of behavioral chaining can also be seen in the next example:

Clyde is a nine-year-old learning disabled student who is mainstreamed in a regular classroom the entire day except for 40 minutes per day for math remediation—his math level is 2.2. Although Clyde's reading is at an appropriate level, he has difficulty with basic math (addition, subtraction, multiplication). He has, however, learned how to use a calculator correctly. In fact, his teacher commented that if he were permitted to use a calculator in class, he would be "within range" of the other students in class. An additional problem is that Clyde "does not appear motivated" to do his math in class.

Since his teacher felt that Clyde could do better in class in his math work, but was more "comfortable" in the resource room, she decided to increase his interest and motivation in doing math work in class by permitting him to use his favorite calculator to redo his written math work and check/correct his previous answers. He liked the plan.

The behavioral chain in this example can be represented as:

Behavior A   Behavior B
(Working on math   (Using calculator
work sheet)   to check answers)

Behavior C —————————→Behavior B
(Copying math problems   (Using calculator
from chalkboard   to check answers)
and answering them)

Behavioral chaining is an effective way of teaching both complex behaviors or activities and behavior sequences. Since reinforcement does not always follow the completion of each part of the chain, it is important that the behavior modifier praise the child as often as possible when he or she completes various components in the chain.

CONTINGENCY CONTRACTING

We often find behavior modifiers who work with various exceptional children preferring to establish programs in the form of an agreement between the target child (or, in some cases an entire class of students) and themselves. This agreement is called a *behavioral contract* (e.g., O'Banion & Whaley 1981; Tharp & Wetzel 1969). The contract is in written form and describes in detail the target behavior(s) to be performed and the reinforcer(s) to be provided (Kazdin 1980). If both parties agree to the contents of the contract then they each sign and date it. Two more aspects of a behavioral contract should be mentioned. First, if both parties agree, there should be some consequence for failure on the part of the child to perform the target behavior(s). Similarly, there should be some consequence on the part of the behavior modifier for failure to deliver the reinforcer(s). In both instances, all persons involved in the behavioral contract should agree to these consequences. Second, as an optional addition to the contract, both parties could agree to add a bonus for performing the target behavior more often, sooner, and/or for longer periods of time than what appears in the contract (Stuart 1971).

Once a contract is agreed upon and signed by all parties the behavior modifier should chart the percentage of times or number of times per hour, day, week, month, or training session that the child achieves the contract requirements. The behavior chart described in Chapter 2 could be used.

Behavioral contracts do not need to be very complex. Three examples of behavior contracts appear in Figures 4.4, 4.5, and 4.6. The contract in Figure 4.4 is for students in a self-contained classroom program for emotionally handicapped, normal intelligence children. The classroom program is divided into four levels, varying in terms of amount of student freedom of movement, classroom structure, teacher

FIGURE 4.4
Example of a contingency contract used in a self-contained classroom

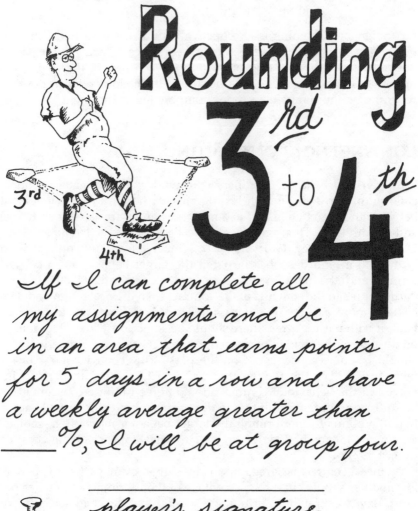

Rounding 3rd to 4th

If I can complete all my assignments and be in an area that earns points for 5 days in a row and have a weekly average greater than ____%, I will be at group four.

player's signature

coach's signature

FIGURE 4.5
Example of a behavior contract between parent and child

CONTRACT

Between (Son's Name), and (Father's Name)

Son agrees to:
1. Carry out garbage pail each day.
2. Work six hours on Saturday every week. Work will consist of anything that he is capable of doing, such as hoeing, weeding, washing the car, or helping father and so forth.

Father agrees to:
1. Pay four dollars ($4.00) per week for above work each week (Saturday).

Both parties agree to the following conditions:
1. Penalty for failing to carry out garbage after being reminded will be reduction of 25¢ for each failure.
2. Penalty for not working on Saturday when work is available will be 40¢ per hour unless condition is covered by another condition.
3. When no work is available due to bad weather or father unable to supervise, $1.00 per Saturday will be paid.
4. Re-evaluation after a trial period of three weeks.
5. If son is sick there will be no penalty reduction on garbage detail, and $1.00 will be paid for Saturday. A total of $2.00 will be paid under this condition.

Signed: _____
Father

Signed: _____
Son

From Dinoff, M., & Rickard, H. C. (1969). Learning that privileges entail responsibilities. In *Behavioral Counseling: Cases and Techniques*, edited by John D. Krumboltz and Carl E. Thoresen. Copyright © 1969 by Holt, Rinehart and Winston, Inc. Reprinted by permission of CBS College Publishing.

supervision and monitoring, amount and availability of privileges, and degree of mainstreaming into regular classes. Students from one level agree to work for a certain weekly average percentage of tokens (points) in order for them to be permitted to go into the next less restrictive classroom program (Drossman 1982).

GROUP REINFORCEMENT

Many times, within a classroom setting, community group home environment, community work station, or institutional setting, it is preferable to establish a reinforcement program for a whole group rather than a particular individual. This is called *group reinforcement programing*.

FIGURE 4.6
Sample behavior contract used in the classroom

Date
_____

Contract no.
_____

Mrs. Harris will initial a smiley card for Andrew each time he does one of the following:

1.   Comes into school, hangs up his wraps, and takes his seat without arguing or fighting with another child.
2.   Eats his lunch and has his noon recess without arguing or fighting with another child.
3.   Clears his desk, gets his wraps, and goes to the bus without arguing or fighting with another child.

When Andrew has received 15 signatures from Mrs. Harris and has had his cards signed by one of his parents, he may choose one of the following rewards:

Read a story to someone.
Be first in line for lunch.
Pass out supplies.
Get notes from the office.
Bring a treat from home for the class.
Go to the library for free reading.
Choose a book for Mrs. Harris to read to the class.
Choose a friend for a math game.
Bring a carrot for Chopper and get a chance to hold him.
Be a student helper in math for 30 minutes.

I, Andrew, agree to the terms of the above agreement,

_____

I, the classroom teacher, agree to provide Andrew with the reinforcers specified above if Andrew keeps his part of the agreement. I also agree not to provide Andrew with any of the above reinforcers during the term of the contract if he does not earn the necessary signatures.

_____

I, Andrew's parent, agree to sign each card that Andrew brings home, to post the cards where Andrew can see them, and to help Andrew keep track of the number of signatures he has earned. Andrew can earn 15 minutes of extra "stay up" time by bringing home 3 signatures.

_____

WE UNDERSTAND THAT THIS IS NOT A LEGALLY BINDING CONTRACT, BUT RATHER A FIRM COMMITMENT OF GOOD WILL AMONG PARTIES WHO CARE ABOUT EACH OTHER.

From Counseling Methods, edited by John D. Krumboltz and Carl Thoresen. Copyright © 1976 by Holt, Rinehart and Winston. Reprinted by permission of the publisher, CBS College Publishing.

Group reinforcement procedures can take many forms. Two approaches will be discussed briefly. One approach involves having the entire group on a reinforcement schedule whereby only when all members of the group perform the target behavior will they, in turn, receive reinforcement according to the designated schedule. In this approach, even if some members of the group engage in the target behavior, they will not be reinforced until and unless all members perform the target behavior. When this point is reached, all members receive the reinforcement (e.g., leaving for recess, going for a snack, watching a cartoon or movie on video tape machine, going on a field trip, and so forth). An example of this approach follows.

> *Mrs. Robinson, a fifth-grade teacher for educable mentally handicapped students noticed that many of her students were not handing in any of their daily assignments. She found this unacceptable and decided that there were going to be five assignments each day that the students should hand in. In order to increase the chances that all students would hand in their required work, she consulted with the school psychologist, who suggested that she establish a group reinforcement program. She told the students that each time someone handed in an assignment, he or she would receive one point. If a student accumulated twenty points at the end of the week (a criterion level of 80%), he or she would have the opportunity to go on a field trip the following Friday afternoon—providing that every other student also accumulated at least twenty points for handing in their assignments. In order to help everyone in class know how well each person was doing, she made a poster with each student's name on it and put a check mark by a student's name each time he or she handed in an assignment. If students accumulated more than twenty points each week, they were permitted to spend their extra tokens on various reinforcers in the class "goodie store."*

A second approach involves establishing a token economy system in the group setting, where each student receives the same reinforcement when he or she accumulates a certain number of tokens. A case example follows involving an elementary school learning disabled class.

> *The teacher's goal was to increase task completion during the morning. Each student received six assigned tasks to be completed during the morning period before lunch. The teacher initially took a baseline on the percentage of tasks completed by her students during this period over three weeks. These data showed that on the average, only about 34% of the tasks assigned to the class were being completed each day. She decided to implement a group reinforcement program in order to increase the chances of students completing more tasks each day.*
>
> *Students were able to earn one point for each of the six assigned tasks they completed each morning. Then, just 20 minutes before lunch, those students who earned six points were allowed to choose a free-time activity*

for 20 minutes. Students who earned three to five points were able to have five minutes of free time, while those students who earned less than three points were required to complete their unfinished work during this 20-minute period.

Although group reinforcement approaches are effective, they should not be used as a substitute for working directly with a particular exceptional child who has one or more specific behavior or learning problems. These approaches, however, could be used for changing those behaviors in a group setting that a substantial number of exceptional children demonstrate in that setting.

MODELING

Behavior change that results from the observation of another person has been typically referred to as *modeling* (e.g., Bandura 1969; Bandura & Walters 1963). The modeling procedure consists of an individual called the *model* (e.g., teacher, aide, parent, peer, or therapist) and a person called the *observer* (i.e., the exceptional child). The observer typically observes the model performing the desirable target behavior in a familiar setting where the model experiences reinforcement for engaging in the behavior. Another approach to modeling involves having the behavior modifier first demonstrate the target behavior and then reinforce the child for successfully imitating the target behavior of the behavior modifier. This has also been called *imitation learning.* Modeling or imitation learning often reduces the amount of time a child needs to learn a particular behavior. For example, sometimes a child can learn a SAP much faster if the whole SAP is first modeled for the child by the behavior modifier; the child, in turn, is reinforced for approximating what the behavior modifier did. Children also learn quickly by observing other children perform a behavior—especially when that child receives reinforcement contingent on the behavior.

There are two distinct types of modeling. The first, *live modeling,* involves the actual or live demonstration of the target behavior while the child is observing. The second form, *symbolic modeling,* involves the presentation of the model either through film, video tape, or imagination. In most of our work with exceptional children, we would probably use live modeling more often than symbolic modeling.

Although modeling is an effective way of teaching children, there are certain preconditions that need to be met for it to be helpful. First, the child should be able to *attend* to the various aspects of the modeling situation. This means, among other implications, that the exceptional child should be able to sit and watch the modeling event over its duration. Second, the child must be able to *retain* what he or she has learned from observing the model. Third, the child should be able to *motorically reproduce* the modeled behavior. Fourth, the child should be *motivated* to perform the target behavior that he or she observed (Bandura 1969; Rimm & Masters 1979). If any of these factors are absent in a child, then the behavior modifier should consider using other behavior modification approaches for strengthening target behaviors. As an alternative, the behavior modifier may want to teach the child some of the behaviors associated with these preconditions. For example, if the child's eye contact is low in frequency, the behavior modifier might want to use the eye contact behavioral prescription in Chapter 6 to strengthen this behavior. If the child has difficulty matching or motorically reproducing what he or she observed, then the behavior modifier could use the imitation learning behavioral prescription in Chapter 6 to strengthen this behavior, too.

RELAXATION TRAINING

No matter how hard some children try, they still find it very difficult to relax their bodies. Teachers, for example, report these children as being "tense," "nervous," "upset," "troubled," "anxious," "uptight," or "uncomfortable." Sometimes, this tenseness in children is associated with fears or phobias, depression, aggressive behavior, compulsive acts, and psychophysiological or psychosomatic complaints or problems (see, for example, Morris & Kratochwill 1983c). A factor in many of these activities is that these children cannot (or do not know how to) relax.

In such cases, we teach the child how to relax his or her body using relaxation training steps like those presented in Table 4.1. These steps represent a modified version of a technique developed by Jacobson (1938) for inducing deep muscle relaxation. The wording of each step should be adapted to each child's developmental level and exceptionality. The whole prescriptive procedure usually takes about 20 to 25 minutes to administer—with each step taking about 10 seconds with a 10- to 15-second pause between each step (Morris & Kratochwill 1983b). During the first few relaxation training sessions, it is often helpful for the behavior modifier to model the steps in the relaxation procedure with the child or children so that they can observe how to correctly reproduce a particular step. The behavior modifier may also want, at first, to physically guide the child in performing the steps, gradually fading out the assistance. Each step presentation should also be geared to the child's ease in performing that step (Morris & Kratochwill 1983b). Relaxation training can take place on an individual basis or in a group setting. In the latter case, the relaxation training should be paced to the slowest child. In all cases, relaxation training should take place in a quiet, sound attenuated, softly lighted area or room. The child or children should be sitting in folding lounge chairs, lying on mats, or lying

TABLE 4.1
Program for teaching relaxation to children

Steps in Relaxation

1. Take a deep breath and hold it (for about 10 seconds). Hold it. Okay, let it out.
2. Raise both of your hands about half way above the chair or mat, and breathe normally. Now, drop your hands down.
3. Now hold your arms out and make a tight fist. Really tight. Feel the tension in your hands. I am going to count to three and when I say "three" I want you to drop your hands. One . . . Two . . . Three.
4. Raise your arms again, and bend your fingers back the other way (toward your body). Now drop your hands and relax.
5. Raise your arms. Now drop them and relax.
6. Now raise your arms again, but this time "flap" your hands around. Okay, relax again.
7. Raise your arms again. Now relax.
8. Raise your arms above the couch (chair) again and tense your biceps until they shake. Breathe normally, and keep your hands loose. Relax your hands. (Notice how you have a warm feeling of relaxation.)
9. Now hold your arms out to your side and tense your biceps. Make sure that you breathe normally. Relax your arms.
10. Now arch your shoulders back. Hold it. Make sure that your arms are relaxed. Now relax.
11. Hunch your shoulders forward. Hold it, and make sure that you breathe normally and keep your arms relaxed. Okay, relax. (Notice the feeling of relief from tensing and relaxing your muscles.)
12. Now turn your head to the right and tense your neck. Relax and bring your head back again to its natural position.
13. Turn your head to the left and tense your neck. Relax and bring your head back again to its natural position.
14. Now bend your head back slightly toward the chair. Hold it. Okay, now bring your head back slowly to its natural position.
15. This time bring your head down almost to your chest. Hold it. Now relax and let your head come back to its natural resting position.
16. Now open your mouth as much as possible. A little wider; okay, relax. (Mouth must be partly open at end.)
17. Now tense your lips by closing your mouth. Okay, relax.
18. Put your tongue at the roof of your mouth. Press hard. (Pause) Relax and allow your tongue to come to a comfortable position in your mouth.
19. Now put your tongue at the bottom of your mouth. Press down hard. Relax and let your tongue come to a comfortable position in your mouth.
20. Now just lie (sit) there and relax. Try not to think of anything.
21. To control self-verbalization, I want you to go through the motions of singing a high note—not aloud! Okay, start singing to yourself. Hold that note, and now hard. Relax. (You are becoming more and more relaxed.)
22. Now sing a medium tone and make your vocal cords tense again. Relax.
23. Now sing a low note and make your vocal cords tense again. Relax (Your vocal apparatus should be relaxed now. Relax your mouth.)
24. Now close your eyes. Squeeze them tight and breathe naturally. Notice the tension. Now relax. (Notice how the pain goes away when you relax.)
25. Now let your eyes relax and keep your mouth open slightly.
26. Open your eyes as much as possible. Hold it. Now relax your eyes.
27. Now wrinkle your forehead as much as possible. Hold it. Okay, relax.
28. Now take a deep breath and hold it. Relax.

TABLE 4.1 (continued)

29. Now exhale. Breathe all the air out . . . all of it out. Relax. (Notice the wondrous feeling of breathing again.)
30. Imagine that there are weights pulling on all your muscles making them flaccid and relaxed . . . pulling your arms and body into the couch.
31. Pull your stomach muscles together. Tighter. Okay, relax.
32. Now extend your muscles as if you were a prize fighter. Make your stomach hard. Relax. (You are becoming more and more relaxed.)
33. Now tense your buttocks. Tighter. Hold it. Now relax.
34. Now search the upper part of your body and relax any part that is tense. First the facial muscles (Pause 3 to 5 seconds) Then the vocal muscles. (Pause 3 to 5 seconds) The neck region. (Pause 3 to 5 seconds) Your shoulder . . . relax any part which is tense (Pause) Now the arms and fingers. Relax these. Becoming very relaxed.
35. Maintaining this relaxation, raise both of your legs (about a 45° angle). Now relax. (Notice that this further relaxes you.)
36. Now bend your feet back so that your toes point toward your face. Relax your mouth. Bend them hard. Relax.
37. Bend your feet the other way . . . away from your body. Not far. Notice the tension. Okay, relax.
38. Relax. (Pause) Now curl your toes together as hard as you can. Tighter. Okay, relax. (Quiet . . . silence for about 30 seconds.)
39. This completes the formal relaxation procedure. Now explore your body from your feet up. Make sure that every muscle is relaxed. (Say slowly)—first your toes, your feet, your legs, buttocks, stomach, shoulder, neck, eyes, and finally your forehead—all should be relaxed now. (Quiet—silence for about 10 seconds). Just lie there and feel very relaxed, noticing the warmness of the relaxation. (Pause) I would like you to stay this way for about one more minute, and then I am going to count to five. When I reach five, I want you to open your eyes feeling very calm and refreshed. (Quiet—silence for about one minute.) Okay, when I count to five I want you to open your eyes feeling very calm and refreshed. One . . . feeling very calm; two . . . very calm, very refreshed; three . . . very refreshed; Four . . . and Five.

Source: Adapted in part from Jacobson (1938), Rimm (1967 personal communication), and Wolpe and Lazarus (1966); reprinted from R. J. Morris and T. R. Kratochwill, *Treating Children's Fears and Phobias: A Behavioral Approach.* New York: Pergamon Press, 1983, 135–36.

on pillows—they should not be sitting in desk chairs. Taking the child's developmental and emotional level into consideration, the behavior modifier might say or adapt the following:

> *I am going to teach you how to become very relaxed. In doing this, I am going to ask you to tense up and relax . . . sets of muscles. . . . That is, I am going to ask you to tense up and relax different sets of muscles so that there is a [warm and soothing] effect of relaxation over your whole body.* (Pause) *Okay, now I would like you to. . . . (Morris & Kratochwill 1983b, pp. 133–34).*

Although this training has been found to increase the level of relaxation in children, the reader should note that some children cannot relax using this training method. No matter how motivated they are, they find it difficult to respond—or find the training instructions too complex to comprehend or carry-out. One way of resolving this problem is to adapt the instructions further. A second way, suggested by Cautela and Groden (1978), would be to use shaping to assist children in learning how to tense and then relax particular muscle groupings. They also suggest using various squeeze toys to help teach these children to tense and then relax their muscles, and suggest the use of certain air flow toys (whistle, harmonica, bubble pipe, etc.) to teach the breathing steps portion of the relaxation training prescription.

SELF-CONTROL

Self-control is a procedure in which the child becomes the primary agent in directing and controlling his or her behavior in order to lead to preplanned and specific behavior changes and/or consequences (Gold-fried & Merbaum 1973; Hallahan, Lloyd, Kauffman & Loper 1983; Kanfer 1980; Karoly & Kanfer 1982; Richards & Siegel 1978). It has only been since the mid to late 1970s that self-control has contributed substantially to our work with exceptional children (see, for example, reviews by Hallahan et al. 1983; Kendall & Hollon 1979; Litrownik 1982; Shapiro 1980).

Self-control actually encompasses numerous intervention methods, each having as its common base (1) the recognition of the contribution of cognitive processes to behavior change, and (2) the view that individuals can regulate their own behavior. A third common base involves the presence of a behavior modifier "to instigate or motivate" the child to begin a behavior program, and to teach him or her how, when, and where to use it (Kanfer 1980).

The essence of the self-control approach involves (1) having the child discuss with the behavior modifier and be aware of the negative thinking styles that may be preventing him or her from working effectively or lead him or her to becoming emotionally upset, (2) developing with the child specific self-statements, rules, or strategies that the child can use to carry out his or her activities or tasks successfully, and (3) providing the child with reinforcement and feedback for his or her use of self-control and performance of the target behavior (e.g., Meichenbaum & Gerest 1980). On the basis of this general approach, a target behavior or task or activity is identified and a self-control training sequence is developed.

Self-Control Training Sequence

1. The trainer performs the task while asking questions aloud about the task, giving self-guiding instruction, and making self-evaluations of performance.

2. The child imitates the trainer's overt self-instruction while doing the task.

3. The trainer performs the task while modeling self-instruction in a whisper.

4. The child imitates the trainer's performance with whispered self-instruction.

5. The trainer models covert self-instruction while performing the task.

6. The child imitates the trainer's performance and covert self-instruction. (Hallahan et al. 1983, p. 119)

Before initiating this sequence, the behavior modifier should make sure that the child has mastered all of the component skills that are necessary for the successful performance of both the target behavior and the self-control strategy. The behavior modifier should also make sure that the child receives reinforcement and feedback when the self-control procedure is used and the target behavior is performed. Last, the program should be continued until the criterion level for success (see Chapter 2) has been achieved.

Self-control represents a potentially very effective approach for changing the behaviors of many exceptional children. The relative effectiveness of this approach, however, is tied not only to the amount and quality of structuring provided by the behavior modifier, but also to the receptiveness and interest or motivational level of the exceptional child in implementing the procedure and, in fact, wanting to change his or her behavior.

STUDY QUESTIONS

1. Choose a child to whom you would like to teach a desirable behavior (perhaps the child you chose on p. 42). Determine whether you want to strengthen a behavior or develop a new behavior. Then develop a treatment using the questions outlined on pp. 67–68.

2. What is *prompting* and why is it used? (Review p. 72 to check your answer.)

3. Write out a SAP procedure for teaching a child to do one of the following: tie shoes, eat with a spoon, put on a T-shirt. Compare your program with the one listed on pp. 139–41, 132–35, or 136–38. (Review pp. 74–79 to check your answer.)

4. List the five important points to remember in developing a new behavior in a child.

a.

b.

c.

d.

e.

(Review pp. 77–78 to check your answer.)

5. What is behavioral chaining and how is it used? (Review pp. 79–83 to check your answer.)

6. How does behavioral chaining differ from a successive approximation procedure? (Review pp. 79–81 to check your answer.)

7. What is contingency contracting and how is it used? (Review pp. 83–85 to check your answer.)

8. How does group reinforcement differ from individual reinforcement procedures? (Review pp. 85–88 to check your answer.)

9. How would one use modeling to teach an imitative child to throw a ball? (Review pp. 88–89 to check your answer.)

10. What are the important preconditions for effective modeling? (Review pp. 88–89 to check your answer.)

11. How would you teach relaxation training to a very tense child? (Review pp. 89–92 to check your answer.)

12. Define self-control. (Review p. 92 to check your answer.)

13. How would you teach self-control to a child who has not mastered multiplication? (Review pp. 92–93 to check your answer.)

Chapter 5

REDUCING UNDESIRABLE BEHAVIORS IN CHILDREN

The use of procedures for reducing undesirable behaviors is described in this chapter. The development of a treatment plan is followed by a discussion of the use of an extinction procedure and the reinforcement of an incompatible desirable behavior. Time out from reinforcement procedures is discussed next, followed by a response cost system, a contact desensitization procedure for reducing children's fears, situational control of children's behavior, an overcorrection procedure, and the use of physical punishment. The chapter ends with a brief discussion of which procedure the behavior modifier should initiate first.

DEVELOPING A TREATMENT PLAN

We have seen repeatedly that an exceptional child's behavior is very much influenced by what happens to the child immediately after he or she performs a particular behavior, and we have learned that when his or her behavior leads to satisfying or reinforcing consequences it will, in most cases, recur the next time the same situation cues or antecedent events are present. Similarly, we find that when a target behavior is followed by dissatisfying or unpleasant consequences, a child's behavior is less likely to recur the next time the same situation cues are present. This can be diagrammed in the following way:

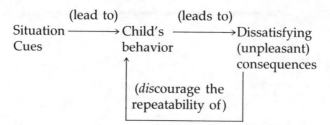

In this chapter, we describe procedures for reducing undesirable behaviors in exceptional children. As in any behavior modification procedure, a behavior program plan must be completely formulated *before* any intervention is started. Listed here is an outline for developing a program plan, which is somewhat similar to the one presented in Chapter 4. It should be used by the behavior modifier to help him or her plan out exactly what will happen when the child shows or does not show the undesirable target behavior.

Outline For Developing A Behavior Program Plan

1.   What is the undesirable target behavior?

2.   What method of observation will be used?

3.   What should be recorded on the behavior chart?

   a.   Circle one:

   Number of times the behavior occurred
   Percent of times the behavior occurred
   Number of minutes the behavior occurred

   b.   Circle one:
   Days (target behavior recorded on a daily basis during days child is in resource room or on program days)

   Sessions (target behavior recorded in individual training sessions or class periods)
   Hours (target behavior recorded during specific times or blocks of hours during the day)
   Weeks (target behavior recorded weekly)
   Months (target behavior recorded monthly)

4.   How long will the baseline period be?

5.   What will be the criterion for success?

6.   What *specifically* will be done when the target child makes an undesirable response?

7.   What *specifically* will be done when the target child makes a desirable response?

8. After the criterion for success is achieved by the child, will it be necessary to fade out the behavior program? If so, how will this be accomplished?

9. Will there be a follow-up observation period to determine if the child has maintained the criterion for successful behavior change? If so, when specifically will the follow-up period(s) take place?

10. Does the child need to learn to transfer the reduction in the target behavior to other settings? If so, is transfer training being planned? If not, what are the reasons transfer training is not being planned? If transfer or generalization is planned, what *specifically* will be done to accomplish this, and when will it begin?

11. Have the use of reinforcement methods, self-control, or other positive procedures been *thoroughly examined and/or tried* before the implementation of the planned behavior reduction program? If so, which reinforcement or other procedures have *not* been found to be successful in reducing the undesirable target behavior?

12. Is the program plan proposed in Question 6 the *least restrictive* behavior reduction program that can possibly be proposed at the present time? If not, specify which other less restrictive procedure has been used, and specify the reasons a more restrictive procedure is being proposed at the present time.

13. Any additional comments about the behavior program?

Questions 4 through 9 define what the behavior program plan will be. The behavior modifier should be able to answer each of these questions based on material presented in previous chapters and from information contained in this chapter. Question 5 requires a rather subjective answer—determined by the needs, expectations, and desires of the behavior modifier, the child's family and peers, and/or society.

Question 8, as we discussed in Chapter 4, relates to how one terminates a behavior program. In many cases, when our goal is to reduce the frequency of occurrence of a target behavior to zero or an "acceptable level," the program can just be withdrawn when the criterion for success is met. In those cases, however, when a reinforcement method is used concurrently with the behavior reduction method, to strengthen one or more behaviors other than the behavior targeted for reduction, then a plan is needed to show how the complete behavior program will be faded out. Another factor to consider when withdrawing a behavior reduction program is that it is quite conceivable that a positive relationship developed between the child and the behavior modifier during the tenure of the behavior modification program (see, for example, Goldfried & Davison 1976; Goldstein 1980; Morris & Magrath 1983). Not only is the particular intervention program being withdrawn when the child reaches criterion, but a positive relationship is also being withdrawn. Abruptly terminating the relationship could possibly lead to negative side effects. The child could, for example, become disruptive or increase the frequency of the very behavior that was successfully changed. The general rule, therefore, is to ask oneself the question "If I stop this program completely when [child's name] reaches criterion, what effect will this have on the frequency of occurrence of the child's target behavior or any other aggressive, disruptive, or inappropriate behavior that the child might show?" If the answer suggests that there might be an effect on the child's behavior(s), then the program and/or the behavior modifier's relationship with the child should be faded out gradually.

Question 9 relates to the same comments made in Chapter 4, namely, the "success" of a behavior modification program can be determined at many points. What the behavior modifier needs to determine is whether the success of a program includes follow-up, i.e., whether the behavior modifier and the colleagues involved in providing services to the child feel that it is important to know whether the child maintains the behavior reduction over time.

The topic area covered in Question 10 regarding the transfer of training or generalization will be discussed later in this book (Chapter 7). Suffice it to mention at this point, however, that this question covers a very important issue (Ollendick & Cerny 1981; Smith 1981). For example, let us suppose that a child is noncompliant in class, on the playground, and at home. Her teacher decides to develop a behavior reduction program for one aspect of her noncompliant behavior—specifically, teaching her how to follow instructions in class the first time they are given by the teacher or aide at least 90% of the time. She works with the child on the program and finds within seven weeks she has met the success criterion. The teacher learns, however, that the child is still noncompliant at home and on the school playground. The question that arises then is should the teacher transfer the program to the other settings. This question is not an easy one to resolve, and the best approach is to have all the people involved in providing services to the child decide if the behavior reduced in the classroom should be transferred to the other settings—and whether the behavior program used by the teacher is appropriate for these other settings.

Questions 11 and 12 relate to the area of ethical and legal issues in the use of behavior modification with exceptional children. This topic is discussed later in Chapter 8. What is important to mention now, however, is that over the past ten to fifteen years a movement has developed in behavior modification that has focused on ethical approaches regarding the use of behavior modification procedures. The movement began, in part, as a reaction against the use of certain behavior reduction programs (e.g., physical punishment) with some severely mentally retarded and autistic children and some psychotic adults (see, for example, Bragg & Wagner 1968; Lucero, Vail & Sherber 1968; Miron 1968, 1970). What has emerged from this literature on ethical issues related to the use of behavior modification techniques is the position that *reinforcement and other positive behavior change procedures should always be emphasized in the modification of undesirable or maladaptive behaviors*. This means (1) that reinforcement and/or other positive behavior modification procedures should *first* be used in the control of an undesirable behavior before proceeding to the use of behavior reduction methods and (2) that reinforcement for desirable behaviors should *always* accompany the use of behavior reduction procedures. Thus, reinforcement and other positive behavioral procedures, not behavior reduction methods, constitute the major application of behavior modification (e.g., Kazdin 1980; May, Risley, Twardosz, Friedman, Bijou & Wexler 1975; Morris & Brown 1983; Ollendick & Cerny 1981). The behavior reduction methods discussed in this chapter should therefore, for the most part, be used only after reinforcement and the other positive behavior change procedures discussed in Chapters 3 and 4 have been tried and found to be unsuccessful.

Question 12 in the above behavior program plan outline refers to the types of behavior reduction methods that should be used first. As a general guide *the behavior modifier should always use the least restrictive behavior modification procedure that is available*. Only after the least restrictive procedure has been found to be ineffective should the behavior modifier then consider using more restrictive behavior reduction methods (see, for example, May et al. 1975). This topic is discussed further in Chapter 8 with a guide to procedures that vary in the level of restrictiveness.

Once the behavior program plan is established, the behavior modifier is ready to begin intervention.

THE USE OF EXTINCTION

Children tend to perform certain undesirable behaviors because they are (or have been) reinforced for performing them. Thus, just as it is possible to strengthen a desirable behavior by reinforcing the child each time the behavior occurs, it is also possible to reduce an undesirable behavior by making certain that the behavior modifier does not reinforce the child when he or she performs the target behavior. *Extinction refers to the removal of those reinforcing consequences which normally follow a particular behavior* (e.g., Kanfer & Phillips 1970; Skinner 1953).

In order to use this procedure, the behavior modifier *must* be in a position to do the following:

1. Identify those consequences that are reinforcing or maintaining the child's undesirable behavior

2. Determine whether those consequences will follow the child's behavior

3. Control the occurrence of the reinforcement

4. Be consistent in the use of the procedure each time the behavior occurs—not varying the application of the procedure at any time (see, for example, Azrin & Holz 1966; Kazdin 1980; Reynolds 1968).

If these conditions cannot be met, then another behavior reduction procedure should be considered for possible use. For example, in a classroom setting a teacher may know very well that his or her negative attention ("Please stop doing that," "It's hard for me to continue when you act that way," "Let's wait for Danny to stop talking," etc.) is what is maintaining or reinforcing a child's loud outbursts in class. The teacher, however, may be unable to say for sure that he or she will not ignore the child's undesirable behavior each and every time it occurs during the entire school day. Other behaviors that teachers may not be able to ignore—even though they may be maintained by teacher attention—are self-injurious behavior, property destruction, physical assaults on other children, stealing, and inappropriate sexual activities.

To understand what could possibly be reinforcing the child's behavior, the behavior modifier should apply the observational approach discussed in Chapter 2 for the identification of situation cues and consequences. For example, the behavior modifier should try to determine what happens both immediately before and after the undesirable behavior occurs. One of the most common reinforcing consequences for a child's undesirable behavior is the adult (or peer) attention that the child receives.

After the behavior modifier determines what is reinforcing the target behavior, the behavior modifier should make sure that the child will not receive this reinforcer when he or she performs the behavior. In addition, the behavior modifier should not expect the child's behavior to decrease immediately when the extinction procedure is first introduced—in fact, we should first expect an increase in the occurrence of the undesirable behavior before we begin to notice a decrease (e.g., Kelleher 1966). Each of us knows this to be true from our own life experiences. For example, if one walks into one's kitchen at night and turns the light switch to *on*, but does not receive reinforcement by having the light go on, the person's first reaction would be to flip the switch from *on* to *off* to *on* to *off* to *on* repeatedly until he or she was "sure" the light would not go on. The person then might stop flipping the switch (behavior is on extinction) and go and find a new light bulb—

or call an electrician. Here, the person's reaction—as is the case with children—was first to increase the occurrence of the flipping-the-switch behavior and then decrease it because reinforcement did not follow. The following case example illustrates the use of extinction with a three-and-a-half-year-old autistic child named Phil.

> *Phil has recently begun to cry loudly and scream whenever his mother puts him to sleep at his regular bedtime. His mother paid little attention to his crying, believing that he would stop eventually. During the first few evenings, she was right. He stopped crying and screaming after about 15 minutes, and then she looked in on him to make sure he was all right.*
>
> *Toward the end of the week, however, he did not stop crying after 15 minutes, so she decided to enter his room to make sure he was safe. He stopped crying as soon as she opened the door, and began crying after she closed the door. Twenty minutes later he was still crying, so she went back into his room, picked him up, and tried to comfort him for a few minutes.*
>
> *As soon as Phil quieted down, she placed him back in his bed and left the room. He began crying again—finally going to sleep 2½ hours later. This pattern of crying followed by mother's intervention continued for five more days until the mother sought help from her pediatrician who, in turn, referred her to a university clinic.*
>
> *The psychologist at the clinic sent an observer into the home to determine objectively what happened between mother and child at the child's bedtime. The mother and father were asked to "do what you normally do" for the next three nights and not change the normal routine. The mother was also asked to record how many minutes it took Phil to fall asleep (or stop crying for 45 consecutive minutes) after putting him to bed. Over the three-night period, Phill fell asleep (or stopped crying for 45 minutes) after an average of 165 minutes.*
>
> *For the fourth night, Mrs. Barker was told to resist any temptation to enter Phil's room while he was crying unless she was sure he had injured himself. She was also told to remove any toys or objects from his room which could possibly injure him if he became very angry at night. Mrs. Barker followed these instructions, although very hesitantly.*
>
> *The first night Phil cried and screamed for almost five hours—stopping, at times, for about 10 to 15 minutes—before he finally fell asleep. When she was sure he was asleep, she went into his room and was glad to see everything was all right. The second night Phil cried for three hours, and by the eighth night he cried for only 15 minutes. Within two weeks, he no longer cried or screamed before going to sleep. A chart of Phil's progress appears in Figure 5.1.*
>
> *The Barkers were pleased that Phil could now fall asleep without any "fuss." Mrs. Barker was happy to know that she could now put him to bed, spend more time with him before he fell asleep, and not be afraid that he was going to start crying once she left the room.*

FIGURE 5.1
Chart showing the reduction in Phil's crying in bed using an extinction pro-
cedure

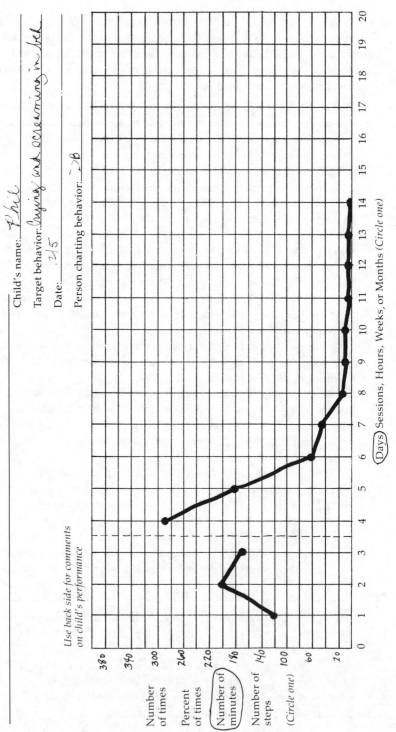

Extinction is an effective procedure for reducing various undesirable behaviors, but its use is very limited (e.g., Kazdin 1980; Repp 1983; Smith 1981). As mentioned earlier, it should only be used when the behavior modifier is able to (1) identify specifically what is reinforcing the child, (2) be certain that the reinforcer follows the target behavior, (3) control the occurrence and nonoccurrence of the reinforcement, and (4) be consistent in the application of the procedure. It should be pointed out here that meeting these conditions is not necessarily easy. For example, a teacher may feel that he or she has identified the consequences (reinforcement) for a student banging on his desk with his textbook each time at the beginning of class when he goes to sit down—the consequences being the teacher showing a startled reaction and looking up at the student. But, in fact, the consequence for the student was that he liked hearing the reverberating noise that came from inside his desk each time he banged it with his book.

REINFORCING INCOMPATIBLE DESIRABLE BEHAVIORS

We often find that for every undesirable behavior a child demonstrates, there is a directly opposite or more appropriate desirable behavior that could take its place. For example, isolate play can be replaced by interactive or cooperative play, out-of-seat running can be replaced by in-seat sitting, thumbsucking can be replaced by having the child do other activities with his or her hands, repeated loud bursts of screaming or "strange" noises can be replaced by long periods of quiet, and spilling food at the table can be replaced by careful handling of food. Thus, *we can reduce some undesirable behaviors by reinforcing the child for performing behaviors that are incompatible with (or prevent the occurrence of) the undesirable behaviors.*

In using this procedure, we are not just extinguishing one undesirable behavior and reinforcing another desirable behavior; rather we are teaching the child to perform a behavior that is incompatible with his or her performance of the undesirable behavior (e.g., Repp 1983; Smith & Snell 1978; Smith 1981). A child cannot mumble and talk clearly at the same time, run around in the classroom and sit in his seat at the same time, slap her face with both hands and hold a teddy bear with both hands at the same time, and so forth. The successful use of this procedure, therefore, depends on (1) how adept the behavior modifier is in identifying a behavior that is incompatible with the undesirable behavior and (2) whether the behavior modifier can find a reinforcer that is powerful (and attractive) enough to outweigh the positive factors associated with the child's performance of the undesirable behavior. Obviously, as the frequency of desirable behavior increases, the frequency of undesirable behavior decreases.

The following examples illustrate the use of this procedure.

Sarah is a sixteen-year-old mildly mentally retarded girl who is in a self-contained classroom. The goal was to decrease the frequency of her not following her teacher's instructions or directions in class, and to increase the frequency of her following her teacher's instructions or directions within 15 seconds of the time that they were given. Using a stopwatch, her teacher took a baseline for one week on the number of seconds it took Sarah to follow her teacher's instructions or directions. The data showed that it took an average of 35 seconds for her to respond.

Sarah's teacher developed a reinforcement program where he gave Sarah a "happy face" sticker for her sticker book each time she responded within 15 seconds. At the end of the day, Sarah was then allowed to take the sticker book home to show her parents, who praised her for her good work at school. Sarah received no attention from her teacher when she responded after the 15 second period. Her teacher just ignored her. Within eight days from the beginning of this intervention, Sarah's average response time decreased to below 15 seconds.

In the next example, reinforcement of incompatible behavior is used with a highly verbal, hyperactive five-year-old child.

Bill was brought to the clinic by his parents, who reported that for the last six months he had been "virtually uncontrollable" in the home. He climbed on furniture and on guests who came into the home, did not sit still at the dinner table, spilled food, "constantly" ran in and out the back door, and did not fall asleep until late in the evening.

Mr. and Mrs. Thomas were asked to choose one particular situation that was especially annoying to them and that they would like to deal with first. They chose Bill's behavior at mealtime. Specifically, the target behavior was sitting at the dinner table kicking the legs of the chair or moving from side to side in the chair.

The Thomases were asked to observe Bill for five days at each dinner meal and to record separately with a stopwatch the number of minutes he spent performing the target behavior. They discovered that on the average he spent about 15 minutes moving around in his chair and kicking it during a 20-minute meal.

They were next asked to choose a reinforcer that was very attractive to Bill and to give bits of this reward to him after he sat quietly for 20 seconds (sitting quietly is incompatible with kicking the chair legs and moving around in the chair). This was to occur for the next three days.

The Thomases returned on the fourth day and reported that Bill's undesirable behavior had begun to decrease—although he was still moving around for, on the average, about 12 minutes. They were then instructed to continue the procedure for another four meals. Upon their return, they said that he was now down to about 8 minutes per meal. They were then told to vary the use of his favorite rewards (various sweet desserts) and to increase the sitting quiet time interval to 40 seconds for the next seven days.

Bill seemed to adjust easily to this new schedule and the different rewards. Within five days he was sitting quietly at the dinner table for 15 minutes, and by the end of the week he was quiet for almost 17 minutes. His behavior at the table continued to improve, and at the end of three and half weeks he was sitting still for practically the whole meal (19 minutes). His parents had also begun to withdraw gradually the use of his favorite desserts and, instead, to praise him for behaving so quietly.

As can be seen from these examples, the most favorable aspect of this procedure (especially when one compares it to some of the other procedures described in this chapter) is that the behavior modifier is strengthening a desirable (adaptive) behavior while reducing an undesirable behavior.

TIME OUT FROM REINFORCEMENT

A very effective way of reducing a child's undesirable behavior involves removing the child from an attractive and reinforcing situation (or withdrawing a reinforcing activity or event from the child for a certain time period *immediately following* the child's performance of the target behavior. This procedure is called *time out from reinforcement*, or just *time out* (e.g., Ferster 1957; Kanfer & Phillips 1970). Each time the child shows the undesirable behavior, we take the child out of the reinforcing situation and place the child in a situation where, presumably, his or her undesirable behavior will not be reinforced (e.g., Ollendick & Cerny 1981).

The type of situation in which the child is placed is very important. If, for example, the child performs the target behavior and the behavior modifier sends the child to another room away from where the behavior occurred, the behavior modifier may think that this is sufficient. But the other room may contain many interesting toys, books, and magazines, a radio or record player, and so forth that the child can listen to, read or play with; the probability, therefore, that removal to this room will have any effect on the child's undesirable behavior is quite low. The situation or area to which the child is sent should be, whenever possible, devoid of interesting and distracting objects (as well as potentially dangerous objects) and should be far enough away from the reinforcing situation so that the child cannot hear or see what is going on. *The time out area, therefore, must have many fewer positive aspects associated with it than the reinforcing area.* If a time out area is not readily available, the behavior modifier can place the child in a chair (facing the wall) in a remote corner or section of a classroom, living room, kitchen, dormitory room, dayroom, and so forth. Or, the behavior modifier can construct or purchase a "portable" time out room such as the one described in Appendix F or construct a partition or screen that can be placed in a corner to section off the area.

There are three types of time out procedures with each involving the removal of the child from the reinforcing situation (see, for example, Bijou & Baer 1979; Kazdin 1980; Repp 1983; Ross 1981; Smith 1981; Whitman, Scibak, & Reid 1983). The first procedure is called *contingent observation*, where the child who shows the undesirable behavior is instructed to step away from the reinforcing situation (e.g., free play, class activity, athletic event, etc.) for a specified period of time, and to sit in a chair or stand in the area away from the reinforcing situation and watch the other children as they behave in an appropriate manner. During this period of time, the behavior modifier interacts with and reinforces the other children in the group who are showing the types of desirable behavior that the behavior modifier would like to see the target child engage in. The child then rejoins the group or activity after the specified period has elapsed. A second time out procedure is called *exclusion time out*, where the child is removed from a reinforcing situation and placed in a situation that has a lower reinforcement value (or, is less attractive than the reinforcing situation) each time the child performs the undesirable behavior. This exclusion procedure does not involve taking the child out of his or her immediate environment (i.e., placing the child in a vacant room); rather, the behavior modifier removes the child from the reinforcing activity or event and places the child, for example, in a corner on a chair and facing the wall, on a chair behind a screen or partition, or on a chair with his or her back to the group.

A third time out procedure is called *seclusion time out*. This is the most restrictive of the three procedures and involves removing the child from a reinforcing situation and placing him or her in a supervised isolation area (e.g., vacant room, cubicle, etc.) that is separate from the reinforcing situation. The room in which the child is placed must be well ventilated, well lighted, and not locked (e.g., Accreditation Council for Services for Mentally Retarded and Other Developmentally Delayed Persons 1978), and the child must be monitored on a regular basis to make sure that no dangerous conditions exist. As a general rule, seclusion time out should not be used unless (1) the setting from where the child was removed has been shown to be reinforcing, attractive, and or satisfying to the child, and (2) the setting in which the child is secluded has been found to be unattractive, dissatisfying, and unpleasant for him or her.

A child should be allowed to return to the reinforcing situation as soon as the undesirable behavior has stopped or within a few minutes (usually 3 to 10 minutes). There are some instances—for example, where a child becomes physically assaultive—that the child might have to be placed in a time out area for a longer time. If this is the case, then the child should be monitored or checked every 10 minutes to make sure the child is safe. As a general rule, however, no child should be permitted to stay in the time out area for an extended period of time and, under *no* conditions is it advisable for a child to stay in any time out area for longer than 60 minutes (see, for example, Accreditation Council for Services for Mentally Retarded and Other Developmentally Delayed Persons 1978).

When the child is brought to the time out area, the behavior modifier should carry out this activity matter-of-factly with as little verbal, emotional, and physical interaction as possible. Similarly, while the child is brought back to the reinforcing situation, the behavior modifier should make every effort to interact with him or her only in a matter-of-fact fashion. Then, when they are back in the reinforcing situation, the behavior modifier should respond to the child in his or her normal way. Whenever possible, the behavior modifier should reinforce the child for behaving in a desirable way when the child is in the reinforcing situation. *Children learn to reduce their undesirable behavior more readily when they observe that satisfying consequences follow some of their behaviors and dissatisfying consequences follow other behaviors.*

The following case example illustrates the use of seclusion time out.

Darby is an eight-year-old moderately retarded girl who is verbal, interactive, and overweight. She enjoys her special education class and looks forward to going to school each day. One of Darby's main problems in school is that she hits other students and occasionally pinches them. Her teacher had tried in vain to change Darby's behavior, using many different positive behavior change procedures. She then decided to use a time out procedure.

The teacher observed Darby for a five-day baseline period and counted the number of times she hit or pinched another student. The teacher then told Darby that she would lose the privilege of staying in the classroom whenever she hit or pinched another student. Within 10 minutes, Darby hit another student while they were painting. The teacher went to Darby, told her, "You do not hit people!" took her hand, and brought her outside the classroom and into an adjacent small vacant room which had only two chairs in it. Darby started crying just as her teacher left the room.

Five minutes later, the teacher returned to the room and said, "You can come out now," and accompanied Darby back to the classroom. Once back in the classroom, the teacher made it a point to praise Darby for acting appropriately with other students. The time out procedure was continued over a five-week period until Darby's undesirable behavior was no longer a problem. During this five-week period, the teacher also praised Darby whenever she saw her playing with other students and not hitting or pinching them.

Another time out procedure, called *withdrawal of reinforcement,* does not require the behavior modifier to remove the child from the reinforcing situation. Instead, the behavior modifier removes what is reinforcing to the child. For example, if a child hits his or her face in a self-injurious manner and also enjoys physical stimulation and contact by the behavior modifier, the behavior modifier could use the withdrawal of stimulation and contact each time the child hits himself or herself (e.g., Tate & Baroff 1966). The withdrawal of contact with the reinforcing situation, as well as its presence during periods without hitting, will help the child learn which behavior will produce dissatisfying consequences and which behaviors will lead to continued satisfying consequences.

The reinforcing situation should be returned to the child when the target behavior (e.g., self-injurious behavior, tantrum, hitting, loud outbursts, screaming) stops, or within 3 to 10 minutes. Moreover, the reinforcing situation should be returned in the same matter-of-fact manner in which it was withdrawn. Once the reinforcement is back, however, the behavior modifier should again respond to the child in his or her normal way and praise the child for continuing to perform desirable alternative behaviors.

It is important to remember that a time out procedure should

- Only be used when the environment or setting from which the child is removed is very reinforcing to the child

- Be administered in a matter-of-fact way immediately following the occurrence of the undesirable behavior

- Not be used indiscriminately by the behavior modifier for any undesirable behavior—only for the target behavior

- Not be used for purposes of detention or to provide the child with a quiet area where he or she can "calm down"

- Be applied consistently each time

- Not be continued if there is no noticeable reduction in the occurrence of the target behavior over a three- to five-week period

- Not be used if actual physical force is needed to carry out the procedure, if the child becomes combative easily, or he or she expresses a desire or interest in being in the time out area

RESPONSE COST

Many behavior modifiers find that once a token economy system is established with a child or group of children, a procedure is "built into" the system for reducing undesirable behaviors. This procedure is called *response cost* (e.g., Kazdin 1977). Specifically, by placing a price on the occurrence of an undesirable behavior we find a reduction in the frequency of that behavior.

The system that we use is very much like the economic and legal sanctions that adults live under in most Western cultures. For example, if a person is caught by the police speeding on an expressway, the person will likely be fined (i.e., some of the offender's income will be taken away by society) and, in some states in the U.S., a certain number of points will either be charged against or taken away from the offender. This is also what happens in a response cost behavior reduction program, i.e., the child is typically charged points or tokens or receives a salary cut for performing certain undesirable behaviors. Specifically, *response cost consists of the removal or withdrawal of a particular quantity of tokens (reinforcers) from a child each time he or she engages in an undesirable target behavior.*

In most cases, a response cost system is added to an existing token economy program in order to reduce the frequency of target behaviors that have not been decreased successfully using reinforcement-based procedures (e.g., differential reinforcement of other behaviors; reinforcement of incompatible behaviors). A response cost procedure, therefore, should only be added to a token economy program after the behavior modifier has determined that more positive approaches have been ineffective in reducing the frequency of the child's undesirable behavior.

The following case example illustrates the application of this procedure.

> *Sharon is a ten-year-old educable mentally handicapped girl who attends public school and is mainstreamed approximately 75% of the school day. Although she is quite well behaved at school, her parents report that she is a "behavior problem" at home. Their success with stopping her hitting of her younger brother and her negativism ("No!" "I won't do that!") has been minimal.*
>
> *After consulting the school psychologist and her special education resource teacher, they initiated a token economy system in the home for Sharon for about one month (they decided not to include Bobby, their younger son, since they felt he was too young for such a program). Sharon received tokens for various activities and exchanged tokens for various*

"rewards and things." After about one month, Sharon was also charged tokens each time she hit Bobby (10 tokens) and each time she talked back to her parents in a negative way (1 to 5 tokens, depending on the severity of her negativism).

Sharon liked "being paid" for doing various activities around the house and being able to exchange the tokens for different foods and other items. She did object, however, to being charged for "doing bad things," although she admitted that she would not like these "things" done to her. The token system was arranged so that the extent of Sharon's undesirable behavior during the day was reflected in how many tokens she had left at the end of the day. On those days that Sharon behaved especially badly, she would not have any tokens left at the end of the day; on those days that she showed a few undesirable behaviors, she would end up with a few tokens to spend; and, on those days when she was especially well behaved, she had many tokens to spend.

Sharon's undesirable behavior decreased to a minimal level within five weeks, although there were still occasional outbursts toward her parents. Her parents decided to keep the system going in the house and modify it as her undesirable behavior decreased even more.

A procedure similar to the one presented in this case example could be established within a classroom setting for a child or children showing such behaviors as: spitting, cussing, hitting, shoving, pushing, screaming, and so forth (Kazdin 1977). The critical factor in establishing a response cost program is the pricing of the undesirable behaviors. As in the case of token economy systems, we do not want our prices to be too low (and, possibly, not deter a child from engaging in the target behavior) or too high (resulting, perhaps, in the child not having any tokens remaining at the end of the day).

As a general rule, a child who is on a response cost program should be able to have a few tokens left at the end of the day, even though the child showed the undesirable target behavior(s) on that day. This behavior reduction program should not be used as a punitive procedure. It is an educational/therapeutic procedure and, as such, should have positive features associated with it. Once the child has zero tokens left—and does not have the opportunity to earn more on that day—the behavior modifier cannot establish a deficit or negative economic system, i.e., the child can *not* owe tokens or be charged tokens that he or she does not have. If the situation arises where the child has zero tokens left and engages in the undesirable behavior without being charged, this indicates that there is something wrong with the economic system that was established—and it should be changed immediately. If the child's behavior does not decrease in frequency over a three to six week period with the response cost procedure, then another behavior modification procedure should be used.

Since the effectiveness of this procedure is related, in part, to the ratio of tokens earned for desirable behavior to tokens lost for undesirable behavior, the behavior modifier should critically evalute the program on a weekly basis. Specifically, the behavior modifier should make sure that the number of tokens charged for reinforcers is consistent with the number of tokens earned as well as with the number of tokens removed for undesirable behavior. In this regard, the Point System Summary Chart in Appendix C may be of assistance to the reader in keeping track of how well the system is working.

A response cost procedure is obviously not for every child who is on a token economy system. The child should be verbal and capable of understanding *why* certain behaviors lead to the receipt of tokens and other behaviors lead to the taking away of tokens. Finally, this procedure should not be instituted until the normal token system is well established, and the behavior modifier should make sure that the child does not regard the whole token system as unpleasant—whether the child receives tokens for desirable behavior or has tokens taken away.

CONTACT DESENSITIZATION FOR FEARS

Fear is a very strong emotion and is associated with many signs of anxiety—for example, rapid pulse rate, tense muscles, irritability, and "butterflies" in the stomach (Morris & Kratochwill 1983b). When a child experiences fear in a situation where there is no obvious danger, his or her fear is irrational. When the child begins to avoid a nondangerous feared situation, the child's fear then becomes a *fear reaction* (or phobic reaction).

Fear reactions are very common in children. Some are so common that we often view them as "normal" (e.g., fear of dogs and other animals, the dark, ghosts, bugs). Some fear reactions are fleeting, while others persist over time. When a child's fear becomes intolerable, however, or prevents him or her from carrying out normal, everyday activities at school or home or from visiting nondangerous places, then reducing the child's fear becomes necessary (Morris & Kratochwill 1983b). Here is a case example of a child whose fear began to interfere with his everyday life activities.

Tommy is a six-year-old boy who has a severe neurological disorder causing his right leg to "give-out" and cause him to fall without warning and to have mild seizures a number of times per month. Medication did not seem to appreciably control these events. Sometimes the ataxia in his legs and his seizure activity occurred at night and at other times during the school day or in the morning before school, causing Tommy to sometimes miss the school bus. He enjoyed school tremendously and often became upset when he missed school.

He often associated getting dressed in the morning with his ataxia and seizures and blamed his missing the bus on his difficulty in getting dressed following and during his falling and seizures. In order to avoid the fear and tension he experienced each morning regarding whether he would be able to be dressed for school and meet his bus, Tommy began going to bed each night with all his clothes on (excluding shoes) for the next morning, i.e., he changed his clothes, bathed, and dressed each evening before bedtime wearing clean clothes for the next day. He slept very still at night in order not to mess up his next day's clothes. In addition, he always made sure that he wore very long soccer socks so that they could fit over his knees. By engaging in these dressing activities at night, Tommy avoided the frustrating and unpleasant situation of possibly experiencing falling and seizures in the morning and then missing the bus because he was not dressed. (Morris & Kratochwill, 1983b, p. 7)

One of the most successful procedures for reducing fears in children is called *contact desensitization* (Ritter 1968). In this procedure, the behavior modifier, through his or her contact with the child, carries out a series of steps to help the child become *desensitized* to the feared object, situation, or event.

The desensitization process is accomplished by gradually exposing the child in small steps to the feared object or situation *after* each step has been modeled first by the behavior modifier. After modeling a step, the behavior modifier helps the child perform that step—touching the child to help guide him or her, encouraging the child with various motivating statements, and praising the child for making progress. The behavior modifier then gradually removes his or her prompts until the child can perform the step alone (Morris & Kratochwill 1983b; Ritter 1968). The behavior modifier should make sure that he or she has established a good, positive relationship with the child, and conveys interest and understanding toward the child, before initiating this procedure.

The desensitization procedure consists of three major components: (1) identification of the target behavior, (2) construction of a graduated hierarchy of steps toward the feared object or situation, and (3) treatment proper (Morris & Kratochwill 1983b).

As is the case with any behavior being modified, the target behavior should be specifically identified by the behavior modifier. A behavior checklist that has been used in identifying fears in children is presented in Appendix B. It is also important for the behavior modifier to identify not only what the child is afraid of, but the situation(s) in which the fear reaction occurs.

After the behavior modifier has identified a child's fear as well as the situations in which it occurs, the next step is to develop a graduated hierarchy. It should be constructed with a great deal of care, and should start with the least fearful step that the child can perform (without any trouble) and proceed gradually to the most fearful step. Here is an example of a hierarchy used with mentally retarded and autistic children who were afraid to go into a swimming pool:[1]

1. Let's begin by walking into the pool room to the white marker (one-quarter of the way to the pool).

2. Walk to the yellow marker on the floor (half of the way).

3. Walk to the red marker on the floor (three-quarters of the way).

4. Walk to the green marker by the edge of the pool.

5. Sit down right there (by the edge of the pool).

6. Let's see you put your feet in the water, while I slowly count to 9. 1 . . . 2 . . . 3

7. . . . 4 . . . 5 . . . 6

8. . . . 7 . . . 8 . . . 9

9. Get up and walk into the water to the red marker and stay there until I count to 6. 1 . . . 2 . . . 3

10. . . . 4 . . . 5 . . . 6

11. Walk to the green marker (halfway down ramp) and stay there until I count to 6. 1 . . . 2 . . . 3

12. . . . 4 . . . 5 . . . 6

13. Walk to the yellow marker (bottom of ramp: 2' 6" deep) and stay there until I count to 9. You can hold onto the edge. 1 . . . 2 . . . 3

14. . . . 4 . . . 5 . . . 6

15. . . . 7 . . . 8 . . . 9

16. Let's see if you can stand there without holding on (only if person held on in previous step).

17. Walk out to the red marker (3' from edge) and then come back to me.

18. Splash some water on yourself; hold on to the edge if you like.

19. Do that without holding on (only if person held on in previous step).

20. Splash some water on your face; you may hold on to the edge if you like.

21. Do that without holding on (only if person held on in previous step).

22. Squat down and blow some bubbles in the water. You can hold on if you like.

23. Blow bubbles without holding on (only if person held on in previous step).

24. Put your whole face in the water. You may hold on if you like.

25. Do that again without holding on (only if person held on in previous step).

26. Put your whole body under water. You can hold on if you like.

27. Do that again without holding on (only if person held on in previous step).

28. Walk out into the water up to your chin (if pool depth permits).

29. Hold onto this kickboard and put your face in the water.

30. Hold onto the kickboard and take one foot off the ground.

31. Hold onto the kickboard and take both feet off the ground.

32. Put your face in the water again and take your feet off the bottom.

33. Let's go down to the deep end of the pool. Sit on the edge and put your feet in the water.

34. O.K. Now climb down the ladder.

35. Now hold onto the edge right here by the green marker.

36. While still holding on, put your whole body under water.

37. Hold onto the kickboard.

38. While still holding on put your face in the water.

39. Do that again, but now put your whole head under water.

40. O.K. Now climb out of the pool and come over to the blue marker. Jump in the water right here (at pool depth of 3'6" or 5' depending on person's height).

Most hierarchies contain twenty to forty items. It is not unusual, however, for those hierarchies that represent a narrowly focused childhood fear to have fewer hierarchy items. Regardless of the number of items, the final hierarchy should represent a slow and smooth gradation of steps (Morris & Kratochwill 1983b).

Following the formation of the hierarchy, the behavior modifier initiates the actual behavior intervention program. The behavior modifier models the first step on the hierarchy and then encourages the child to imitate him or her. The child is then physically guided by the behavior modifier, encouraged, and praised for his or her progress. This procedure is continued for each step on the hierarchy. After the child develops confidence in performing some of the early steps (after he or she has practiced them many times with the behavior modifier's assistance), the behavior modifier can gradually withdraw his or her modeling and guidance, although he or she should continue praising and encouraging the child. The behavior modifier should continue the modeling, guiding, encouraging, and praising on the later steps. A prescriptive program describing this procedure is presented in Chapter 6 (pp. 124-25).

SITUATION CONTROL

In many instances, a behavior modifier is not interested in reducing or eliminating a child's target behavior; rather, the behavior modifier wants to teach the child to perform the behavior *only* in certain situations. This is called *situation (or stimulus) control* (e.g., Skinner 1953). In some situations, therefore, the target behavior is desirable; in others it is undesirable. *The goal of intervention using situation control is to restrict the child's target behavior to those situations in which it is desirable.*

For example, instead of permitting a boy to urinate in his pants in class, we would prefer to teach him where and under what circumstances he should perform this behavior. Specifically, we would want him to be standing in front of a toilet with his pants down before he performed this activity. Similarly, we would not want a girl to disrobe in the middle of the school playground; rather, we would want to teach her, for example, to remove her clothes only in those situations in which her teacher says, "*(Name)*, get undressed and get your gym clothes on." In another instance, it may be appropriate for a child to run and jump in the schoolyard during playtime, but it is not desirable for that child to run and jump in the classroom during math work or social studies workbook time.

To assist the child in learning where and when he or she can and cannot perform the target behavior, we have to help the child discriminate between permissible situations (PERM) and nonpermissible situations (not-PERM). The best way to teach the child is first to make sure that PERM and not-PERM are obviously different. For example, whenever possible the immediate surroundings of PERM should be different from not-PERM. The color of the walls and floor in PERM should be different from not-PERM, the types of activities that usually go on in PERM should be different, and the instructions from the behavior modifier preceding PERM should differ from not-PERM. Finally, if the time of day for PERM can be arranged so that it differs from not-PERM, this would also be advisable.

Next, the behavior modifier should reinforce the child for performing the behavior in PERM and never reinforce him or her for performing the target behavior in not-PERM. The behavior modifier should also make sure that the child does not receive reinforcement from other sources in not-PERM. Alternately, the behavior modifier may want to use in not-PERM one of the other procedures discussed in this chapter. For example, the behavior modifier could use a time out procedure, a response cost program (assuming the child is on a token economy system), or reinforce a behavior that is incompatible with the undesirable behavior. Whichever method is used in not-PERM, the behavior modifier should continue reinforcing the child in PERM.

The next case illustrates the use of a situation control procedure with an autistic child.

Carlos is a sixteen-year-old autistic student who is in a self-contained classroom. The goal was to reduce his spitting in the classroom. Carlos is a very large, athletic, and active young man who often spits in the classroom and outside while pacing or running. Carlos' spitting behavior was not directed toward people, but appeared to be a habit. Carlos' teacher first took a baseline, counting the number of times he spit in the classroom. Baseline data showed that Carlos sometimes spit as many as 14 times a day when in class. His teacher decided that she did not want to completely eliminate Carlos' spitting behavior, since she felt it was socially acceptable for him to spit outside the classroom or while he was exercising outdoors. Thus, her goal was to teach Carlos that it was appropriate to spit outside the classroom (PERM) and that it was inappropriate to spit when in the classroom (not-PERM).

To accomplish this goal, she developed the following plan. First, she made sure that Carlos was reinforced frequently for behaving appropriately in the classroom. For every 10 minutes of remaining on task, attending to task, and following directions, Carlos earned 5 minutes to listen to records.

Immediately following each spitting incident in the classroom, a staff person told Carlos in a firm voice, "No spitting in class." A staff person then escorted Carlos to an area outside the classroom and again told him in a firm voice, "You spit outside." Carlos was then brought back into the classroom and required to clean the area where he had spit. Carlos was then returned to his assigned academic activity, and after working for several minutes without spitting, was praised for working appropriately. When

Carlos was outside on the playground during free time, and a staff person observed him spitting, he was immediately praised. After several weeks of this intervention, Carlos' teacher reported that his spitting in the classroom was completely eliminated. Interestingly, the frequency of his spitting in PERM also decreased, but not to the level of not-PERM.

Before situation control is taught to a child, the behavior modifier should be sure that the child (1) is able to pay attention to the behavior modifier, (2) can at least minimally attend to situational differences between PERM and not-PERM and (3) is able to follow simple commands (e.g., "Come to me"; "Sit down!"). If the child cannot perform all three of these activities, the child should be taught them first. As the child learns to discriminate successfully when and where to perform the target behavior, the behavior modifier—if it seems necessary—can begin gradually to lessen the distinct differences between PERM and not-PERM. The differences, however, should never be made so small that the child again has trouble discriminating between the two types of situations.

OVERCORRECTION

Overcorrection is a relatively new behavior modification procedure that has been used with a variety of handicapped and special needs children. It is a procedure that includes both an educational and a response suppression component (Foxx & Azrin 1972). The method can best be described in the following way:

The general rationale of overcorrection [OC] is (1) to educate the person to accept responsibility for his misbehavior through Restitutional OC procedures that require him to restore the disturbed situation to a vastly improved state and (2) to require the offender to practice appropriate modes of responding through Positive Practice OC procedures that require him to behave appropriately in the situations in which he normally misbehaves (Foxx & Martin 1975, p.153).

Thus, there are two major components of an overcorrection procedure: (1) *restitution*, where the child corrects the environmental effects or impact of his or her problem behavior to a vastly improved state, and (2) *positive practice*, where the child is required to intensely practice appropriate types of behavior in the environmental setting in which he or she showed the behavior problem. For example, if a student knocks down her desk chair in class as she is going out for recess, she might first be instructed to pick up her chair and place it by her desk and then align all of the desk chairs and desks around her desk (restitution) and, second, to practice getting up from her chair and placing the chair back next to her desk and practice walking by her chair and not touching it (positive practice). In those instances where a child's maladaptive behavior or behavior problem does not disrupt aspects of his or her immediate environment—for example, in those cases where the child is engaging in stereotypic behavior or self-injurious behavior—then the positive practice component may only be used (Marholin, Luiselli, & Townsend 1980).

Overcorrection has been used effectively with reducing the occurrence of such target behaviors as stealing, enuresis, encopresis, screaming, vomiting, disrobing, throwing objects, mouthing objects, thumbsucking, hand movements, body rocking, head hitting or banging, noncompliance, and aggressive and disruptive behavior in a variety of settings (e.g., Ferretti & Cavalier 1983; Marholin et al. 1980; Ollendick & Matson 1978).

During the time that the child is engaging in the overcorrection procedure, the behavior modifier should not provide him or her with any praise or other reinforcement. In addition, the child may need to be prompted or receive assistance at first in the carrying-out of the components of the procedure. Such prompting, however, should be faded out as soon as possible. *The overcorrection procedure should be administered in a matter-of-fact manner with minimal prompting by the behavior modifier under conditions where the child does not receive any reinforcement.* Once the procedure has been completed with the child, he or she should return to the regular environment or environmental routine, and the behavior modifier should respond or interact with him or her in the normal manner.

The relative effectiveness of overcorrection depends on a number of factors: (1) the procedure should occur, as in other behavior reduction methods, immediately following the occurrence of the maladaptive behavior, (2) the nature or content of the procedure should be directly related to the type of maladaptive behavior shown by the child, (3) the child should not receive reinforcement during the time of the procedure—setting up a time out situation, and (4) the child should carry out the procedure without pausing (Ferretti & Cavalier 1983). In addition, the behavior modifier should consider two other factors. First, if the child strongly resists engaging in the procedure, and if verbal and/or physical prompting has been found to be ineffective or causes the child to be combative, then a decision must be made as to the appropriateness of the procedure for that child. For example, if actual physical force is needed to have the child carry out the procedure, then the behavior modifier should consider using another behavior reduction procedure. Second, the behavior modifier should decide in advance regarding the feasibility or appropriateness of using this procedure in the particular setting in which they work with the child. For example, a teacher might ask, "Given the constraints on my time and only one aide in my class, can I effectively carry out this procedure?"

Although this procedure has been found to be very effective in reducing a variety of maladaptive behaviors, the reader should note that it is a behavior reduction procedure and, thus, should be used within the same constraints as any other procedure for reducing the frequency of a behavior (see Chapter 8).

THE USE OF PHYSICAL PUNISHMENT

The next procedure is the least preferred by the author and the least recommended. It involves the use of physical punishment. The use of such punishment very often results in unpleasant or unwanted side effects. Some potential side effects are the following:

1. Punishment often suppresses a child's undesirable behavior, but does not change it. Once a child realizes or observes that physical punishment will no longer follow the undesirable behavior, the behavior is likely to recur.

2. Although punishment may reduce or eliminate a particular behavior, other undesirable behaviors may develop.

3. Punishment often produces emotional responses in the child such as unnecessary anxiety and fear responses. These, in turn, could interfere with the child's new learning in, for example, the classroom setting or in interacting positively in social situations.

4. The behavior modifier who administers the punishment may become the recipient of aggression and hostility from the child. This side effect would also influence the nature of the relationship between the behavior modifier and the child—possibly leading the child to become fearful of and also avoid or try to escape from the behavior modifier.

5. A generalization gradient may develop, whereby the child not only avoids performing the undesirable behavior, but also avoids participating in various activities in the punishment situation (or he or she may avoid entering the situation completely).

6. Punishment may have no effect on the child's undesirable behavior, or it may even lead to an increase in the behavior—especially where the child views the attention he or she receives from the behavior modifier as a reinforcement for the undesirable behavior.

7. Through modeling, the child may learn that he or she can also control people by using punishment (or his or her perception of what punishment is). That is, the child may learn to imitate the aggressive behavior or punishing activity of the adult behavior modifier.

It is not clear from the research literature that these or other side effects *always* occur (e.g., Kazdin 1980), and there are some instances where physical punishment (e.g., a painful event like a slap or a loud noise; a squirt of lemon juice in the mouth; a squirt of water on the face) may have to be used since all other procedures have been found to be ineffective. Before the behavior modifier applies this procedure, he or she should consider the following questions:

1. What are the risks involved for the child, for myself, and/or for the school, institution, clinic, or hospital where I work? (If the procedure is used, the behavior modifier should make sure that he or she has the parents' written consent for the use of this procedure and that the institution's, school's, clinic's, or hospital's administration has approved the use of the procedure.

2. Have all other possible procedures been shown to have no or little effect on the child's behavior?

3. Do the potential positive benefits of using the procedure in terms of possible behavior reduction outweigh the possible negative side effects?

4. Is the child's behavior so undesirable that it needs to be changed?

Once these questions are answered, and the decision has been made to use the procedure, the behavior modifier should apply the physical punishment in a *consistent fashion* and *immediately* following the occurrence of the undesirable behavior. The behavior modifier should also make sure that he or she reinforces the child throughout the day for performing various desirable behaviors as well as those behaviors which are incompatible with the undesirable behavior. It is also helpful to pair a preliminary cue (e.g., a neutral mechanical sound, or the verbalization "No") with the punishment within a classical conditioning paradigm. In this way, the behavior modifier may be able to use the cue (or conditioned stimulus) once in a while instead of the physical punishment to reduce the behavior.

WHICH PROCEDURE TO USE?

After reading about each of the procedures described in this chapter, the question that arises for a behavior modifier is, "Which procedure should I use?" The question is not an easy one to answer, but certain guidelines can be provided. *Whenever possible, a behavior modifier should first use the most positive procedure.* In this regard, the first choice would be the use of the reinforcement of incompatible behavior procedure. This is clearly the most preferred procedure. Instead of this method, the therapist could initiate an extinction procedure, but this is not recommended when there is an obvious incompatible behavior available that can be taught to the child. The behavior modifier, however, could combine the use of extinction and a DRO reinforcement procedure. If neither of these procedures is effective in reducing the exceptional child's behavior, and a token economy system has been established, then the behavior modifier could use the response cost procedure. A time out procedure or over correction could also be initiated. Physical punishment should be used only after all previous procedures have been used unsuccessfully, and only after the various questions listed previously regarding punishment have been carefully considered. Most important, however, no matter which procedure is chosen, the behavior modifier should make sure that he or she (and the behavior modification assistants) are *consistent* in the application of each procedure.

STUDY QUESTIONS

1. Choose a child whose undesirable behavior you would like to reduce. Based on the material presented in this chapter, formulate a behavior program plan using the outline listed on p. 96–97.

2. What are the ethical issues associated with the use of behavior reduction methods? (Review pp. 98–99 to check your answer.)

3. What are the major limitations associated with the use of an extinction procedure? (Review p. 103 to check your answer.)

4. What should you first expect to happen to a child's undesirable behavior when you begin an extinction procedure? (Review p. 100 to check your answer.)

5. List five undesirable childhood behaviors and their corresponding incompatible desirable behaviors.

Undesirable Behavior	*Incompatible Behavior*
a.	
b.	
c.	
d.	
e.	

6. What two factors largely determine the success of a treatment program involving the reinforcement of incompatible behavior modification procedure?

    a.

    b.

    (Review p. 103 to check your answer.)

7. Why is the type of situation in which the child is placed important in a time out procedure? (Review p. 105 to check your answer.)

8. A response cost procedure should only be used when a _____ is in existence. (Review p. 109 to check your answer.)

9. What should be avoided in establishing a response cost program? (Review pp. 110-111 to check your answer.)

10. What are the three major components of contact desensitization?

    a.

    b.

    c.

    (Review p. 112 to check your answer.)

11. Contact desensitization consists of behavior modifier touch, encouragement, praise, and _____. (Review p. 112 to check your answer.)

12. When should a behavior modifier use the situation control procedure? (Review p. 115 to check your answer.)

13. Why should the PERM differ from the not-PERM? (Review pp. 115-16 to check your answer.)

14. What is meant by *overcorrection?* (Review pp. 117-18 to check your answer.)

15. What are the two components of the overcorrection procedure? (Review p. 117 to check your answer.)

16. List four potential side effects of the use of physical punishment.

    a.

    b.

    c.

    d.

    (Review p. 119 to check your answer.)

17. What procedure should be combined with the use of punishment? (Review p. 120 to check your answer.)

18. No matter which procedure a behavior modifier uses, the behavior modifier should make sure that he or she is _____. (Review p. 121 to check your answer.)

NOTES

1. Based on a study by Morris, R.J., & Morisano, E. (1974). *The treatment of aquaphobia in retarded persons via contact desensitization.* Unpublished study. Syracuse University.

Chapter **6**

PRESCRIPTIONS FOR TEACHING PARTICULAR TARGET BEHAVIORS

In this chapter a series of behavioral prescriptions for teaching various target behaviors to exceptional children is presented. There are two categories of prescriptions: specific and general prescriptions. These prescriptions are intended to aid the behavior modifier in developing expertise in changing various behaviors shown by different exceptional children. Prescriptions are included for social and self-help skills, as well as fear reduction, aggression control, language training, and reducing stereotypic behavior.

USE OF THE BEHAVIORAL PRESCRIPTIONS

Over the past twenty to twenty-five years, a great deal of clinical research and case studies has been published on the use of behavior modification procedures with exceptional children (see, for example, reviews by Graziano & Mooney 1984; Matson & Andrasik 1983; Matson & McCartney 1981; Morris 1978; Smith 1981; Snell 1978; Whitman et al., 1983). On the basis of this work we find that there is now sufficient information available to allow us to develop prescriptions regarding the modification of various behaviors exhibited by these children. The prescriptions presented in this chapter are in two categories: (1) *specific prescriptions*—where the operations involved in changing a target behavior are presented in a step-by-step manner and (2) *general prescriptions*, where the operations involved in modifying the child's behavior are more global and the behavior modifier needs to adapt them to his or her particular situation.

Many of the specific behavioral prescriptions presented in this chapter are designed for those exceptional children who do not show (or demonstrate only minimally) the target behavior being taught. For those children who can perform some (but not all) of the steps listed in a particular behavioral prescription, the behavioral modifier may have to modify the program to adapt it to the particular child. Changes in a prescription may also be necessary for other reasons. The behavior modifier, however, should arrange any revised prescriptive program so that it (1) proceeds in gradual steps and (2) gives the behavior modifier the opportunity to guide the child through some of the difficult steps before the child is requested to perform those steps by himself or herself.

Throughout the use of each prescriptive program, the behavior modifier should reinforce the child for any progress. If more tangible reinforcers are used (e.g., tokens, activities, food or drink), then the child should be praised, too. If tokens are used as reinforcers, make sure that the child is thoroughly familiar with the tokens and what can be "purchased" with the tokens after the training session, class period, etc., is over. The behavior modifier should also chart the child's progress, circling the appropriate phrase on the vertical line of the chart (e.g., "Percent of Times" or "Number of Steps") and circling "Sessions", etc. on the horizontal line of the chart. The behavior modifier should also keep a record of the child's progress during each training session or class period so that he or she can readily transfer this information to the child's chart at the end of the time period.

Before applying a behavior program like the specific prescriptions that follow, the behavior modifier should read through the program in its entirety and make sure that he or she thoroughly understands the steps as well as the comments made at the end.[1]

SPECIFIC PRESCRIPTIONS

PROGRAM FOR EYE CONTACT TRAINING[2]

The behavior modifier should work with each child on an individual basis at least once per day, 5 to 10 minutes per session.

Training Setting

Eye contact training should take place in a quiet room, devoid of any distractions. Ideally, the room should contain two chairs and a table. It should be well lighted, sound attenuated, and not very large. The two chairs should face each other and the table should be placed to the side of the behavior modifier's chair. The table will be used to record correct and incorrect responses on the tally sheet and to keep the child's rewards out of his or her reach. The child's chair should be small enough to enable the child's feet to touch the floor.

Equipment and Materials Needed

1. A stopwatch or a large clock with an easily observable second hand. The stopwatch or clock should be placed outside the child's reach and clearly in view of the behavior modifier—if possible, the large clock should be hung on the wall behind the child.

2. Two wrist (golf) counters of different colors or a tally sheet and pencil.

3. A graph to chart the child's progress. The vertical line should state "Percent of Correct Eye Contacts," and the horizontal line should state "Sessions."

Procedure

Baseline level.   Before training begins, you should conduct five baseline observation sessions. Bring the child to the room and sit the child down opposite you.

1. Say the command, "[*Name*], look at me."

2. If the child makes direct eye contact with you within a 10-second period, *say nothing and do not give him or her anything as a reward.* Just record a correct response on the tally sheet by placing a plus sign on the sheet or by pressing one of the wrist counters one time.

3. If the child does not make direct eye contact with you within the 10-second period, *say nothing and do not give anything as a reward.* Just record an incorrect response on the tally sheet by placing a minus sign on the sheet or by pressing the other wrist counter one time.

4. After 10 seconds have elapsed, say the command again. Continue this 10-second sequence until the designated 5- to 10-minute treatment time has ended.

5. Be sure to add up the number of correct (+) and incorrect (−) responses for each session. After the session is over, *calculate and then record the percent of correct eye contacts* on the child's chart and compare his or her performance with the previous sessions.

Treatment Phase. This phase is conducted in essentially the same way as the baseline phase except we reward the child for correct responses (with social praise for correct responses as well as small amounts of the child's favorite food, candy, or drink—whenever possible nonedible and nonliquid reinforcers should be used).

1. Before each training period begins, determine which type of reward the child would prefer. Offer the child three or four of his or her favorite types of food and see which one he or she seems to like best at that time. This should be the reward that you start using for that particular session. If the child seems to become bored with that reward or unresponsive, switch to the next preferred item.

2. If the child makes direct eye contact to the command "[*Name*], look at me," then say, "Very good (or "Good boy"/"Good girl") . . . I am so happy," and give the child a bit of the favorite food or drink. Then record a correct response on your tally sheet (+) or wrist counter.

3. If the child does not make direct eye contact in response to your command "[*Name*], look at me," then *say nothing and do not give him or her anything as a reward*. Record an incorrect response on your tally sheet (−) or other wrist counter.

4. This sequence of giving the child a reward or nothing each time he or she looks at you, as well as recording correct and incorrect responses, should be continued until the 5- to 10-minute treatment time has ended.

5. After the session, add up the number of correct and incorrect responses. Then *calculate and record the percent of correct eye contacts* on the child's chart and compare his or her progress with the previous sessions.

6. The training phase should continue until the child reaches at least 90% or above correct eye contacts per session for three consecutive sessions.

If the child does not respond at all initially to your instruction to "Look at me," you should use a *prompting procedure*. Prompting helps the child learn what the desirable behavior is. First, you should give your instruction, "[*Name*], look at me." Then, you should gently grasp the child's head with your hands and slowly turn it so that he or she is looking at your eyes. Reward and praise the child when the child looks at you. The next time, the child should be given the opportunity to look at you without prompting. If he or she does not look at you, again say

"[Name], look at me," and gently move the child's head until the child's eyes meet yours. Prompting is continued until the child learns what behavior he is supposed to perform in the particular situation. It is important, however, to be sure that you lessen your assistance as the child makes progress toward performing the correct behavior. After awhile you will notice that he or she will make the desired response without your assistance—although it may take a number of sessions.

PROGRAM FOR IMITATION LEARNING[3]

Each child should be worked with on an individual basis at least once per day, 10 minutes per session.

Training Setting

Imitation training should take place in a quiet room, devoid of any distractions. Ideally, the room should not contain any furniture except two chairs and a small table. The two chairs should face each other and the table should be placed to the side of the behavior modifier's chair. The table will be used to record correct and incorrect responses on the tally sheet and to keep the child's rewards out of his or her reach. The room should be well lighted, sound attenuated, and not very large. The child's chair should be small enough to enable the child's feet to touch the floor.

Equipment and Materials Needed

1. A stopwatch or a large clock with an easily observable second hand. The stopwatch or clock should be placed outside the child's reach and clearly in view of the behavior modifier—if possible, the large clock should be hung on the wall behind the child.

2. Two wrist (golf) counters of different colors or a tally sheet and pencil.

3. A graph to chart the child's progress. The vertical line should state Percent of Correct Imitations and the horizontal line should state Sessions.

Procedure

Baseline. Following eye contact training (three successive sessions with 90 percent or greater eye contact response), the child should be brought to the same room and seated opposite the behavior modifier.

1. Say the command, "[*Name*], do this!" At the same time, the first of the 15 responses presented here should be modeled by the behavior modifier.

   - Raise both arms

   - Place hands on chest

   - Place hands on knees

   - Touch nose with one hand

   - Touch stomach with both hands

   - Touch ears with both hands

   - Place hands over eyes

   - Place both hands on top of head

   - Stretch both hands to the sides

   - Protrude tongue

   - Clap hands

   - Touch elbow with hand

   - Nod head

   - Tap chair

   - Stamp feet

2. This response should be performed until the child imitates your response, or for a maximum period of 10 seconds.

3. If the child imitates you, *say nothing and do not reward the child*, but record his or her success on one of the wrist counters or on the tally sheet.

4. If the child does not imitate, say nothing and do not reward, and record an incorrect response on the tabulation sheet or on the wrist counter.

5. After 10 seconds has elapsed, you should perform the next response. If the child imitates you correctly, you should record a correct response. If the child does not imitate you, record an incorrect response.

6. Continue saying one command every 10 seconds until the end of the 10-minute session.

7. Be sure to add up the number of correct and incorrect responses for

each session. After each session, calculate and then record the *percent of correct imitations* for that session on the graph.

Treatment. This phase is essentially the same as baseline; however, correct responses are rewarded with small amounts of food or liquids and social praise ("Very good! Good boy[girl]!")—food and liquids, however, should only be used when other types or categories of reinforcement are found to be ineffective.

1. Before each treatment period begins, determine which type of reward the child prefers. This should be the reward that you start using for that particular session. If the child seems to become bored with that reward or unresponsive, switch to the next preferred item.

2. If the child makes a correct imitative response to the command "[Name], do this," then say "Very good! Good boy [girl]!" and give him or her a bit of the favorite food or drink. Then record the correct response.

3. If the child gives an incorrect or no response, say nothing and do not give anything as a reward.

4. This sequence of giving the child a reward or nothing each time he or she has the opportunity to imitate you, as well as recording his or her correct and incorrect responses, should be continued until the 10-minute treatment time has ended.

5. After the session, add up the number of correct and incorrect responses. Then calculate and record the percent of correct imitative responses on the child's chart and compare his or her progress with the previous sessions.

6. The treatment phase should continue until the child reaches 90% or above correct imitations for three consecutive sessions.

If the child initially does not respond to your instructions to "Do this," you should use a *prompting procedure*. Prompting helps the child learn what the desirable target behavior is. First you should give your instruction, "[Name], do this," and show the response to be imitated. Then you should gently assist the child in performing the desired behavior. Upon completing the behavior, the child should be rewarded and praised as if he or she had actually performed the behavior by himself or herself. The next time, the child should be allowed to try the response alone. If the child does not perform the behavior, prompting should again take place—though with a lessened grasp on the child. Reward should again follow this behavior. Prompting is continued until the child learns what has to be done in the situation. Most important, however, is to make sure that you lessen your assistance as the child progresses. The child should have ample opportunity to perform the response by himself or herself in the amount of time alloted. After awhile you will notice that the child will make the desired response exactly as you performed it—although it may take a number of sessions.

Additional Comments

1. If possible, you should try to avoid presenting the imitative responses in the same order in each session.

2. A suggested tally sheet for imitation training appears in Table 6.1.

3. After the child has reached 90% or above correct imitations, you may want to begin teaching him or her more complex imitations. A few more complex imitations are listed here:

   • Stand up and sit down

TABLE 6.1
Tally sheet for imitation training

+ = child imitated behavior and was reinforced

○ = child did not imitate behavior

Δ = child attempted to imitate, but did not respond as accurately as in the past, therefore *no* reinforcement

S = (shaping) child attempted to imitate and was reinforced since response was more accurate than in the past

Child's name: _____

Date: _____

Session no.: _____

	Trial 1	Trial 2	Trial 3
1. Raise both arms			
2. Place hands on chest			
3. Place hands on knees			
4. Touch nose with one hand			
5. Touch stomach with both hands			
6. Touch ears with both hands			
7. Place hands over eyes			
8. Place both hands on top of head			
9. Stretch both hands to the sides			
10. Protrude tongue			
11. Clap hands			
12. Touch elbow with hands			
13. Nod head			
14. Tap chair			
15. Stamp feet			

- Stand up and twirl around, sit down

- Stand up, jump up and down, sit down

- Stand up, walk to wall, tap wall with hand, sit back down in chair

- Stand up and move chair back and forth, sit down

- Stand up, go to door, touch door with one hand, go back to chair and sit down

PROGRAM FOR INDEPENDENT EATING

Throughout the program, praise the child for his or her progress. Identify an effective reinforcer for the child. Make sure that you have made up a chart to graph the child's progress. The vertical line should state Number of Steps and the horizontal line, Sessions.

1. Put the child's hand around the handle portion of the spoon and gently wrap your hand over the child's.

2. Assist the child in scooping the food and bringing the food to his or her mouth. Scoop food in a motion toward the child.

3. After the child receives the food, continue to hold his or her hand gently and direct his or her hand (and the spoon) back to the food.

4. Repeat steps 2 and 3.

5. While repeating steps 2 and 3, gradually begin to loosen your grip on the child's hand just before he or she puts the food in his or her mouth. Maintain this loose grip until after the child has received the food, then return the child's hand (spoon) to the food with the original amount of guidance.

6. Repeating steps 2 and 3, gradually loosen your grip on the child's hand just after the child puts food on the spoon. *Don't let go of the child's hand, just loosen your grip.* Maintain the loose grip until after the child has received the food, then redirect the child's hand and the spoon to the food with the original amount of guidance.

7. Repeat step 6, but in addition loosen your grip on the child's hand when you return the child's hand to the plate.

8. Repeat step 6, except loosen your grip even more when you return his or hand to the plate. *Don't let go of his or her hand.*

9. Repeat step 8 except also loosen your grip even more just before the child places the spoon in his or her mouth.

10. Repeat step 9, except this time let go of his or her hand completely just as the spoon enters his or her mouth. Retake the child's hand with your loose grip *immediately after* he or she receives the food in his or her mouth.

11. Repeat step 10 except now place your hand just under the child's wrist *immediately before* the child places the spoon in his or her mouth. Again, there should be no support while the spoon is in the mouth. Retake the *child's* hand with the loose grip and bring it back to the plate.

12. Repeat step 11, except move your hand under the child's wrist about three-quarters of the way up between the plate and his or her mouth.

13. Repeat step 12, except move your hand under the child's wrist about halfway between the "scoop" and his or her mouth.

14. Repeat step 13 except move your hand under the child's wrist about one-quarter of the way up between the plate and the child's mouth.

15. Repeat step 14 except move your hand under the child's forearm about three-quarters of the way between the plate and the child's mouth.

16. Repeat step 15 with your hand under his or her forearm about half of the way.

17. Repeat step 15 with your hand under his or her forearm about one quarter of the way.

18. Repeat step 17 except move your hand to the child's wrist after the food enters his or her mouth and then guide his or her hand back to the plate.

19. Repeat step 18 except place your hand under his or her forearm after the food enters the mouth. At this point, there should be firm pressure on the child's hand only when scooping the food. There should only be gentle forearm pressure for all other movements.

20. Repeat step 19 except move your hand to the child's wrist while the child is scooping food. (You may have to gently guide him or her at first by grasping his or her hand.)

21. Repeat step 20 except move your hand to just under the child's elbow *immediately after* he or she scoops the food. After he or she receives the food, keep your hand under his or her elbow, guiding the spoon back to the plate.

22. Repeat step 21 except let go of the child's hand and arm completely

about three-quarters of the way up from the scoop to the child's mouth. Continue guiding the return of the spoon to the food by placing your hand under the child's elbow.

23. Repeat step 22 except let go of the child's hand and arm half way between the scoop and his or her mouth.

24. Repeat step 23 except let go of the child's hand and arm one-quarter of the way between the scoop and his/her mouth.

25. Repeat step 24 but let go completely just after he or she makes the scoop. You may have to touch his or her hand gently to signal him or her to move the spoon to the child's mouth. The child's return to the plate should still be elbow guided.

26. Repeat step 25 except place your hand on the child's elbow while the child is scooping.

27. Repeat step 26 except let go of the child's elbow on the return trip to the plate. (You may have to touch the child's hand gently to signal him or her to return spoon to food.)

28. Repeat step 27 except let go of the child's elbow completely. (You may have to guide the child's hand at various points at first.) As the child continues to practice this step, gradually remove any prompting.

If the child drops the spoon at any point after he or she has held the spoon without assistance (step 11), the food and then the child should be immediately removed from the table. One hour later, the child should be given another opportunity to feed himself or herself using this program.

Chart on your graph the last step that the child successfully completed at the end of each session.

Additional Comments

1. While using this program it is a good idea to use a bib that has a pouchlike lip at the bottom. This type of bib usually catches most of the food that spills out of the spoon.

2. If the child has repeated difficulty holding the spoon over a number of sessions, you may want to consider modifying the spoon's shape to further help him or her. For example, you can enlarge the handle of the spoon by wrapping adhesive tape around it. Then, as the child develops skill in holding the spoon, you can gradually remove some of the tape until the child is again using a spoon with a "normal" handle. Other modified spoons are available commercially from medical supply stores that sell prosthetic devices. *If at all*

possible, you should only use a modified spoon on a temporary basis. As the child develops expertise in using the modified spoon, you should gradually begin introducing him or her to the use of a normal spoon.

PROGRAM FOR INDEPENDENT DRESSING: PANTS

Use loose fitting pants with an elasticized waist. Throughout the program, praise the child for any progress. Also, reward the child at each step with small amounts of the reinforcement being used. You will also need a chart to record the child's progress. The vertical line should state Number of Steps and the horizontal line, Sessions.

1. Place pants completely on the child.

2. Pull pants up to *just below* the child's waist. Place your hands gently over the child's hands on either side of his or her pants and help the child pull up the pants as you say, "[*Name*], pull up your pants." Praise the child for pulling up his or her pants.

3. Repeat step 2 except gently move your hands to the child's wrists.

4. Repeat step 2 except move your hands to the child's forearms to guide him or her gently.

5. Repeat step 2 except remove your hands from the child's forearms *(you may have to gently prompt him or her at first on this and later steps).*

6. Pull pants up to the child's hips. Then have the child pull the pants up the rest of the way. Remember to say, "Pull up your pants," and to praise the child when the child is successful.

7. Pull pants up to the child's knees. Then have him or her pull the pants up the rest of the way.

8. Have the child sit down with the pants up to the knees. Then have him or her stand up and pull the pants up the rest of the way. Remember to say, "Pull up your pants," and to praise the child.

9. Have the child sit down. Place the pants *just over* his or her feet up to the ankles. Have him or her pull the pants up to the knees. Then have the child stand up and pull the pants up the rest of the way.

10. Have the child sit down. Place the pants *just over* his or her toes. Have the child pull the pants up to the knees. Then have him or her stand up and pull them up the rest of the way.

11. Have the child sit down. Place one of the child's feet into one of the pant legs until the toes show. Then have the child place his or her other foot through the other pant leg and pull the pants up to the knees, then stand up and pull the pants up the rest of the way.

12. Have the child sit down. Place the pants in front of the child with the opening of one pant leg just touching the toes of one foot. Then have him or her first pull the pant leg up until the toes show, then place his or her second foot in the other pant leg, then pull them up to the knees, and stand up and pull them up the rest of the way.

13. Have the child sit down. Place the pants in front of the child. Have the child grab the pants with his or her hands on both sides of the pants, place one foot through one pant leg, then the other foot through the other pant leg, pull them up to the knees, and stand up and pull them up the rest of the way.

14. Repeat step 13.

Remember to praise the child each time he or she successfully completes a step and to say to the child, "[Name], pull up your pants" right before the child begins to pull his or her pants up. You may have to prompt the child a few times at various points to help the child completely learn a particular step. Chart on your graph the last step that the child successfully completed at the end of each session.

PROGRAM FOR INDEPENDENT DRESSING: SHIRT

Use a loose fitting, short-sleeve T-shirt. (It is a good idea to use initially a shirt that is bigger than the child's normal size.) Throughout the program, praise the child for any progress. Also, reward the child at each step with small amounts of his or her favorite reinforcement. You will also need a chart to record the child's progress. The vertical line should state Number of Steps and the horizontal line, Sessions.

1. Place the shirt completely on the child.

2. Repeat step 1 except pull the shirt down to stomach level. Place your hands gently over the child's hands on either side of his or her shirt and help the child pull the shirt down as you say, "[Name], put on your shirt." Praise the child for pulling down the shirt.

3. Repeat step 2 except gently move your hands to his or her wrist and guide the child in pulling down the shirt.

4. Repeat step 2 except gently move your hands to his or her forearms and continue to gently guide the child.

5. Repeat step 2 except remove your hands completely from the child's forearms (you may have to prompt him/her gently at first on this and later steps until the child masters grasping and pulling down the shirt). Remember to say, "Put on your shirt."

6. Repeat step 5 except have the child pull down the shirt from midway between his or her stomach and chest.

7. Have the child pull down the shirt from chest level.

8. Have the child pull down the shirt from just below the armpits.

9. Have the child pull down the shirt from just over the back of the shoulders (the front of the shirt should be over the chest region).

10. Have the child pull down the shirt from just above the back of the neck. This can be accomplished by first having the child slowly swing his or her arms to the sides, then having the child bring his or her arms back to the front of the shirt, and finally pulling it down.

11. Have the child pull down the shirt from the back of the head. (This can be accomplished by having the child grab the neck region of the shirt and pull it down to his or her shoulders; then have the child repeat step 10. The child should still have both arms through the sleeves of the shirt. *You may have to guide the child gently through this and later steps.*)

12. Have the child pull down the shirt from the top of his or her head.

13. Have the child pull down the shirt from the front of his or her head (the child should now have both arms through the sleeves of the shirt, and the shirt should be across the child's upper arm region.)

14. Have the child grab the waist opening of the T-shirt at the back and bring the T-shirt to the front of his or her head; then have the child repeat step 13.

15. Have the child's arms placed three-quarters of the way through the sleeve. Have the child push his or her arms through and then repeat step 14.

16. Have the child's arms placed half way through the sleeve. Have the child push his or her arms through and repeat step 14.

17. Have the child's arms placed one-quarter of the way through the sleeve. Have the child push his or her arms through and then repeat step 14.

18. Place the shirt with the child's hands just at the arm opening. Have the child push his or her arms all the way through and then repeat step 14.

19. Place the shirt with one of the child's arms just inside the shirt (shirt should be situated at child's chest region) and the other hand already through sleeve at forearm region. Have the child get one

hand through the sleeve and then push both hands through and repeat step 14.

20. Place the shirt with one of the child's arms not inside the shirt (shirt should be at stomach region) and the other hand already through sleeve at forearm region. Have the child get one hand through the sleeve and push both hands through and then repeat step 14.

21. Hold the shirt out in front of the child and guide the child in placing one of his or her arms through a sleeve to the forearm; then encourage the child to repeat step 20.

22. Have the child hold the shirt open at the waist so that he or she can insert one arm into the shirt and push it through the sleeve to his or her forearm; then have him or her repeat step 20.

23. Have the child lift up the back of the shirt at the waist to make an opening at the bottom of the T-shirt. Insert one arm and repeat step 22.

24. Have the child pick up the T-shirt from the table or chair and repeat step 23.

Remember to say, "[Name], put on your shirt," and to praise the child each time the child successfully completes a step and puts on his or her shirt. You may have to prompt the child a few times at various points to help the child develop expertise in putting on his or her shirt.

Chart on your graph the last step that the child successfully completed at the end of each session.

After the child has mastered putting on a large T-shirt, introduce a slightly smaller T-shirt and encourage him or her to put this T-shirt on. Upon meeting with success, you should gradually proceed in having the child put on T-shirts which are closer to (and then finally) the child's size.

PROGRAM FOR INDEPENDENT DRESSING: SOCKS

Use loose-fitting socks. Throughout the program, praise the child for any progress. Also, reward the child at each step with small amounts of the child's favorite reinforcement. You also need a chart to record the child's progress. The vertical line should state Number of Steps and the horizontal line, Sessions.

1. While the child is sitting, place one sock completely on him or her.

2. Pull a sock up to just above his or her ankle. Place your hands gently over the child's hands on either side of the sock and help the child pull up his sock as you say, "[Name], put on your socks." Praise the child for pulling up his sock.

3. Repeat step 2 except this time gently move your hand to the child's wrist and then help him or her pull up his or her sock.

4. Repeat step 2 except move your hands to his or her forearm and gently guide the child.

5. Repeat step 2 except remove your hands completely from the child's forearm. (You may have to prompt the child at first on this and later steps.)

6. Pull the sock up to the child's ankle region. Say, "Put on your socks." (You may have to prompt the child and gently guide the child in completing this activity.)

7. Repeat step 6 except have the child pull up the sock from just below the child's ankle.

8. Repeat step 6 except have the child pull up the sock from just above the heel.

9. Repeat step 6 except have the child pull up the sock from just below the heel.

10. Repeat step 6 except have the child pull up the sock from the middle of the foot.

11. Repeat step 6 except have the child pull up the sock from just above the toes.

12. Repeat step 6 except have the child pull up the sock from the toes.

13. While the child is holding the sock, have the child place his or her toes in the sock opening; repeat step 12.

14. Have the child pick up the sock with both hands and bring the sock to his or her toes; repeat step 13.

15. With the sock in front of the child, instruct the child to put on the sock; repeat step 14. (You may have to prompt the child a few times at various points to help the child complete the activity.)

Remember to say "[Name], put on your socks," and to praise the child each time the child successfully completes a step. Chart on your graph the last step that the child successfully completes at the end of each session.

PROGRAM FOR INDEPENDENT DRESSING: TYING SHOES[4]

Use a shoe with a shoestring which is *longer than average* for the child's shoes. Each half of the shoestring should be a different color (e.g., red and white). Throughout the program, praise the child for any progress. Also reward the child at each step with small amounts of his or her favorite reinforcement. Make sure that you chart the child's progress; the vertical line should state Number of Steps and the horizontal line, Sessions.

1.   Place the shoe on a table in front of the child. The heel of the shoe should be directly in front of the child and the toe of the shoe away from the child. (The child should be seated.)

2.   Help the child take the left (red) shoestring and place it to the left of the front of the toe of the shoe. (You may have to prompt him or her at first on this and later steps. If the child prefers handling the right shoestring first, adjust the program to the child's preference.)

3.   Next, help the child take the right (white) shoestring and place it to the right of the front of the toe of the shoe.

4.   Repeat steps 2 and 3. Next, have the child pick up the red shoestring, cross it over the white string, and place it down to the right of the white string.

5.   Repeat step 4. Then have the child pick up the white string and bring it down toward the center of the shoe so that the tip of the string is touching the tongue of the shoe. (Make sure the strings are still crossed.)

6.   Repeat step 5. Then have the child place the white string under the red string (beneath the crossed strings) and pull it toward the toe of the shoe.

7.   Repeat step 6. Next, have the child pick up the red and white strings and pull them out towards the sides away from each other (red to right, white to left), and then have the child place them down.

8.   Repeat step 7. Have the child pick up the middle of the red string and bring it to the tongue of the shoe (a large loop should result from this action).

9.   Repeat step 8. Then have the child pick up the middle of this white string and bring it to the tongue of the shoe (a second large loop should result from this action).

10.   Repeat step 9. Next, have the child pick up the tip of the white loop with his or her right hand and place it across the red loop. Then have the child continue holding the white loop with the right hand.

11.   Repeat step 10. Have the child pick up the tip of the red loop with his or her left hand and place it across the white loop. (Make sure the loops are still crossed.) The child should continue holding both loops.

12. Repeat step 11. Have the child place the red loop under the white loop and pull it away from the center of the shoe, and then put both loops down.

13. Repeat step 12. Then have the child pick up the red and white loops and pull them slowly out toward the sides away from each other. The child should then put them down.

Remember to praise the child each time the child successfully completes a step. You may have to prompt the child a few times at various points to help him or her complete each step. You may also have to help him or her practice these steps *many times* before the child develops expertise in tying his or her shoes. Next, have the child practice on shoes which have almost normal length shoestrings. Make sure you offer guidance when it seems necessary and that you reward the child for being successful. Gradually withdraw your help. Next, have the child practice on shoes with normal length shoestrings, assisting when necessary, until the child develops complete expertise. Finally, have him or her practice on shoes that are on his or her feet, assisting when necessary, until the child has mastered tying his or her own.

Chart on your graph the last step that the child successfully completes at the end of each session.

An alternative way of teaching the child to tie shoes is to reverse the above program and first teach him or her to tie a bow. Using this reversal procedure, you would guide the child through steps 1 through 12 of the program. Then you would help the child do part of step 13 and encourage the child to do the rest on his or her own. You would then reward the child when the child is finished. Next, you would guide the child through the first twelve steps again, and when you reached the last step, the child would be encouraged to do more of this step on his or her own. Again, you would reward the child when the child was finished. This procedure of backward chaining would be continued throughout all the remaining steps until the child can begin step 1 and perform all of the succeeding steps on his or her own. In every instance, you would only reinforce the child when he or she finished step 13.

PROGRAM FOR INDEPENDENT DRESSING: PUTTING ON A ZIPPERED COAT

Use a loose-fitting jacket which has an easily workable zipper. Throughout the program, praise the child for any progress. Also reward the child at each step with small amounts of his or her favorite reinforcement. Make sure that you chart the child's progress. The vertical line should state Number of Steps and the horizontal line, Sessions.

1. Place the jacket completely on the child. Do not zipper the jacket.

2. Place the jacket on the child, except have the child's right arm placed only three-quarters of the way through the sleeve. Say to the child, "[Name], put on your coat," and gently guide the child in pushing his or her hand through the sleeve opening and placing the coat completely on the shoulders.

3. Place the jacket on the child, except have the child's right arm placed only halfway through the sleeve. Say "[Name], put on your coat," and gently guide the child in pushing his or her hand through the sleeve opening and placing the coat on the shoulders. (Begin gradually to reduce your guidance.)

4. Place the jacket on the child, except have child's right arm placed only one-quarter of the way through the sleeve. Then have the child push the arm through the rest of the way, placing the coat on the shoulders. (Again, gradually withdraw your assistance.)

5. Place the child's right hand just at the arm opening of the jacket. Have the child push the arm all the way through. (Again, you may have to guide him or her at certain points.)

6. Repeat step 5, except this time have the child's left arm placed three-quarters of the way through the sleeve. Say, "[Name], put on your coat," and guide the child if necessary, in putting the coat on.

7. Repeat step 5, except this time have the child's left arm placed halfway through the sleeve. Then encourage the child to put on the coat. (Again, you may have to guide him or her at certain points.)

8. Repeat step 5, except this time place the child's left arm one-quarter of the way through the sleeve. Then encourage him or her to put on the coat.

9. Repeat step 5, except this time have the child's left hand just at the arm opening of the jacket. Then have him or her push all the way through until the coat is on both shoulders.

10. Place the jacket front side up (unzipped) on top of a table (or on a chair) and say to the child, "[Name], put on your coat." Then gently guide the child through steps 1 through 9. Practice this five consecutive times, gradually withdrawing your assistance. If the child has any difficulty with a particular step, review the step with him or her until the child can successfully put on the coat.

Once the child has learned to put his or her coat on without continued assistance, you should begin to teach the child how to zipper the coat. Again, praise the child for any progress. Also reward the child at each step with small amounts of his or her favorite reinforcement. Make sure you use a coat that has a zipper that moves easily.

11. Let the child put on the coat to your statement "[*Name*], put on your coat." Then you should pull the zipper all the way up.

12. Let the child put on the coat. Then pull the zipper up to just above his or her chest level. Place your hand gently over the child's hand and help the child pull up the zipper as you say, "[*Name*], pull up your zipper."

13. Let the child put on his coat. Then pull the zipper up to just above his or her chest level. Gently place your hand over the child's hand until the child grasps the zipper. Then move your hand to the wrist and guide him or her in pulling up the zipper as you say, "[*Name*], pull up your zipper."

14. Repeat step 13 except move your hand to his forearm to guide the child.

15. Repeat step 13 except this time remove your hand from the child's forearm (you may have to prompt the child at first on this and later steps). Make sure you say, "[*Name*], pull up your zipper."

16. Let the child put on his or her coat. Then pull the zipper to the chest level and encourage the child to pull the zipper up the rest of the way. (Again, you may have to prompt the child a few times.)

17. Repeat step 16 except this time have the child pull up the zipper from midway between the waist and chest.

18. Repeat step 16 except this time have the child pull up his zipper from just above the waist level.

19. Repeat step 16 except have the child pull up the zipper from waist level. (If the child's coat goes beyond his waist level, he or she should next be encouraged to pull up the zipper from his or her hip region.)

20. Repeat step 16 except have the child pull the zipper all the way up from the bottom of the zipper.

21. Let the child put on his coat. Then help him or her grasp the two parts of the unhooked zipper, one part in each hand, and then help him or her connect them. Then have him or her zip the coat up all the way, to your statement "Pull up your zipper."

22. Repeat step 21, except this time gradually withdraw your assistance in helping him or her connect the two parts of the zipper. Do not hold the child's hand too firmly. Make sure you praise the child when he or she is successful.

23. Repeat step 21, except this time place your hands over the wrists and assist the child in connecting the two parts of the zipper. As soon as the zipper is connected, withdraw your help and tell the

child to "Pull up your zipper." Make sure you praise him or her for being successful.

24. Repeat step 21, except this time place your hands on the child's forearms and gently guide the child in connecting the two parts of the zipper.

25. Repeat step 21, except this time encourage the child to connect the two parts of the zipper with little if any assistance from you. (You may in the beginning have to guide the child then gradually withdraw all your assistance until the child is completely successful alone.) You may have to practice this step a number of times before the child develops expertise in zipping up the zipper.

Remember to say, "[Name], put on your coat [pull up your zipper]" and to praise the child each time he or she successfully completes a step. You may have to prompt the child a few times at various points to help him or her complete the activity.

Chart on your graph the last step that the child successfully completes at the end of each session.

PROGRAM FOR INDEPENDENT WALKING

Before initiating this program,[5] the child should be seen by a physician for a thorough examination to determine if there is any physical reason why he or she cannot (or should not) learn to walk. Throughout the program, praise the child for any progress. Also reinforce the child at each step with small amounts of his or her favorite reinforcement. You will need a graph to chart the child's progress. The vertical line should state Number of Steps and the horizontal line, Sessions.

Materials Needed

Two sturdy wooden chairs with spaced slot backs and weights (e.g., a 50-pound bag of sand) anchored to each chair. The chairs should be back to back in the middle of a room. The room should be well lighted and devoid of any distractions for the child. Two behavior modifiers are needed for this program, and they should sit on the chairs so that they are facing one another.

1. Place the child between the two chairs on the floor in a sitting position. (There should be a distance of about two feet between the two chair backs.) Say to the child "[Name], stand up," and gently guide his or her hands to the first rung of one of the chairs. Then, while the child is holding onto the rung, gently help the child pull himself or herself up by lifting him or her under each arm. (Both

behavior modifiers should participate in helping the child stand up—each behavior modifier holding one side of the child.)

2. Repeat step 1 except this time guide the child's hands to the next rung on the same chair while saying to the child, "[*Name*], stand up." Then help the child stand up (make sure the child is still holding on to the rung). The behavior modifier may have to hold the child's hands in order to help him or her maintain balance.

3. Repeat step 1 except guide the child's hands to the top rung and gently help the child pull himself or herself up. Make sure the child is holding on to the rung. If necessary, the behavior modifier should hold the child's hands on the rung to help the child maintain balance.

4. Repeat step 3. Make sure that the child is holding on to the chair with both hands. (The behavior modifiers may have to hold their hands over the child's hands to help the child maintain balance.)

5. While the child is standing between the two behavior modifiers and holding on to the top rung of the first behavior modifier's chair, the second behavior modifier should then say, "[*Name*], come to me," and gently guide the child's hand across to the top rung on the opposite chair. After the child places his or her hands on the second chair, the second behavior modifier should reward the child with the child's favorite reinforcement. (If the child drops down to the floor, repeat step 3, rewarding the child only after he or she successfully completes step 3.)

6. Repeat step 5 for the child's other hand (the child's upper body should now be facing the second behavior modifier). The second behavior modifier should also gently guide the child's feet and torso so that they are facing the second behavior modifier's chair.

7. Repeat steps 5 and 6 using the first behavior modifier so that the child can transfer back to that chair.

8. Repeat steps 5 through 7, gradually withdrawing the physical guidance by the behavior modifier. (Both behavior modifiers should continue to say, "[*Name*], come to me," before each transfer from one chair to the other, and continue to reward the child with reinforcement for successful transfers.) You may have to prompt the child at various points to help him or her learn how to transfer. Make sure that each behavior modifier says, "[*Name*], come to me," only when the behavior modifier wants the child to transfer in his or her direction.

9. Repeat steps 5 through 7 until the child completes 10 consecutive unassisted transfers.

10. Increase the distance between the chairs to 30 inches. Then repeat steps 5 through 7 until the child has made 10 consecutive successful unassisted transfers.

11. Increase the distance between the chairs to 36 inches. Then repeat steps 5 through 7 until the child has made 10 consecutive successful unassisted transfers. (If the child can no longer reach the other side by just stretching out his or her arms you may have to provide some support for the child until the child learns to move his or her feet to reach the other chair.)

12. Increase the distance between the chairs to 42 inches. Then repeat steps 5 through 7 until the child has made 10 consecutive successful unassisted transfers. (Once again, you may have to guide the child at first to help the child learn to move his or her feet.)

13. Increase the distance between the chairs to 48 inches. Then repeat steps 5 through 7 until the child has made 10 consecutive successful unassisted transfers.

14. Increase the distance between the chairs to 54 inches. Then repeat steps 5 through 7 until the child has made 10 consecutive successful unassisted transfers.

15. Increase the distance between the chairs to 60 inches. Then repeat steps 5 through 7 until the child has made 10 consecutive successful unassisted transfers.

16. Turn the chairs around so that they are facing each other. The chairs should be about 60 inches apart. The behavior modifiers should sit in a normal way on the chairs. The child should be placed next to one behavior modifier. The other behavior modifier should then say, "[Name], come to me." When the child walks to the behavior modifier, he or she should be rewarded. The second behavior modifier should then say, "[Name], come to me," and also reward the child for walking to the behavior modifier. (You may have to prompt the child at various points to help the child walk from one behavior modifier to the other.) Repeat this step until the child has made 10 consecutive successful unassisted transfers.

17. Increase the distance between the chairs to 72 inches, and repeat step 16 until the child has made 10 consecutive successful unassisted transfers.

18. Increase the distance between the chairs to 84 inches and repeat step 16 until the child has made 10 consecutive successful unassisted transfers.

19. Increase the distance between the chairs to 96 inches, and repeat step 16 until the child has made 10 consecutive successful unas-

sisted transfers. (By this time the child should be walking independently and freely rewarded for walking around.)

Remember to reinforce the child each time he or she successfully transfers from one chair to the other. Gentle guidance is often helpful in aiding the child in the initial learning of a particular step.

Chart on your graph the last step that the child successfully completes at the end of each session.

PROGRAM FOR INDEPENDENT TOOTHBRUSHING

Use a toothbrush which is appropriate for the child's size (you should check with a dentist to determine whether the child should use a soft, medium, or hard toothbrush, as well as what the configuration of the toothbrush should be). Throughout the program, praise the child for any progress. Also, reward the child at the end of the session with an appropriate amount of his or her favorite reinforcement. You should also chart the child's progress.The vertical line should state Number of Steps and the horizontal line, Sessions. (*Note:* This program assumes that the child can grasp and hold a toothbrush and toothpaste by himself or herself.)

1. Bring the child to the washroom and place his or her toothbrush and a tube of open toothpaste directly in front of the child. Tell the child, "Pick up the tube of toothpaste and place some toothpaste on the toothbrush. Then, place the toothpaste back down." If the child follows this instruction, go to step 10. If he or she *does not* follow this instruction, gently cover his or her hands with yours and guide him or her in spreading the toothpaste on the toothbrush and then place the toothpaste down (the toothbrush should be placed in the child's preferred hand).

2. Repeat step 1, except loosen your grip on the child's hands.

3. Repeat step 1, except loosen your grip even more, but *do not let go of the child's hand.*

4. Repeat step 1, except place your hand just under the child's wrist *immediately* before he or she places the toothpaste on the toothbrush. Continue guiding the child from this position and praising him or her (you may have to grasp one of the child's hands initially to help the child spread the toothpaste).

5. Repeat step 1, except move your hand down toward the middle of the child's arm. Continue guiding the child and praising him or her for making progress.

6. Repeat step 5, except remove your hands from the child's arms

immediately before he or she places the toothpaste down (you may have to guide him or her occasionally on this and later steps).

7. Repeat step 5, except remove your hands from the child's arms immediately before the child finishes putting the toothpaste on the toothbrush.

8. Repeat step 5, except remove your hands just as he or she begins placing the toothpaste on the toothbrush.

9. Repeat step 1 (you may have to gently guide him or her at times until he or she develops mastery of this skill).

10. After the child successfully completes step 1 or step 9, he or she should be told, "Now I want you to brush your teeth." If the child does not follow this instruction, then you should gently cover the child's hand with yours and guide the child's hand through the following sequence:

   a. turn the water on in the wash basin to a moderate degree and then bring the child's hand slowly toward the mouth,

   b. touch the toothbrush bristles to the child's teeth and move the toothbrush up and down on the outer surface of the child's front teeth for 5 to 10 seconds (avoid placing undue pressure on the child's gums),

   c. then gently move the toothbrush to one side of the child's mouth (the child's preferred side) and brush this side for 5 to 10 seconds in an up-and-down motion,

   d. then gently move the toothbrush to the other side of his or her mouth and brush this side for 5 to 10 seconds in an up-and-down motion,

   e. then gently move the toothbrush to the bottom surfaces of the top teeth on the child's preferred side and brush them for 5 to 10 seconds,

   f. then gently move the toothbrush to the bottom surfaces of the top teeth on the other side and brush them for 5 to 10 seconds,

   g. then guide the child's hand and toothbrush to the upper surfaces of the bottom teeth on the child's preferred side and brush them for 5 to 10 seconds,

   h. then guide the child's hand and toothbrush to the upper surfaces of the bottom teeth on the other side and brush them for 5 to 10 seconds,

   i. then guide the child in brushing the inside surfaces of the bottom teeth,

j. then guide the child in brushing the inside surfaces of his or her top teeth,

k. then guide the toothbrush out of the child's mouth and back toward the basin,

l. place the toothbrush under the water, rinse it off, and put it down,

m. then encourage the child to spit out the toothpaste that has remained in the mouth,

n. then guide the child in picking up a cup, filling it with water, rinsing out the mouth, and placing the cup back down,

o. and, finally, guide the child in turning off the water and wiping the face and hands with a towel.

11. Repeat the sequence presented in step 10, except loosen your grip on the child's hand.

12. Repeat the sequence in step 10, except loosen your grip even more. *Do not let go of the child's hand.*

13. Repeat the sequence in step 10, except place your hand just under the child's wrist *immediately* before the child places the toothbrush in his or her mouth. Continue guiding the child from this position and praising him or her for doing well. Retake the child's hand after the child is finished using the toothbrush in his or her mouth.

14. Repeat the sequence in step 10, except move your hand just under the child's wrist about three-quarters of the way up between the wash basin and the child's mouth. Retake the child's hand after the child is finished using the toothbrush in his or her mouth.

15. Repeat the sequence in step 10, except move your hand under the child's wrist about half way up between the wash basin and the child's mouth. Retake the child's hand after the child is finished using the toothbrush in his or her mouth.

16. Repeat the sequence in step 10, except move your hand just under the child's wrist about one quarter of the way up between the wash basin and the child's mouth. Leave your hand in this position after the child is finished with the toothbrush in his or her mouth (you may have to regrasp the child's hand occasionally to aid him or her in rinsing the toothbrush).

17. Repeat the sequence in step 10, except move your hand under the child's forearm about three-quarters of the way up between the wash basin and the child's mouth. Leave your hand in this position after the child is finished with the toothbrush in the mouth (again,

you may have to guide the child gently through the remainder of the sequence).

18. Repeat the sequence in step 10, except move your hand under the child's forearm about half way up between the wash basin and the child's mouth. (Again, leave your hand in this position throughout the remainder of the sequence, although you may have to retake the child's hand at certain times to further guide the child).

19. Repeat the sequence in step 10, except move your hand under the child's forearm about one-quarter of the way between the wash basin and the mouth. Leave your hand in this position throughout the remainder of the program.

20. Repeat step 10 (you may have to gently guide the child through various parts of the sequence until the child develops expertise in brushing his or her teeth).

21. Repeat steps 1 and 10 (again, you may have to guide the child occasionally until he or she develops complete mastery of these skills).

Remember to praise the child each time he or she completes a step and successfully brushes his or her teeth. Chart on your graph the last step that the child successfully completes at the end of each session. After the child has mastered brushing the teeth, you may want to begin teaching him or her how to take off and replace the cap to the toothpaste, as well as how to use dental floss. Also, be sure to bring the child to the dentist for regular check-ups.

PROGRAM FOR INDEPENDENT FACE WASHING

Throughout the program, praise the child for any progress. Also, reward him or her at the end of each session with an appropriate amount of his or her favorite reinforcement. You should also chart the child's progress. The vertical line should state Number of Steps and the horizontal line, Sessions.

1. Bring the child to the bathroom and stand the child in front of the sink. Say, "[Name], wash your face." Then turn the water on. (This program assumes that the child is familiar with having water on his or her face. If the child is not familiar with this, the behavior modifier should take the time to place small amounts of water gently over his or her face until the child feels comfortable with having the water on the face.)

2. Bring the child to the bathroom and have the child stand in front of the sink. Say, "[Name], wash your face." Then guide the child in

turning on the appropriate amount of hot and cold water to achieve a warm water temperature. Assist the child in cupping his or her hands, in bringing his or her cupped hands under the water, and then patting his or her face with the water (this process should be performed in one continuous motion).

3. Repeat step 2. After the child pats his or her face with the water, continue to hold the child's cupped hands and gently direct them back to the water.

4. Repeat step 3.

5. While repeating step 3, gradually begin to loosen your grip on the child's cupped hands just before he or she places water on his or her face. Maintain the loose grip until after the child has placed the water on his or her face; then return his or her hands to the water with the original amount of guidance.

6. Repeat step 3, but this time gradually loosen your grip on the child's hand just after the child gets water in his or her hands. Don't let go of the child's hands, merely loosen your grip. Maintain this loose grip until after the child has patted his or her face with the water, then redirect the child's hands to the water with the original amount of guidance.

7. Repeat step 6, except also loosen your grip on the child's hands as you return them to the water.

8. Repeat step 7, except this time loosen your grip on his or her hands even more, without letting go of the child's hands entirely.

9. Repeat step 8, except let go of his or her hands *just as* the child splashes the water on his or her face, retaking the child's hands with your loose grip *immediately after* he or she finishes splashing his or her face.

10. Repeat step 9, except place your hand just under his or her wrist *immediately before* he or she pats water on his or her face. There should be no support of his or her hands while the child is splashing his or her face but you should retake the child's hands with the loose grip and bring them back to the water.

11. Repeat step 10, except move your hand under the child's wrist about three-quarters of the way between the water and his or her face.

12. Repeat step 10, except move your hand under the child's wrist about half way between the water and his or her face.

13. Repeat step 10, except move your hand under the child's wrist about one-quarter of the way between the water and his face.

14. Assist the child in cupping his or her hands and bringing his or her cupped hands under the water. Then, as you guide the child's hands (at the wrist) to the child's face, move your hand to his forearm about three-quarters of the way between the water and his or her face.

15. Repeat step 14, except move your hand under the child's forearm about half way between the water and his or her face.

16. Repeat step 14, except move your hand under the child's forearm about one-quarter of the way between the water and his face.

17. Repeat step 14, except this time move your hand to the child's wrist *right after* the child splashes the face.

18. Repeat step 14, except place your hand under the child's forearm right after he or she splashes the face. (At this point there should be firm pressure on the child's hands only as he or she begins to cup the water. Gentle forearm pressure should be present for all other movements.)

19. Repeat step 14, except move your hand to the child's wrist just as he or she is cupping his or her hands. (You may have to guide the child gently at first by gripping his or her hands.)

20. Repeat step 14, except move your hand to just under the child's elbow just as the child cups his or her hands. After this, continue to have your hand under the child's forearm and gently guide the child through the other motions.

21. Repeat step 20, except let go of the child's forearm completely about three-quarters of the way from placing water in the child's hands. Continue guiding the return of his or her hands to the water by placing your hand under the child's elbow.

22. Repeat step 20, except let go of the child's hand and arm half way between the water and the child's face.

23. Repeat step 20, but let go of the child's hand and arm one-quarter of the way between the water and the child's face.

24. Repeat step 20, but let go completely just after the child places water in his or her hands. You may have to touch the hand gently to signal the child to move the hands to his or her face. The child's return to the water should still be elbow guided.

25. Repeat step 20, except do not guide the child's arm back to the water. (You may have to prompt the child occasionally.)

Remember to say, "[Name], wash your face," and to praise the child for the successful completion of each step. Chart on your graph the last step that the child successfully completes at the end of each session.

If you wish to teach the child to wash his or her face with soap and/ or a wash cloth, you can extend this program using the same graduated format. You can also apply this program (after minor modification) to teaching the child to wash other parts of the body (e.g., neck, underarms).

At the end of each session assist the child in turning off the water and in using a towel to dry the face and hands. As the child progresses, gradually withdraw your guidance in these activities—until he or she can perform them by himself or herself.

PROGRAM FOR INDEPENDENT HAIR COMBING

Make sure that you use a comb which can be easily handled by the child. Throughout the program praise the child for any progress. Also reward the child at each step with small amounts of the child's favorite reinforcement. You will also need a chart to record the child's progress. The vertical line should state Number of Steps and the hoizontal line, Sessions. (*Note:* This program assumes that the child can grasp a comb.)

1. Pick up the comb and place it in the child's hand, cupping your hand over the child's hand. Say to the child, "[*Name*], comb your hair."

2. Repeat step 1 and guide the child's hand and comb to the child's hair.

3. Repeat step 2 (again saying, "[*Name*], comb your hair"); then, while holding his or her hand over the comb, comb the child's hair in accordance with your preference.

4. Repeat step 3 except slightly loosen your grip on the child's hand.

5. Repeat step 3 except loosen your grip even more.

6. Repeat step 3 except gradually move your hand to the child's wrist and continue guiding his or her hair combing.

7. Repeat step 6 except move your hand to the child's wrist. Loosen your grip slightly so that he or she can have the opportunity to move the comb.

8. Repeat step 6 except move your hand just under the child's elbow. Continue guiding him or her whenever it seems necessary.

9. Repeat step 8 except remove your guidance completely. (You may have to guide the child occasionally.)

Remember to say "[*Name*], comb your hair," and to praise the child each time he or she successfully completes a step. You may have to prompt the child a few times at various points to help him or her reach complete mastery.

Chart on your graph the last step that the child successfully completes at the end of each session.

PROGRAM FOR COMMAND FOLLOWING: "COME TO ME"

Throughout the program, praise the child for any progress. Also, reward the child at each step with small amounts of the child's favorite reinforcement. Chart the child's progress. The vertical line should state Number of Steps and the horizontal line, Sessions.

1. Stand face to face with the child at a distance of two feet. Say, "[Name], come to me!" At the same time, gesture to the child that you want him or her to come to you by stretching out your arms in front of you and slowly bringing them back toward your chest. If the child does not come to you, repeat the command and reach for the child's forearms and slowly pull him or her toward you. Repeat this prompting procedure until he or she comes to you without assistance. (Although you should continue using gestures, you should gradually withdraw your assistance as the child progresses in coming to you on command. In this way, the child will learn to perform the behavior alone.)

2. Repeat step 1, except stand three feet from the child. If he or she does not come to you, repeat the command and reach for the child's forearms and slowly pull the child toward you. (Repeat this prompting procedure until the child comes to you without your assistance. Continue using gestures but gradually withdraw your prompting until the child comes to you without any assistance.)

3. Repeat step 1, except stand four feet from the child. (If the child does not come to you in response to your command, repeat the prompting procedure and then gradually withdraw your prompts until he or she comes to you without any assistance.)

4. Repeat step 1, except stand five feet away from the child. (If necessary, use the prompting procedure to assist the child in following your command. Be sure to withdraw your prompts gradually as the child learns to come to you.)

5. Repeat step 1, except stand six feet from the child. (If necessary, move toward the child and use the prompting procedure to bring the child to you.)

6. Repeat step 1, except stand nine feet from the child. (You may have to use prompts at first in this and the remaining steps.)

7. Repeat step 1, except stand 12 feet from the child.

8. Repeat step 1, except stand 20 feet from the child (or at the opposite side of the room).

Remember to praise the child each time he or she shows even the slightest amount of progress. Chart on your graph the last step that the child successfully completes at the end of each session.

PROGRAM FOR COMMAND FOLLOWING: "SIT DOWN"

For this program you will need a chair which is appropriate for the child's size. (The child should be able to sit comfortably in the chair with his or her feet touching the floor.) Throughout the program, praise the child for any progress. Also, reward him or her with small amounts of his or her favorite reinforcement. You will also need a chart to record the child's progress. The vertical line should state Number of Steps and the horizontal line should state Sessions.

1. Stand face to face with the child at a distance of two feet. Say, "[*Name*], sit down!" While you are saying the command, gesture to the child to sit down—that is, outstretch your hands in front of you and move them downward toward the floor. If the child does not follow your command, say the command again and gently place your hands on his or her shoulders and assist the child in sitting down. Repeat this prompting procedure (gradually withdrawing your assistance) until the child responds to your command without any prompting. (For some children you may have to help them learn to bend their knees before they can learn to sit down.)

2. Repeat step 1 except stand three feet away from the child. If the child does not follow your command and gesture, place your hands on the child's shoulders and gently sit him or her down. Repeat the prompting procedure until he or she performs the behavior without any assistance.

3. Repeat step 1 except stand four feet from the child. If he or she does not respond to your command and gesture, repeat the command and the prompting procedure and then gradually withdraw your prompts until he or she follows your command without any help.

4. Repeat step 1 except stand six feet from the child. If he/she does not respond to your command and gesture, repeat the command and the prompting procedure by reaching over to him or her and gently sitting him or her down. Be sure to withdraw your assistance gradually as the child learns to follow the command.

5. Repeat step 1 except stand twelve feet away. (If necessary, move toward the child and use the prompting procedure until he or she can follow the command without any prompting.)

6. Repeat step 1 except stand sixteen feet away (or at the opposite side of the room). You may have to use prompting until he or she performs the behavior without any assistance.

Remember to praise the child each time he or she successfully shows even the slightest amount of progress. Chart on your graph the last step that he or she successfully completes at the end of each session.

PROGRAM FOR COMMAND FOLLOWING: "PUT THAT DOWN"

Stand the child next to a table (the table should be on the child's dominant side) and place a small box or object on the table. Throughout the program, praise the child for any progress. Also reward the child at each step with small amounts of the child's favorite reinforcement. You will also need a chart to record the child's progress. The vertical line should state Number of Steps and the horizontal line, Sessions.

1. Stand face to face with the child at a distance of two feet. Place the small box or object in the child's dominant hand. Say to the child, "[Name], put that down!" While you are saying the command, gesture to the child to put the box down—that is, point to the box in the child's hand and then point to the place where you want him or her to place it. If the child does not follow your command, repeat the command and then gently reach for the child's dominant hand and lead it down toward the table. Then slowly help the child open his or her hand and assist the child in placing the box on the table. Finally, gently guide the hand away from the table. Repeat this prompting procedure (gradually withdrawing your assistance) until the child responds to your command without any prompting.

2. Repeat step 1 except stand three feet away from the child. If he or she does not follow your command, reach for his or her dominant hand and gradually bring it down toward the table and help him or her place the box on the table. (Make sure you use the gesture when you give the command.) Repeat the prompting procedure until the child performs the behavior without any assistance.

3. Repeat step 1, except stand five feet away. If the child does not respond to your command and gesture, repeat the prompting procedure and then gradually withdraw your prompts until he or she follows your command without any help.

4. Repeat step 1, except stand eight feet away. (If necessary, move toward the child and use the prompting procedure. Be sure to withdraw your assistance gradually as the child learns to place the box down.)

5. Repeat step 1, except stand 12 feet away. (If necessary, move toward the child and use the prompting procedure until he or she can follow the command without any prompting.)

6. Repeat step 1, except stand 16 feet away (or at the opposite side of the room). You may have to move toward the child and use prompting until the child performs the behavior without any assistance.

Remember to praise the child each time the child successfully shows even the slightest amount of progress. Chart on your graph the last step that the child successfully completes at the end of each session.

To help the child learn to follow this command when he or she is holding various types of objects, place different items in the child's hand and repeat step 6 of the program. Praise the child and reward him or her for successfully following your command.

PROGRAM FOR REDUCING A CHILD'S FEAR

This program[6] assumes that the child is afraid of *something which can be seen* by the behavior modifier (e.g., animals, elevators, darkness, strangers, going into the water in a swimming pool, high places). Throughout the program praise the child for any progress. You should also chart the child's progress. The vertical line of the chart should state Number of Steps and the horizontal line, Sessions.

1. If you are uncertain what the child is afraid of, talk with the child and help him or her describe exactly what he or she is afraid of. Then, identify the target behavior as clearly as possible. In order to use this program, you should be able to see the feared object.

2. In order to help the child overcome the fear, you should develop a graduated series of steps (hierarchy) toward the feared object— *starting with the least fearful step,* which the child is willing to make (and has no trouble making), and gradually moving down to the most fearful step that the child prefers not to make. *The development of the hierarchy is one of the most important steps in this program.* Make certain that it represents a very gradual gradation toward the feared object.

3. Write out the hierarchy steps on a sheet of paper and show them to a friend or colleague. This person should agree that the hierarchy represents a gradation toward the feared object. If there is some

disagreement with a few of the steps in the hierarchy, modify those steps.

4. Number the vertical line of your chart to correspond to the number of steps in your hierarchy. The horizontal line should state Sessions. Each session should last not more than 20 minutes, with two to five sessions per week (one session a day).

5. Expose the child to the first, least fearful step on the hierarchy. Tell the child that you are now going to perform the first step on the hierarchy (instead of using these words, you would just say what the first step is), and after you are finished the two of you will do the same activity again. Thus, after you *model* each step, you should *gradually ease* the child into performing that same step (with you participating, too). You should also *encourage* the child throughout his or her performance of the step, *praise* him or her for even the slightest progress, and *physically help* the child practice that step. After performing a particular step, the child should feel fairly confident that he or she can perform it again.

6. If the child successfully completes this first step, you should then proceed to the next step. Do not rush the child through any steps. Always model the step first, then encourage his or her participation, praise the child and physically help the child perform the step. If the child does not successfully complete the first step, this indicates that the hierarchy is not graduated enough and/or you have not successfully identified the least fearful step which the child is willing to perform (and has no trouble performing).

7. At the end of a session, record the last step that the child has successfully completed. Chart the child's progress, and give praise and show your happiness for the success the child has made.

8. At the next session, start the child at the beginning of the hierarchy and proceed through the steps that he or she has already successfully completed. As the child repeatedly practices these earlier steps, gradually withdraw your modeling and physical help, although you should continue encouraging and praising him or her. When you reach the last step that the child successfully completed in the previous session, model that step again and then proceed with the rest of the procedure. *Before beginning a new session always review the earlier steps which have been successfully completed. Start the new session with the last step that the child successfully completed in the previous session.*

9. If the child is hesitant to perform a particular step, or just refuses to perform a step, do not force the child. Go back a step and model it

and then have the child perform the step. Then go to the next step and have the child imitate what you did (again, encouraging, praising, and assisting him). If the child still fails that step, go back to the last step successfully completed and have the child repeat that step. Then, stop the session. *It is important to always end each session with the successful completion of a step.* If a child repeatedly fails a step, break it down into smaller graduated components and have the child perform each step as he or she would any other step on the hierarchy. To help you modify a step, you should also ask the child what about the failed step is difficult to perform. Then, adjust the particular step accordingly. At the next session, have the child go through those steps already mastered, and then start the contact desensitization procedure on the last step that he or she successfully completed, followed by his or her exposure to the revised steps. Further modification of the steps and added behavior modifier contact and reassurance may be necessary.

Remember, always praise the child for any progress, and use modeling, encouragement, and physical help to assist him or her in mastering a particular step. *Never* require the child to do anything that he or she truly does not want to do. If the child is having difficulty progressing from one step to another, develop in-between steps to help the child gradually progress to the next step.

PROGRAM FOR TOILET TRAINING

This program assumes that the child can obey simple commands (e.g. "Sit down!"). It is advisable for the child to know how to pull down and up his or her pants and wash his or her hands. Throughout the program praise the child for any progress, and reward him or her with small amounts of the child's favorite reinforcement. You should also keep a daily tally sheet of the child's progress and transfer this information to the child's chart at the end of each day. Circle Number of Times (wet/ BM) on the vertical line and Days on the horizontal line. You will also need a potty chair appropriate for the child's size (for larger children you can use an insert for a normal commode or even the regular commode). When necessary, use a urine deflector for boys.

The daily tally sheet should resemble the observation sheet presented in Table 2.3 with the following modification: record a " + " when the child is dry, a " + + " when the child has not had a bowel movement (BM), a " − " when the child is wet, a " − − " when the child has had a BM. Thus, if the child is dry at 8:00 A.M. and did not have a BM, you would record the following: " + , + + ." If the child is wet at 8:30 A.M.

but did not have a BM, then you would record the following: "−, + +," etc. You should keep two charts on the child—one for Number of Times (urinated) and the other for Number of Times (BM).

Before using this program, the behavior modifier should make sure that he or she has a sufficient amount of time to carry out the program in its entirety. The program demands a great deal of therapist involvement and time—as well as consistency.

1. Prepare a Daily Tally Sheet resembling the one in Table 2.3. The times listed for each observation should be 10 minutes apart, starting from the time that the child wakes up in the morning to the time that the child goes to bed.

2. The first 7 to 10 days should consist of baseline observation. The therapist should check the child every 10 minutes throughout each day and record when the child is dry or wet or has or has not had a BM. When the therapist goes to check the child, he or she should say, "Let's see, [Name], if you are dry." Do not say anything if the child is dry or wet.

   At the end of each day, you should record on each chart the respective total number of times that the child wetted or had a BM. To make sure that the baseline period is representative of the child's "normal" toilet habits, be certain that the child is not sick during this period and is eating solids and drinking liquids regularly.

3. At the end of the 7- to 10-day baseline period, review the child's daily tally sheets and determine the time(s) when the child is *most frequently* wet during the day and *most frequently* has a BM. Then, determine the *next most frequent* time(s) that the child wets/has a BM, and so on until you have accounted for 80 percent or more of the times that the child wets or has a BM. For example, you may discover that the child most frequently urinates between 9:30 A.M. and 10:00 A.M. and between 12:00 noon and 12:30 P.M. Similarly, he or she may most often have a BM between 2:00 P.M. and 3:00 P.M. Next, he or she may wet frequently between 1:00 P.M. and 1:45 P.M. and between 4:00 P.M. and 5:00 P.M., and has a BM between 10:30 A.M. and 11:00 A.M. and between 6:30 P.M. and 7:00 P.M.

4. After you have determined the "pattern" to the child's toileting habits, you are ready to begin treatment. Continue checking the child every 10 minutes, and again say to him, "Let's see, [Name], if you are dry." But this time, instead of saying nothing *when he or she is dry*, say the following: "Good boy [girl], you are dry. I am so proud of you. Remember, when you have to go, you should use the potty [toilet]." Then give the child a reward (or token). Make sure the child knows that you are pleased with him or her and that he or she is thoroughly familiar with the toilet and its location. *If the child is*

wet say the following: "No! Bad boy [girl]. You went in your pants. You should go in the potty [toilet], *not* in your pants." Then take the child to the potty (toilet) and say, "This is where you go."

5. When the frequent time periods occur (e.g., between 10:00 and 10:30 A.M.), bring the child to the potty every ten minutes and sit with him or her for three to five minutes—giving the child time to initiate the passage of urine or a BM. If he or she goes in the potty—even the slightest amount—express your happiness and joy: kiss the child, hug the child, pat the child on the back, shout "Hurray!" and also reward the child with his or her favorite reinforcement. When the child finishes, and when it is appropriate, help him or her wipe. Then, have the child pull up his or her underpants and pants (or, pull down her skirt), and repeat the procedure at the next 10-minute period. If the child does not go in the potty, have him or her replace his or her clothing and then return to play or other activity. Check the child again at the next 10-minute period, bring the child back to the potty, and repeat the same procedure—depending on whether the child goes or does not go in the potty.

    When treatment begins you should also make up two new charts to record the child's successes on the potty. The first should state on the vertical line Number of Times (urinated in potty), and the second should state Number of Times (BM in potty). The horizontal line for both charts should state Days. Record the child's number of successes on the appropriate chart at the end of each day.

6. As the child's "in potty" successes begin to increase, you should start monitoring the child every 20 minutes instead of every 10 minutes. As the child approaches 60 percent "in potty" successes, start monitoring him every 40 minutes instead of every 20 minutes. Continue to remind the child that when he or she has to "go potty" he or she should proceed by himself or herself and go on the potty—whenever the child goes by himself or herself he or she should be praised and rewarded generously.

    When the child's "in potty" successes reach 80 percent, you should begin monitoring him or her every 50 minutes. Continue throughout this period to encourage him or her to go to the potty by himself or herself whenever he or she has to go. Praise and reward him or her whenever he or she goes by himself or herself. After he or she reaches 90 percent or above success in the potty, you should monitor him or her every 60 to 90 minutes. After he or she reaches 100 percent success, you should monitor him or her every 90 to 120 minutes and gradually withdraw your monitoring as his or her 100 percent success rate remains constant over a number of weeks.

    Remember to praise the child for any progress in successfully going on the potty. Also, make sure that the child is changed as soon as possible after he or she has either wet or had a BM in his or her pants. Change his or her clothes in a matter-of-fact manner, making sure that you attend to him or her (and perhaps reward him or her) as little as possible. *Do not rush the child to become toilet trained.* Many children react in the opposite way when a behavior modifier pushes them to become toilet trained.

Do not continue this program when the child is sick. Many times, a child's sickness will prevent him or her from controlling his or her urine and/or bowels. Wait until the child feels better again. If, however, the child indicates to you that he or she wants to use the potty when he or she is sick, allow him or her to do this and reward him or her for practicing his or her new toilet habits.

Initially, boys should be allowed to sit while urinating. After they have developed expertise in learning to use the potty, they should then be taught to stand to urinate (and direct their urine stream) and to sit for a BM. Both girls and boys should be taught to wipe themselves well only after they have developed mastery in their new toileting habits.

If the child develops or has enuresis, you should not deal with this problem until he or she is completely toilet trained. Programs (and devices) which can be used for treating enuresis, as well as alternative programs for toilet training children, are mentioned in Appendix F.

The success of this program depends on the consistency of the behavior modifier (and his or her assistants or colleagues) throughout the child's day, as well as how the behavior modifier relates to the child. As the child progresses in his or her toilet habits and begins to be "dry" for a day or more, you may find that occasional accidents occur. Do not say to the child, "No! Bad boy (or girl). You went in your pants. . . ." Rather, accept the event as an accident and help the child change his or her clothes. If, however, the accidents become frequent, you may have to begin monitoring the child more often and remind him or her to use the toilet when he or she feels he or she has to pass urine or have a BM. Continue to reward him or her for using the toilet.

PROGRAM FOR TEACHING A CHILD TO RECOGNIZE HIS/HER NAME

Throughout the program, praise the child for any progress. Also reward the child at each step with small amounts of his or her favorite reinforcement. Each session should be limited to not more than ten minutes once or twice daily. Since this program makes use of different colors, make sure the child is not partially or totally color blind. You will also need a chart to record the child's progress. The vertical line should state Number of Steps and the horizontal line, Sessions.

1. Write the child's name with red crayon on a piece of white card-board. Put the name on a table in front of the child and say "[*Name*], point to your name." You may have to guide the child at first in this activity.

2. Repeat step 1, except this time also place on the table a similar piece of cardboard with another name written on it in a distinctly differ-ent color. (This new name should be approximately the same length and size as the child's name, but should not contain any of, or very few of, the same letters.) You may have to guide the child gently at first to help him or her point to the correct name. Repeat this step until the child can correctly point to his name two con-secutive times.

3. Repeat step 2, except reverse the left-right position of the names (that is, if the child's name was originally to the left of the second name, it should now be placed to the right). You may have to guide the child at first before he or she can correctly choose his or her name two consecutive times.

4. Repeat steps 2 and 3, alternating the left-right position of his or her name until he or she can correctly point to his or her name two consecutive times. Be sure to praise and reward the child for any progress.

5. Repeat step 4, except replace the second name card with a third card which has the same name written in red. Repeat this step until the child correctly identifies his or her name two consecutive times. You may have to gently guide the child at first before he or she can correctly point to his or her name.

6. Repeat step 5, except replace the third name card with a fourth name card. *The new name should also be written in red, be similar. in length, and have a few letters in common with the child's name.* Repeat this step until the child is successful two consecutive times. Be sure to alternate the left-right position of the child's name card.

7. Repeat step 6, except alternate the use of the third and fourth names as well as the left-right position of the child's name. Repeat this step until the child can successfully identify his or her name two consecutive times.

8. This time introduce all three names—each written in red and similar in length. Say to the child, "[*Name*], point to your name." After each try by the child, change the relative positions of the name cards. Repeat this step until the child correctly identifies his or her name two consecutive times. (You may have to guide the child at first in correctly choosing his or her name.)

9. Repeat step 8, except add a fourth name, written in the same color and similar in length to the child's name, but contains many of the letters in the child's name. Again, you may have to guide the child at first in correctly choosing his or her name. Repeat this step until the child correctly identifies his or her name two consecutive times.

10. Repeat step 9, except add a fifth name which is also written in red, not the same length as the child's name, and has many letters in common with the child's name. Repeat this step until the child correctly identifies his or her name two consecutive times.

Remember to praise the child each time he or she successfully identifies his or her name. If the child has repeated difficulty proceeding from one particular step to the next, develop an in-between step(s) to help him or her progress to the next step.

After the child completes step 10, you may want to add and then delete other names of children—again requesting the child to point to his or her name among those presented to him or her. You can also vary the color of his or her name as well as the other names and again ask him or her to point to his or her name.

GENERAL PRESCRIPTIONS

PRESCRIPTION FOR SOCIAL INTERACTION AND COOPERATIVE PLAY

The behavior modifier should first identify specifically what behavior he/she wants the child to learn. To state that he or she wishes to teach a child to socially interact with another child is not specific enough. The *particular* behavior that the behavior modifier wants to strengthen in the child should be stated.

Some researchers have divided the term "social interaction" into four behavioral components: (1) looking at another child, (2) physical proximity to another child, (3) touching another child, and (4) verbalizations with another child. We could also add a fifth component—participation in an activity which produces reinforcement for all of the participants (at least two children); this latter component is often referred to as cooperative play. Although these behavioral components are not necessarily independent of each other, a behavior modifier could, for example, strengthen the ball catching and throwing behavior between two children without strengthening their verbalizations with each other, or their touching of each other.

The next step for the behavior modifier is to specify how the behavioral component will be strengthened.[7] For example, will the behavior modifier use reinforcement (continuous versus intermittent), modeling, prompting, shaping, a social skills training package, and so forth? If reinforcement is used, what reinforcers will be used with the children? Finally, to ensure that the intervention has worked, the behavior modifier should collect data on the child's progress as well as perform a follow-up evaluation and check for generalization.

PRESCRIPTION FOR LANGUAGE TRAINING

Two prescriptions are presented here: the first concerns the establishment of imitative speech and the second involves the acquisition of functional language.[8]

Imitative speech. This prescription assumes that the child is not completely mute (i.e., there is some evidence of gurgling sounds, grunting noises, or babbling). Since a list of the most easily acquired phonemes/sounds has not been published, the behavior modifier should make sure that he or she chooses sounds that allow easy manual prompting and fading (Harris 1975).

Procedure: The child should be brought to a quiet room which is devoid of any distractions. The child should be seated directly in front of and facing the behavior modifier.[9] The child should then be reinforced for emitting any sound within a specified time period (5 to 10 seconds) following the modeling of the sound by the behavior modifier. After the child learns to produce a sound at a stable rate, following the behavior modifier's production of a sound, he or she should begin reinforcing the child for emitting sounds that are closer approximations to those modeled by the behavior modifier. This should occur on a very gradual basis, making sure that the child's frequency of vocal responses does not decrease appreciably.

Next, the behavior modifier should only reinforce the child for imitating those sounds made by the behavior modifier. As the child begins to imitate reliably the original list of sounds, the behavior modifier should then introduce new sounds until these are also modeled appropriately. At this time, he or she can also introduce word-sounds, especially if such sounds were not contained in the original list. The initial word-sounds should not be difficult to form and should contain the phonemes/sounds that were learned previously. Training should take place two to six days per week, 20 minutes to one hour per session. In this regard, it is not clear from the literature that the more time you spend with a child in a session, the faster he or she will learn. It is probably important, however, for the behavior modifier to arrange to see the child in training on as many days during the week as is possible.

Eye contact is also important for effective vocal imitation training. If the child does not have eye contact, then the eye contact prescription outlined earlier in this chapter should be initiated prior to speech training. The behavior modifier should also be certain that the child is not deaf and that the reinforcement chosen is highly attractive to the child.

Functional speech.   This procedure assumes that the child has a stable level of vocal imitation as well as an appreciable level of eye contact—especially eye contact in response to the command "[*Name*], look at me!"

Procedure: A set of approximately four to eight familiar pictures, each containing a clear picture of an animal, object, or person, should be shown to the child concurrent with the behavior modifier naming what is in the picture (e.g., "DOG"). The child should receive reinforcement for imitating the behavior modifier within a five- to 50-second period. After the child is imitating the behavior modifier's words at a heightened stable rate, the behavior modifier should begin to gradually fade out his/her naming of the picture. For example, he or she could begin to soften his/her saying of the word when the picture is shown, and/or delay in saying the word to give the child the opportunity to say the word spontaneously. Each time the child says the word, he/she should receive reinforcement, regardless of whether the word is still being faded out by the behavior modifier.

Next, the behavior modifier should begin asking questions, saying "What is this?" as soon as the picture is shown, and reinforce the child for saying the word without also imitating the behavior modifier's question. At this point, the behavior modifier may have to prompt the verbal response, and gradually fade it out. As the child reaches a stable rate of naming the picture in response to the question, the behavior modifier should gradually begin to introduce new pictures and repeat the previous procedure.

As with imitative speech, the reinforcement used by the behavior modifier should be attractive to the child, and the behavior modifier should work with the child as many days per week as is possible, 20 to 45 minutes per session. The behavior modifier should also be sure that the child is not deaf and that there is no organic reason why he/she cannot acquire language. After the child is responding correctly at a high rate, the behavior modifier can begin to ask new and more difficult questions about particular pictures (e.g., "What candy do you want?").

Following single-word training the behavior modifier can then begin to teach the child how to combine words, to ask questions, and/or to use plural versus singular word forms.

PRESCRIPTION FOR REDUCING AGGRESSIVE BEHAVIOR

The findings from the research literature suggest that there are four approaches to reducing aggressive behavior in exceptional children.[10]

Prescription 1:   Reinforcement of Incompatible Behavior and Use of Extinction. Identify the specific target aggressive behavior that should be reduced. Also, identify one or more nonaggressive behavior that is incompatible with the target aggressive behavior and which you would like to strengthen. Select several different reinforcers for the child. Reward the child immediately after he or she exhibits a nonaggressive behavior or engages in appropriate nonaggressive interactions with others. Praise the student as you give the child the reinforcement. Ignore every instance of the aggressive behavior.

Prescription 2:   Token Reinforcement and the Use of Response Cost. Identify the particular aggressive behavior that should be reduced. Also, identify one or more nonaggressive behavior that you want to strengthen. Decide what medium will be used for tokens. Select and price the reinforcers in relation to tokens that can be earned or charged. Decide on the number of tokens that will be removed following each instance of the aggressive behavior. Reinforce the child with a token immediately after the child exhibits one of the nonaggressive behaviors. Praise the child as you give him or her the token. Remove the specified number of tokens from the child immediately following every instance of the aggressive behavior. At the end of a specified time period, allow the student to exchange his or her tokens for a reward of his or her choice.

Prescription 3:   DRO Plus Time Out. Identify the particular aggressive behavior that should be reduced. Also, identify several nonaggressive behaviors that you want to strengthen. Select a particular time out procedure (e.g., contingent observation, exclusion time out, seclusion time out). Establish an area that the child does not find attractive and that is isolated from others as well as from his or her usual daily activities. Whenever the child exhibits the aggressive behavior, immediately remove the child from the situation and take him or her in a matter-of-fact manner to the time out area. The student should remain in the time out area for a few (3 to 8) minutes or until he or she has calmed down. Return the child to the original situation and reinforce him or her for behaving in a nonaggressive manner.

Prescription 4:· DRO Plus Overcorrection. Identify the particular aggressive behavior that should be reduced. Also, identify one or more nonaggressive behavior that you want to strengthen. Select an appropriate activity for the overcorrection procedure. Whenever the child exhibits the aggressive behavior, immediately stop the child's activity and tell the child that he or she has behaved in an aggressive manner, for example, "We do not hit in this classroom." Provide verbal instructions for the overcorrection procedure. If necessary, use physical guidance to assist the child in carrying out the procedure. Return the child to the ongoing class activity and reinforce him or her for behaving nonaggressively.

PRESCRIPTION FOR REDUCING STEREOTYPIC BEHAVIOR OR SELF-STIMULATION

On the basis of the literature that has been published on the reduction of stereotypic behavior and self-stimulation in exceptional children, the following four prescriptions can be formulated.

Prescription 1: Differential Reinforcement of Incompatible Behaviors Plus the Use of Extinction. Identify specifically the stereotypic behavior that should be reduced. Identify several nonstereotypic/non-self-stimulatory behaviors that are incompatible with the target behavior and that you want to strengthen. Select several different reinforcers for the child. Reinforce the child immediately after the child exhibits one of the nonstereotypic/non-self-stimulatory behaviors. Praise the child as you give him or her the reinforcement. Ignore every instance of the stereotypic or self-stimulatory behavior. Attend to the child again only after he or she has stopped exhibiting the target behavior for several seconds. *Note:* This procedure should *only* be used when the behavior modifier is fairly sure that the child is exhibiting the stereotypic or self-stimulatory behavior to elicit adult attention.

Prescription 2: Differential Reinforcement of Incompatible Behaviors Plus Redirection and Reinforcement. Identify specifically the stereotypic or self-stimulatory behaviors that should be reduced. Also, identify several activities that require nonstereotypic/non-self-stimulatory behaviors. Select several different reinforcers for the child. Whenever the child begins to exhibit the stereotypic or self-stimulatory behavior(s) immediately redirect him or her to one of the activities that require nonstereotypic/non-self-stimulatory behaviors. Reinforce and praise the child for engaging in activities that are incompatible with the stereotypic or self-stimulatory behavior. Also, reinforce and praise the child for exhibiting other appropriate behaviors that are incompatible with the target behavior.

Prescription 3: Differential Reinforcement of Incompatible Behaviors Plus Physical Prompting. Identify specifically the stereotypic or self-stimulatory behavior(s) that should be reduced. Identify several nonstereotypic/non-self-stimulatory behaviors that are incompatible with the target behavior and that you want to strengthen. Select several different reinforcers for the child. Whenever the child begins to exhibit the target behavior, tell him or her "No!" in a firm voice, and physically block his or her behavior. Physically prompt the child to engage in behaviors and activities that are incompatible with the target behavior. Reinforce and praise the child immediately after he or she exhibits nonstereotypic/non-self-stimulatory behaviors.

Prescription 4: Differential Reinforcement of Incompatible Behaviors Plus Overcorrection. Identify specifically the stereotypic or self-stimulatory behavior that should be reduced. Also, identify several non-stereotypic/non-self-stimulatory behaviors that you want to strengthen. Select an appropriate overcorrection procedure (in many cases, a positive practice procedure is appropriate). Whenever the child exhibits the stereotypic or self-stimulatory behavior, immediately stop the child's activity and tell him or her, "No [rocking, slapping, twirling, etc.]" in a firm voice. Provide verbal instructions for the overcorrection procedure. If necessary use physical guidance to encourage the child to carry out the overcorrection procedure. Return the child to the ongoing class activity and reinforce him or her for exhibiting nonstereotypic or non-self-stimulatory behaviors.

NOTES

1. Some of the programs presented in this chapter were developed during the conduct of research and the development of demonstration projects by the author at the Syracuse Developmental Center, Syracuse, New York. The assistance of Drs. Kenneth R. Suckerman and M. Catherine Wheeler in the implementation of these programs is appreciated.

2. This prescription is based on Morris, R. J., and O'Neill, J. H. (1975). Developing eye contact in severely and profoundly retarded children. *Mental Retardation, 13,* 42–43; and Morris, R. J. (1977). A program for establishing eye contact in severely and profoundly retarded children. *Rehabilitation Psychology, 24,* 236–40.

3. This program is based on a study by Baer, D. M., Peterson, R. F., & Sherman, J. A. (1967) The development of imitation by reinforcing behavioral similarity to a model. *Journal of Experimental Analysis of Behavior, 10,* 405–16; and O'Neill, J. H., and Morris, R. J. (1979). The development of imitation in nonimitative, severely retarded children: Contribution of reinforcement and instruction. *Rehabilitation Psychology, 26,* 79–89.

4. This program is based in part on a film by Myerson, L. (Producer). (1967). *Rewards and reinforcements in learning.* Scottsdale, Arizona: Behavior Modifications Productions.

5. This program is based on an article by Meyerson, L., Kerr, N., and Michael, J. L. (1967). Behavior modification in rehabilitation. In S. W. Bijou and D. M. Baer (Eds.), *Child development: Readings in experimental analysis.* New York: Appleton-Century-Crofts.; and a study by Morris, R. J., & O'Neill, J. H. (1974). *Establishing independent walking in severely retarded children.* Unpublished study. Department of Psychology, Syracuse University.

6. This prescription is based on Morris, R. J., and Morisano, E. R. (1974). *The treatment of aquaphobia in mentally retarded persons via contact desensitization.* Unpublished study. Syracuse University; Morisano, E. R. (1980). *A comparison of the effects of contact desensitization and symbolic modeling in the treatment of phobic mentally retarded persons.* Unpublished doctoral dissertation. Syracuse University; and Morris, R. J., and Kratochwill, T. R. (1983). *Treating children's fears and phobias: A behavioral approach.* New York: Pergamon Press.

7. This prescription is based on Morris (1978). For a more detailed discussion of teaching social skills to exceptional children, the interested reader is referred to Ollendick and Cerny (1981), Williams, Hamre-Nietupski, Pumpian, McDaniel-Marx, and Wheeler (1978), and Whitman et al. (1983).

8. This prescription is based on Morris (1978). For a more detailed discussion of language training, the interested reader is referred to Harris, S. L. (1976) *Teaching speech to the nonverbal child.* Lawrence, Kansas: H. & H. Enterprises.; Lovaas, O. I. (1977). *The autistic child's language development through behavior modification.* New York: Irvington Publishers, 1977; and Lovaas, O. I. (1981). *Teaching developmentally disabled children: The me book.* Baltimore: University Park Press.

9. As an alternative to sitting the child in front of the behavior modifier, the child could sit on the behavior modifier's lap, as in Kerr et al. (1965), and/or be played with as discussed by Lovaas et al. (1966).

10. The interested reader is referred to the following source for a more detailed discussion of aggression control: Kazdin, A. E., and Frame, C. (1983). Aggressive behavior and conduct disorder. In R. J. Morris and T. R. Kratochwill (Eds.). *The practice of child therapy.* New York: Pergamon Press.

Chapter 7

PROBLEMS AND DIFFICULTIES CONDUCTING A BEHAVIOR MODIFICATION PROGRAM

This chapter first discusses program development problems and then presents some of the potential difficulties found in carrying out a behavior program plan. This is followed by a discussion of generalization and transfer of training, and a description of some methods for helping a child generalize what he or she has learned. The chapter ends with a review of the steps in conducting a behavior modification program.

PROBLEMS IN ESTABLISHING A PROGRAM

After learning about behavior modification procedures, some behavior modifiers become confused about which behavior they should change first in an exceptional child. For example, should they first modify a desirable or undesirable behavior, an especially difficult and complex behavior, or a simple behavior? Although there is no set pattern to determine which type of behavior a behavior modifier should modify first, we can suggest a general rule. *Until the behavior modifier becomes very familiar with the use of behavior modification procedures, he or she should concentrate on modifying rather simple and straightforward target behaviors.* Then, as he or she develops expertise in using these procedures, he or she can begin tackling more difficult desirable or undesirable behaviors. Some behavior modifiers report that they find it easiest first to try out the use of reinforcement procedures—either strengthening a non-complex desirable behavior or developing a new self-help or social skill in the child.

Even as a behavior modifier becomes more expert at using these procedures, he or she should always *remember not to expect too much, too soon, too fast from a child.* Although each of the procedures described in this book has been found to be effective in the treatment of various children's learning and behavior problems (see, for example, Bijou & Baer 1979; Hammill & Bartel 1982; Kauffman 1981; Kazdin 1980; Krumboltz & Krumboltz 1972; Marholin 1978; Millman, Schaefer, & Cohen 1980; Morris & Kratochwill 1983b; Repp 1983; Ross 1981; Smith 1981; Whitman et al. 1983), it takes time for a particular procedure to have an effect on an exceptional child's behavior. How long a period of time is difficult to say. Some children obviously learn faster than others. Some behavior modifiers apply procedures better than others. Some environments are more conducive to change in a child than other environments. Each of these factors and others influence how long it will take a procedure to have an effect on an exceptional child's behavior. The only advice that we can offer a behavior modifier is to make sure he or she has done the best possible job and not necessarily to expect an immediate change in the child's behavior. If, however, a behavior modifier maintains that he or she has tried to apply a procedure as well as possible and has not found any change in the child's behavior after a significant amount of time, the behavior modifier should consider changing or revising the procedure.

Before changing the procedure, however, the behavior modifier should be sure that the child knows what is expected. For example, if we are interested in developing eye contact in a nonverbal child, the child can learn what is expected of him or her through the behavior modifier's use of a physical prompting procedure. Similarly, a behavior modifier could also use physical prompting to teach a nonverbal child to play cooperatively and interact with other children, to sit in a chair, to attend to an educational task, and so forth. A verbal child, on the other hand, could be told (called a *verbal prompt*) what the behavior modifier expects of him or her or the behavior could be modeled for the child.

In establishing a program a behavior modifier should also be certain that each of the behavior modifiers or assistants involved in working with the exceptional child is thoroughly familiar with the behavioral procedure and is willing to carry out the procedure according to the program plan. That is, there *must* be consistency in carrying out the program. Too often a behavior modifier spends a great deal of time and effort in setting up a behavioral procedure without ever informing others about the program or obtaining their agreement to participate in it. If the other people who work with the child do not participate in the behavioral program, or are inconsistent in its application, they will likely decrease the overall effectiveness of the program. The degree to which the program is affected will be determined largely by the target behavior being changed and the situation in which it is changed. If, for example, a child is being taught by Mrs. Howard to recognize letters and produce their sounds, using a shaping program, and this is not followed through later in the day by Mrs. Thomas or Mr. Smith (who may use another method), it will be more difficult for the child to master this task. Similarly, if time out is used by one behavior modifier to reduce tantrums in the classroom and another person in the classroom prefers to use attention to the tantrums to "help" the child, the child's tantrums are not likely to decrease. On the other hand, if a behavior modifier plans to teach a child a behavior (or reduce a behavior) only in a situation in which the behavior modifier has complete control, then the program is likely to be more successful—although the modified behavior may not generalize or transfer to any other situation (see, for example, Kazdin 1980; Ollendick & Cerny 1981).

Related to the problem of consistency in behavioral programming is the issue of motivation on the part of behavior modifiers and assistants in the whole change procedure. Behavior modifiers differ in their respective motivation to work with a child. Whenever possible, each behavior modifier involved in a behavioral program should have a comparable motivational and interest level in working with a child, and a willingness to contribute the necessary time (and make the necessary sacrifices) to maximize the potential effectiveness of the program.

Before finalizing any treatment program, a behavior modifier should be sure that he or she is comfortable with the use of the procedure being suggested. This is especially true for those procedures described in Chapter 5. Some procedures for reducing behavior may be more acceptable to the behavior modifier, or the facility in which he or she works, than others, and the behavior modifier should be aware of which ones these are. Even under ideal circumstances, a behavioral program is not likely to be effective if the behavior modifier does not feel at ease and confident with it.

DIFFICULTIES IN CARRYING OUT THE PROGRAM

Sometimes after a behavior program has been started a behavior modifier notices that the child or student is refusing to participate—showing, for example, negativism or boredom. This can be caused by many factors:

1. The reinforcer being used may no longer be attractive to the child.

2. The child may view the whole situation as aversive because of various procedures to which he or she has been exposed.

3. The amount and type of reinforcement he or she is receiving for each desirable behavior may not be appropriate.

4. The child may perceive the behavior modifier as disinterested in him or her and in his or her progress.

5. The behavior program is perhaps being applied incorrectly, inconsistently, or not in a systematic fashion.

6. When a behavior reduction program is used, it is not being used in conjunction with a reinforcement program.

If there is a suspected problem with the attractiveness of the reinforcer or with the amount or type of reinforcement being used, the behavior modifier should check the following:

1. The quality of the reinforcement.

2. The schedule of reinforcement that the child or student is on.

3. The immediacy with which the reinforcement is being provided by each of the behavior modifiers as well as the manner in which it is being given to the child.

4. The form of the social reinforcement being used (verbal versus nonverbal; whether the child likes social reinforcers or finds them "neutral" or even aversive).

5. The appropriateness of using token, tangible, or social reinforcers (for example, token reinforcement systems may not be appropriate for some severely mentally retarded or autistic children; social reinforcers may be less effective than tokens with some emotionally handicapped children; e.g., Kazdin 1977, 1980; Repp 1983; Smith 1981; Whitman et al. 1983).

As a general rule, therefore, if the behavior modifier feels that there might be a problem with the reinforcer or reinforcement system being used, it is best to critically evaluate all aspects of the entire reinforcement program—just to make sure that it is being applied correctly and under the best conditions.

The child's negativism and/or boredom may also be an attempt on his or her part to take control—that is, countercontrol—of the situation in which the behavior modification program is being carried out. For example, a child might learn that by being disruptive he or she can stop or temporarily postpone the training period or behavior program. If this appears to be the case, the behavior modifier should initiate—where possible—an extinction procedure, ignoring the child during this period and generously reinforcing him or her on a continuous schedule when he or she is ready to begin the training period or behavior program. The behavior modifier should, however, make sure that this disruptive behavior/negativism/boredom does not become a game for the exceptional child—where the disruption that he or she causes either to the program or personally to the behavior modifier is in fact the reinforcement for the child. If this disruptive behavior continues, the behavior modifier should briefly discontinue the behavior program, and review in detail what went on during the program and what might be contributing to his or her behavior. If changes can be made in the program, they should be made prior to the next training session, school day, or class period. If no changes can be made, and the behavior modifier fully expects the child to continue with his or her negativism or boredom, then the behavior program should be discontinued and a new program plan developed.

Another problem that occasionally develops is related to the use of a particular behavior modification procedure or, more appropriately, the mismatch of a particular procedure with the type of child with whom it is being used. For example, some exceptional children do not have any, or have very few, reinforcement preferences, and for them the use of most reinforcers may actually be like punishment. This is sometimes found with physically abused children who find adult attention or touch to be aversive because of the meaning that such activities had for them in the past. Similarly, some autistic children are not responsive to—and at times actively avoid—adult eye contact and smiles. In addition, as noted in Chapter 6, some children experience negative side effects when physical punishment or a procedure like overcorrection is used. When such negative side effects occur, the behavior modifier *must* ask himself or herself whether the potential benefits of continuing with the program outweigh the observed side effects.

Two additional difficulties that sometimes arise when carrying out a behavior modification program are not related to the specific procedure(s) being used or to the target behavior(s) being changed; rather, they are related to *who* is modifying the behavior and *where* the behavior is being modified. We have already addressed the issue of behavior modifier involvement, expectancy level, and motivation to work with a particular exceptional child or student. If the behavior program is not being carried out within the framework of a positive relationship with the child, then this may influence the successful outcome of the program (see, for example, Morris & Magrath 1983). Related to this is the behavior modifier's concern about the lack of equal or sufficient time to interact with the other children or students for whom he or she is responsible. This has the potential of not only being a problem for the behavior modifier, but for the nontarget children who may feel that they have the "right" to equal time with the behavior modifier. This feeling, in turn, may result in the nontarget children becoming disruptive and/or aggressive (not necessarily toward the target child).

The setting in which the behavior program is being conducted is also important. If, for example, a particular training session (e.g., eye contact training, training in phonics, or math work) is occurring within an environment where the child and/or behavior modifier are being interrupted repeatedly, then this decreases the chances of the program being successful. Whenever possible, scheduled training sessions should be conducted in a quiet area, during a time that the behavior modifier is fairly confident that he or she or the child/student will not be disturbed. Furthermore, during this time the training area should be devoid of objects that may be distracting to the child. The area should also be well lighted, either sound attenuated or away from a noisy street or room, and with few, if any, windows out of which the child can look—if the presence of a window cannot be avoided then it should be covered with a neutral color drapery or a shade. On the other hand, if the behavior modifier feels that it is important for the training to take place in the child's "natural" environment, then he or she should try to anticipate (during the initial phases of training) as many potential interruptions as possible and try to prevent them from occurring.

By monitoring the child's day-to-day, period-to-period progress, the behavior modifier will know whether to intervene in the behavior program. This is another reason it is important for the behavior modifier to chart the child's progress following each period, session, or day. If, for example, through charting the behavior modifier notices that the child is not achieving or progressing toward the criterion for success within a reasonable amount of time, he or she will then know to intervene in the program. Although what is a "reasonable" time period will vary from child to child, and depends on the particular behavior being modified and behavior program being used, the general rule is that if the target behavior does not show some change within three to five weeks or within ten to twenty sessions or class periods then the program should be critically evaluated. It is also important to continue charting the child's target behavior (though not as often) after the child has achieved the criterion for success and the behavior program has been stopped. By doing this follow-up monitoring the behavior modifier will be able to know in a relatively short time whether the child has dropped below the criterion level for success—and whether the behavior program needs to be reintroduced.

In summary, the relative success of any behavior modification program depends greatly on the behavior modifier being sensitive to the potential problems that may develop in carrying out the program. The behavior modifier, however, can avoid some of these problems by soliciting the help of volunteers to increase the number of people who are working with the child or children. Such assistance can be found from local retiree organizations, university undergraduate and graduate programs (in such areas as special education, psychology, educational psychology, nursing, social work, and counseling and rehabilitation), older children in the school or neighborhood, parent organizations, and service and social clubs. Such assistance can greatly reduce a behavior modifier's feeling of frustration with a particular child's progress or behavior program, and, in turn, enhance this person's motivation and involvement with the target child.

GENERALIZATION OF THE EXCEPTIONAL CHILD'S BEHAVIOR

When we modify a child's behavior, we typically do it in a particular situation or within a limited number of situations. Since these situations are associated with learning what to do (or what not to do), we find that the child tends to perform the learned behavior only when these situations occur. In other words, these situations have situational control of the child's behavior. This means, for example, that a child who learns not to hit other children at school may continue hitting other children at home or in the neighborhood. Similarly, a child may learn in the classroom the sound associated with the alphabet in the presence of one teacher and not transfer his or her "knowledge" to another teacher in another classroom—even when it is within the same school setting. And, finally, a child may learn to sit in his or her seat and do the required workbook assignments as long as the reinforcement program is in effect, but start moving around the room and not do his or her seat work after the program has been stopped.

Each of the above examples represents instances where a certain type of generalization did not occur. Although we now know that we can modify many types of academic, social, self-help, and emotional behaviors in exceptional children, these changes are of little importance if they do not, for example, last over time or transfer to other settings. Changes that are to be maintained over time—even after the behavior modification program has been stopped—are usually referred to as *response maintenance generalization*. Changes that are to occur from one environmental situation to another, from one setting to another setting within the same environment, and/or from one person to another person(s) are usually referred to as *situation or setting generalization*. In working with exceptional children, we are concerned with both forms of generalization. And, in some instances, we are concerned with both forms within the same time frame. For example, if we successfully teach cooperative play and social interaction to a child in a classroom setting, we would be concerned with both the maintenance of these social behaviors in the classroom as well as their transfer to such places as the playground, physical education class, art class, and the home environment.

A third type of generalization, *response generalization*, is one that is not as well understood as the other forms of generalization. Response generalization refers to those changes in behaviors that occur in a child that have not been targeted for intervention. These are behaviors that occur as a result of changes found in the target behavior.

Generalization of behavior is *not* a required outcome of a successful behavior modification program (Bijou & Baer 1979). Generalization is a preferred outcome. The reason for this relates back to the assumptions of behavior modification that were discussed in Chapter 1. We learned in Chapter 1 (p. 9) that one of the major assumptions of behavior modification is that the behaviors that children learn are situation specific and do not generalize to other situations. Thus, we should not expect generalization or transfer of training to occur, but these are never the less preferred outcomes of behavior modification intervention. Since we assume that generalization should not occur, and yet maintain that it is a preferred outcome, what needs to be done is to program generalization into the child's behavior program plan. This has become a very important topic of research in recent years, and a number of writers (e.g., Goldstein & Kanfer 1979; Goldstein, Sprafkin, Gershaw, & Klein 1980; Kazdin 1980; Kazdin & Frame 1983; Ross 1980, 1981; Schreibman, Charlop, & Britten 1983) have addressed the issue of how to program generalization into a behavior modification procedure.

Teaching Generalization

As mentioned above, a number of writers have begun to address the issue of generalization training (Goldstein 1981; Goldstein & Kanfer 1979; Kazdin 1980; Ollendick & Cerny 1981). In this section we have listed different methods for teaching various forms of generalization to a child. The reader should note, however, that what is being presented here are only *suggestions* for teaching generalization. A sufficient body of research literature with exceptional children does not yet exist for us to state with any certainty that these methods will work or are appropriate for all children, for all behaviors being changed, under all conditions.

Schedules of reinforcement.   As we mentioned earlier, after a child's behavior is well established using continuous reinforcement, the behavior modifier should switch the child to a fixed and then to a variable schedule of reinforcement. Once a child is on a variable schedule of reinforcement, he or she is being taught to perform the target behavior even though he or she may not be reinforced for it. In essence, we are teaching a child who is on a variable reinforcement schedule to *tolerate* being on extinction most of the time (e.g., Kazdin 1980; Ollendick & Cerny 1981). The effectiveness of this procedure can be immediately seen by just thinking of the number of people who play the slot machines in Las Vegas or Atlantic City. Their behavior is maintained on a variable schedule of reinforcement, and think how many days and weeks they continue to play the slot machines without ever being reinforced or being reinforced at a minimum level.

One of the criticisms of this response maintenance procedure is that the behavior modifier has not really stopped the behavior program; the program has just been "thinned" to the point where the child is performing the behavior at a level that is quite disproportionate to the frequency and amount of reinforcement being provided. Never the less, this is still an effective way of maintaining the child's behavior over time.

Stimulus expansion and stimulus variability. Very often in behavior modification we find that the behavior modifier only works with the child in one particular situation or stimulus setting (e.g., classroom) when, in fact, the goal is for the target behavior also to occur in other stimulus settings (e.g., playground, home, or another classroom). In order to maximize this form of generalization, the behavior modifier should do one or all of the following:

1. As intervention progresses and the child's behavior noticeably changes, begin gradually to bring into the intervention situation other people with whom the child interacts. At first, these people should just observe. Eventually, they should take an active role in the intervention—making sure that they use the same instructions, commands, and so forth as the behavior modifier and carry out the intervention procedure in the *same way* as the behavior modifier. These people should then be encouraged to use the same approach with the child in those situations in which they interact with the child.

2. As the child's behavior noticeably changes and starts to stabilize at an acceptable (but not necessarily final) level, the behavior modifier should bring the child into other situations and apply the intervention procedure. As the child's behavior changes in these situations also, the behavior modifier should bring in those people with whom the child interacts in these new situations. They should then be trained to apply the same procedure as the behavior modifier.

3. If a child shows the same target behavior in more than one situation (e.g., at home, in class, in physical education), all the people involved in these situations should meet before intervention begins and agree on *one* behavior program plan. Each person should then apply the procedure. Regular meetings should be held among these people to discuss the child's progress as well as any problems.

4. As the child's behavior noticeably changes, begin gradually to bring into the intervention situation elements of the other situation(s) in which the target behavior is to occur. Such elements may be nones-

sential people—that is, people with whom the child has a low probability of interacting, but who are still present in the other situation, or people with whom the child has a high probability of interacting, but in whose presence the child does not perform the target behavior—pets, furniture, pictures, background music, and so forth. (Adapted from Goldstein 1981; Goldstein & Kanfer 1979)

Obviously, one cannot expose the child to every conceivable set of circumstances in which the target behavior might occur, but by exposing the child to as many different situations and stimulus elements as possible, the behavior modifier will maximize the gains observed in the training situation.

Fading out the reinforcement schedule.   As we mentioned earlier, one way to establish response maintenance is to move the child into a variable schedule of reinforcement—increasing this schedule as time progresses. The child, however, is still on a reinforcement schedule. Another approach is to fade out the reinforcement schedule as time progresses and the child achieves the criterion for success. Here, pleasant activities and so forth would be increasingly available to the child *without the requirement* that a particular behavior must occur before these activities or rewards are given to the child. Specifically, the previous reinforcers become increasingly available to the child on a *noncontingent basis*—almost as a reinforcement for maintaining his or her behavior at the success criterion level. At the same time the particular reinforcement schedule that he or she is on is faded out.

Self-control.   Using the self-control procedure discussed in Chapter 4, we can teach a child to reinforce himself or herself for continuing to perform the target behavior in not only the training situation (response maintenance) but in other situations (setting generalization), too (e.g., Goldstein, Apter, & Harootunian 1984; Goldstein, Sprafkin, Gershaw, & Klein 1980). This can take place as the child achieves the criterion for success and as the particular behavior program that was used to help the child reach criterion is being faded out.

Bringing in real-life reinforcers.   After the child achieves success in his or her behavior program, the behavior modifier may wish to program the child's new behavior into his or her behavior repertoire or behavior network in the "natural" or real-life environment where the target behavior would normally occur, and where the performance of this behavior, as well as the others in the child's behavior network, are likely to be reinforced by significant people in his or her life (e.g., Goldstein et al. 1984; Goldstein & Kanfer 1979). For example, by teaching an aggressive child to be friendly, not hit other children in class, and to ask such conversational questions as How are you doing today? Do you want to play together after school? and Let's go have lunch together, we might find that the child's peers will pay more attention to him or her and he or she will have more opportunities for other children to want to play with him or her. When this occurs, these natural or real-life reinforcers will likely maintain the target child's behavior criterion for success over time and across situations—permitting the behavior modifier to fade out the behavior program.

SOME REASONS BEHAVIOR MODIFICATION PROGRAMS FAIL

In this section are listed various reasons that have contributed to the ineffectiveness of behavior modification programs. The factors listed are based on unsystematic observations of the implementation of classroom behavior programs, and programs established in residential facilities, as well as on self-reports from behavior modifiers in each of these settings.[1] This list is provided without discussion as a resource for people who plan to use behavior modification procedures to make sure they have controlled for these factors and, perhaps, thereby maximize the effectiveness of the behavior program(s) that they are using or plan to use.

Behavior modification programs fail because of:

- Inconsistency in the application of the procedures among teachers, professionals, and staff.

- Reluctance on the part of the teachers, professionals, or staff to chart the child's progress, and therefore not monitor the relative effectiveness of the behavior program.

- Target behaviors are not identified specifically (e.g., IBSO test is not used) creating uncertainty about which behavior is being modified.

- Negative or unsuccessful prior experiences of staff in the use of behavior modification procedures; creating a negative set or expectation regarding the effectiveness of the behavior program.

- Behavior program produces an initial change in the child's behavior and results in the teacher, professional, or staff easing up on the consistent application of the procedure.

- Lack of staff or parent training in the application of the behavior program before it is initiated.

- Behavior modifier discontinues program early or before the time one should reasonably expect a change in the child's behavior.

- Behavior modifier expects too much, too soon, too fast from the child.

- Classroom, home situation, or other environment not conducive to establishing the behavior program.

- Behavior modifier does not like the child or has low expectations for change.

- Child's repertoire of inappropriate behaviors is so extensive and frequent that by changing one target behavior there will be little impact on the behavior modifier's perception of the effectiveness of the behavior program—the behavior modifier therefore will be disinclined to continue using behavior modification.

- Too many children or students in a classroom to implement the behavior program.

- Not sufficient staff available to assist in carrying out the program.

- The behavior targeted for change in the child is too difficult for him or her to perform.

- Inconsistency between school and home behavior modification programs.

- Difficulty finding or controlling the availability of reinforcers for the child.

- Too long of a delay between performing the target behavior and providing the reinforcement, or between the undesirable behavior and the application of the behavior reduction program.

- Child is on medication that decreases the probability of performing the target behavior, or it changes the nature of the target behavior, or it interrupts the application of the behavior program.

- Rivalry between target student who has a behavior program and other students in class.

- Incorrect identification of antecedents and consequences that contribute to child's behavior.

- Use of too many behavior programs at the same time with the same child.

- False expectation that by using one particular behavior modification procedure for one target behavior, other nontarget behaviors will also change.

- Behavior is expected to generalize despite no attempt to program generalization into the intervention procedure.

- Child's physical handicap interferes with the application of the program.

- Overreliance on behavior modification programs that have been used in the past without tailoring a program to each child's current individual situation.

- Reluctance or refusal to use positive procedures before proceeding to behavior reduction procedures.

- Failure to identify and reinforce a positive alternative and desirable behavior when a behavior reduction program is used.

- Failure to critically evaluate the economic system that was established after a token economy program was developed.

- Child not taught the conditions or settings in which the target behavior is appropriate or inappropriate.

REVIEW OF STEPS IN A BEHAVIOR MODIFICATION PROGRAM

1. Identify the target behavior to be modified. The behavior must be objective and have passed the IBSO test.

2. Choose a plan for observing the target behavior.

3. Develop an intervention program. Have positive programs been tried before using behavior reduction programs?

4. Prepare a progress chart for the child.

5. Establish a criterion for the success of the target behavior.

6. Describe what will specifically occur when the exceptional child performs the desirable behavior, or describe what specifically will occur to teach the child the desirable behavior. Do all behavior modifiers know exactly what to do?

7. Describe what will specifically occur when the exceptional child performs the undesirable behavior, or describe what will specifically occur to teach the child to reduce the undesirable behavior. Do all behavior modifiers know exactly what to do?

8. Decide on the extent of the baseline period. Describe what the behavior modifier will specifically do during baseline.

9. Initiate the baseline phase. Chart the child's target behavior.

10. Initiate the behavior modification program. Continue charting.

11. Monitor the effectiveness of the procedure; make changes in the procedure as appropriate.

12. Program in response maintenance and situation generalization where it is appropriate.

13. Terminate the behavior modification program.

STUDY QUESTIONS

1. In choosing a target behavior, what is the best strategy for a behavior modifier who is using behavior modification procedures for the first time? (Review p. 171 to check your answer.)

2. What should a behavior modifier expect regarding the effectiveness of a behavior modification procedure? (Review pp. 172-73 to check your answer.)

3. Why should different people who work with a child be involved in his or her intervention plan? (Review pp. 172-73 to check your answer.)

4. List four factors which can contribute to a child's refusal to participate in a behavior program.
   a.
   b.
   c.
   d.
   (Review pp. 173-74 to check your answer.)

5. What problems are associated with the use of a behavior modificaiton procedure that is mismatched with a particular exceptional child? (Review p. 175 to check your answer.)

6. Why should a behavior modifier do a follow-up? (Review p. 176 to check your answer.)

7. List three potential behavior modifier problems in the use of behavior modification procedures.
   a.
   b.
   c.
   (Review p. 175 to check your answer.)

8. List three methods of assisting a child in generalizing his or her learned behavior.
   a.
   b.
   c.
   (Review pp. 178-81 to check your answer.)

9. List ten potential reasons that behavior modification programs fail.
   a.
   b.
   c.
   d.
   e.
   f.
   g.
   h.
   i.
   j.
   (Review pp. 181-83 to check your answer.)

10. Review the steps in a behavior modification program and then apply them to the treatment of a particular child.

NOTES

1. Appreciation is due Rebecca A. McReynolds, Ph. D., for her assistance in developing this section.

Chapter **8**

LEGAL AND ETHICAL ISSUES OF BEHAVIOR MODIFICATION

A review of the ethical and legal issues associated with the use of behavior modification procedures is followed by a discussion of a proposed level system regarding the use of positive versus aversive behavior modification methods. The chapter closes with a discussion of a behavior modification peer review system.

ETHICAL ISSUES, RIGHTS, AND BEHAVIOR MODIFICATION

The focus of many discussions of using behavior modification with exceptional children often centers on (1) the issue of controlling people who often have difficulty gaining countercontrol over their environment, and (2) the value or belief by the behavior modifier that these procedures are being used in the "best interests" of a child to help him or her progress socially, academically, emotionally, or developmentally (Morris & Brown 1983).

In addition, concerns have been raised regarding the possible misuse of behavioral procedures, the conditions under which these procedures are used, and whether there is, in fact, infringement on the rights of persons receiving these intervention procedures (e.g., Kazdin 1980). These issues revolve around the notion of *behavioral control*—or the manipulation of other people's behavior through the modification of their environment in order to achieve a particular goal (e.g., the strengthening, developing, or reducing of a target behavior). Braun (1975), for example, has raised the following questions about the use of behavior modification and the issue of behavioral control: "Who shall have the power to control behavior? Towards what end shall the controlling power be used? How shall the power to control behavior be regulated?" (p. 51). To these questions we add: Should the power of control be regulated—if so, under what conditions? Do behavior reduction procedures constitute abusive practices and are they dehumanizing? Even if behavior reduction procedures are effective, does the end result justify the means that are used? (see, for example, Roos 1974 pp. 3–4).

These questions are further complicated by the fact that we are focusing our discussion on the use of these procedures with exceptional children—persons who are often already being controlled by their parents, teachers, and society and who, in most cases, are also being controlled by their school system by being identified as in need of some form of special education services. These children lack rights and control in their participation in their educational programming, and lack the right to decide what the goals of such programming should be, whether they should be in special education, and what should be the format of their curriculum.

One could, therefore, ask the question whether the issue of control addressed in behavior modification is any different than the amount or kind of control exercised by an exceptional child's parents, teachers, or school system regarding what is in his or her "best interests."

This question, as well as those mentioned earlier, is not easy to resolve, and many articles have been published over the past twenty years that have attempted to address the issues surrounding control in behavior modification and the regulation of behavior modification procedures (e.g., Ball 1968; Braun 1975; Farkas 1980; Friedman 1977; Krapfl & Vargas 1973; Roos 1974, 1977). Various legal issues and questions have also been raised (e.g., Friedman 1975a,b; Martin 1975; Shapiro 1974; Wexler 1973,1982).

It is this author's belief that individuals who use behavior modification to change children's behaviors must follow sound ethical practices when applying these procedures. By "ethical practices," we mean that the behavior modifier agrees to follow a particular set of standards, policies, or guidelines established by particular professional groups, organizations, or societies of which he or she is a member (or with which he or she identifies an association) regarding how one should carry out behavior modification procedures. For example, the guidelines for ethical issues for human services published by the Association for Advancement of Behavior Therapy (Table 8.1) are guidelines for the use of behavior modification procedures with both adults and children in a variety of settings (as such, some items may not be apropos for some

TABLE 8.1

Ethical issues for human services

The questions related to each issue have deliberately been cast in a general manner that applies to all types of interventions, and not solely or specifically to the practice of behavior therapy. Issues directed specifically to behavior therapists might imply erroneously that behavior therapy was in some way more in need of ethical concern than nonbehaviorally-oriented therapies.

In the list of issues, the term "client" is used to describe the person whose behavior is to be changed, "therapist" is used to describe the professional in charge of the intervention; "treatment" and "problem," although used in the singular, refer to any and all treatments and problems being formulated with this checklist. The issues are formulated so as to be relevant across as many settings and populations as possible. Thus, they need to be qualified when someone other than the person whose behavior is to be changed is paying the therapist, or when that person's competence or the voluntary nature of that person's consent is questioned. For example, if the therapist has found that the client does not understand the goals or methods being considered, the therapist should substitute the client's guardian or other responsible person for "client," when reviewing the issues below.

A. **Have the goals of treatment been adequately considered?**
   1. To insure that the goals are explicit, are they written?
   2. Has the client's understanding of the goals been assured by having the client restate them orally or in writing?
   3. Have the therapist and client agreed on the goals of therapy?
   4. Will serving the client's interests be contrary to the interests of other persons?
   5. Will serving the client's immediate interests be contrary to the client's long-term interest?
B. **Has the choice of treatment methods been adequately considered?**
   1. Does the published literature show the procedure to be the best one available for that problem?
   2. If no literature exists regarding the treatment method, is the method consistent with generally accepted practice?
   3. Has the client been told of alternative procedures that might be preferred by the client on the basis of significant differences in discomfort, treatment time, cost, or degree of demonstrated effectiveness?
   4. If a treatment procedure is publicly, legally, or professionally controversial, has formal professional consultation been obtained, has the reaction of the affected segment of the public been adequately considered, and have the alternative treatment methods been more closely reexamined and reconsidered?
C. **Is the client's participation voluntary?**
   1. Have possible sources of coercion on the client's participation been considered?
   2. If treatment is legally mandated, has the available range of treatments and therapists been offered?
   3. Can the client withdraw from treatment without a penalty or financial loss that exceeds actual clinical costs?

TABLE 8.1 (continued)

D. When another person or an agency is empowered to arrange for therapy, have the interests of the subordinated client been sufficiently considered?
 1. Has the subordinated client been informed of the treatment objectives and participated in the choice of treatment procedures?
 2. Where the subordinated client's competence to decide is limited, have the client as well as the guardian participated in the treatment discussions to the extent that the client's abilities permit?
 3. If the interests of the subordinated person and the superordinate persons or agency conflict, have attempts been made to reduce the conflict by dealing with both interests?

E. Has the adequacy of treatment been evaluated?
 1. Have quantitative measures of the problem and its progress been obtained?
 2. Have the measures of the problem and its progress been made available to the client during treatment?

F. Has the confidentiality of the treatment relationship been protected?
 1. Has the client been told who has access to the records?
 2. Are records available only to authorized persons?

G. Does the therapist refer the clients to other therapists when necessary?
 1. If treatment is unsuccessful, is the client referred to other therapists?
 2. Has the client been told that if dissatisfied with the treatment, referral will be made?

H. Is the therapist qualified to provide treatment?
 1. Has the therapist had training or experience in treating problems like the client's?
 2. If deficits exist in the therapist's qualifications, has the client been informed?
 3. If the therapist is not adequately qualified, is the client referred to other therapists, or has supervision by a qualified therapist been provided? Is the client informed of the supervisory relation?
 4. If the treatment is administered by mediators, have the mediators been adequately supervised by a qualified therapist?

[Source: Association for Advancement of Behavior Therapy. Ethical issues for human services. *Behavior Therapy*. 1977, **8**, v-vi. Reprinted with permission.]

exceptional children in certain settings). If the reader is not familiar with these guidelines, he or she should take time to carefully study them.

Guidelines have also been published by the Accreditation Council for Services for Mentally Retarded and Other Developmentally Disabled Persons (1978) titled *Standards for Services for developmentally disabled individuals*. These standards, or ethical practices statements, cover such areas as individual program planning and implementation, alternative living arrangements, achieving and protecting rights, research, safety, and sanitation. Listed under "Individual Program Planning and Implementation" are 63 prescriptions and proscriptions to be met when using behavior management or behavior modification procedures with devel-

TABLE 8.2

Examples of items included in the Behavior Management Section of the *Standards for Services for Developmentally Disabled Individuals*

Corporal punishment and verbal abuse (shouting, screaming, swearing, name calling, or any other activity that would be damaging to an individual's self-respect) are prohibited by written policy and are not employed.

Seclusion (defined as the placement of an individual alone, in a room or other area from which egress is prevented, not under observation as part of a systematic time-out program that meets all applicable standards) is not employed.

When food is provided or withheld as part of a behavior management program, its effect on nutrition and dental status is considered.
1. Foods that may be deleterious to health are not used as rewards unless it is documented that alternative rewards have been tried without success.
2. Behavior management programs do not employ, or result in, denial of a nutritionally adequate diet.

The agency has a written policy that defines the use of behavior modification programs, the staff members who may authorize their use, and a mechanism for monitoring and controlling their use.

When maladaptive or problem behaviors are to be modified, the individual's program plan includes provisions to teach the individual the circumstances under which the behaviors can be exhibited appropriately, to channel the behaviors into similar but appropriate expressions, or to replace the behaviors with behaviors that are adaptive and appropriate.
1. Each plan to modify maladaptive behaviors specifies . . . the behavioral objectives of the program . . . the method to be used . . . the schedule for use of the method . . . the person responsible for the program, and . . . the data to be collected to assess progress toward the objectives.
2. Whenever restraint, behavior-modifying drugs, or behavior modification techniques involving the use of time-out devices or aversive stimuli are employed to eliminate maladaptive or problem behaviors, the individual's record documents the fact that less restrictive methods of modifying or replacing the behavior have been systematically tried and have been demonstrated to be ineffective.

Except when used as a time-out device, in accordance with applicable standards, physical restraint is employed only when absolutely necessary to protect the individual from injury to him or herself or to others, and restraint is not employed as punishment, for the convenience of staff, or as a substitute for program.

opmentally disabled persons. A few of the standards that relate specifically to the use of behavior modification are listed in Table 8.2.

The lists in Tables 8.1 and 8.2 clearly demonstrate how various organizations have responded to the concerns of different persons and groups regarding the conditions under which behavior modification services are provided.

Whenever we discuss ethical practices, it is difficult not to include

TABLE 8.2 (continued)

Each behavior modification program that involves the use of aversive conditioning or time-out devices is:

1. Reviewed and approved prior to implementation
2. Conducted only with the written consent of the affected individual and/or the individual's family, as appropriate
3. Described in the individual's program plan
4. When a time-out device is employed, the individual's record documents the fact that the situation from which the individual is removed for time-out provides consistent and positive reinforcement of desired, adaptive behaviors.
5. Removal from a situation for time-out purposes occurs only during the conditioning program and only under the direct observation of the persons conducting the program . . . Removal from a situation for time-out purposes is for not more than one hour, except in extraordinary instances (ordinarily occurring only in the beginning of a time-out program) that are personally approved at the time of occurrence by a member of the individual's interdisciplinary team.
6. Restraints employed as time-out devices are applied only during conditioning sessions and only in the presence of the persons conducting the program . . . Restraints employed as time-out devices are applied for not more than fifteen minutes, except in extraordinary instances (ordinarily occurring only in the beginning of a time-out program) that are personally approved at the time of occurrence by a member of the individual's interdisciplinary team . . . Key locks are not employed on rooms in which individuals are confined for time-out . . . Aversive conditioning is used only in those extreme, last-resort situations in which withholding it would be contrary to the best interests of the individual because his or her behavior is dangerous to him or herself or to other persons and is extremely detrimental to his or her development, and because the individual's failure to respond to positive reinforcement procedures has been documented in his or her record.

From *Standards for Services for Developmentally Disabled Individuals* (1978), pp. 31–35. Reproduced with permission.

philosophical questions regarding people's rights. A rights question arises when an individual causes a change in the behavior of another person by manipulating the person without that person having control over his or her involvement in that manipulation. Here the person is being treated as an object and not as someone who has a choice in establishing a countercontrolling operation (Morris & Brown 1983).

Ethical practices and philosophical issues regarding rights interact when a group of people sharing the same ethics, called the *ethical community*, intervene on behalf of an exceptional child (e.g., Farkas 1980; Vargas 1975). For example, the ethical community (e.g., school board or professional organization) might establish a policy that states "No behavior reduction programs shall be used except those involving reinforcement procedures" or "No special education student should be permitted to engage in self-injurious behavior in school." In each example, the ethical community is acting on its belief that it can determine policy on behalf of the children that it is overseeing; however, the children have not been given the opportunity to offer their opinion or agree with these statements. The children are being treated as objects and not provided with the opportunity to initiate a countercontrolling operation. The ethical community, on the other hand, is doing what it feels is in the "best interests" of the children. How does the ethical community know that it is doing something in the "best interests" of the children? This question is not only relevant to the application or use of behavior modification procedures, but to almost any other psychological, educational, or medical practice. And, obviously, it is a very difficult philosophical question to answer.

LEGAL ISSUES AND BEHAVIOR MODIFICATION

Various legal decisions and related issues over the past decade and a half have had direct implications for the application of behavior modification procedures with exceptional children. For example, for persons who are mentally retarded, autistic, or severely handicapped and living within an institutional or community residential setting, legal decisions have determined specific fundamental rights—the right to balanced meals each day, access to such common activities as watching television, privacy, and shelter. In addition, such laws as Public Law 94-142 (Education for All Handicapped Children Act) assure due process for handicapped children receiving educational services, as well as placement in the least restrictive alternative setting. Because of these decisions as well as many of the ethical issues raised earlier, some writers (e.g., Golddiamond 1974; Ross 1980) have suggested that behavior modifiers obtain a person's informed consent before initiating a particular behavior modification procedure—even when the person is a minor. In most cases, this consent would be obtained in a school setting through the signing of the Individual Education Program (IEP) by parents and the student. In other cases, a special form may be necessary.

A few of the legal decisions that have had a direct impact on the use of behavior modification procedures are presented briefly below. The interested reader is referred to the original cases or to other sources (e.g., Martin 1975; Morris & Brown 1983; Sales, Powell, & Van Duizend 1982) for a more extensive discussion.

Wyatt v. Stickney (1971). This seminal case has defined the majority of rights for all mentally retarded persons living in institutional settings.

The court enumerated many client rights, among which were the following: the right to the least restrictive treatment conditions; the right to be free from isolation (of longer than one hour duration); the right to require informed consent for research; the right not to be subjected to treatments such as lobotomies, electroconvulsive shock, aversive conditioning, or other unusual or hazardous treatment without express and informed consent following consultation with counsel; the right to be paid the minimum wage for institutional maintenance work; the right to a comfortable bed, locker or closet, changes of linen, and privacy; the right to access to a day room with television and other recreational facilities; and, the right to a nutritionally adequate diet. In addition, the court established that no behavior could be extinguished or developed solely for the benefit of the institution.

Morales v. Turman (1973). The court reaffirmed a time limitation on time-out procedures; that time out not exceed 50 minutes.

Pennsylvania Association for Retarded Children (PARC) v. Commonwealth of Pennsylvania (1971). This decision struck down a state statute that said children who were determined to be unable to benefit from education could be refused schooling. The ruling determined that all (handicapped) children, no matter how retarded, could benefit from education and training. Retarded children could not be denied a free public education. The children, it was agreed, were to be placed in the least restrictive alternative setting with the regular classroom being the least restrictive option. Due process procedures were to be followed for all placements. Due process included notification of parents, the right to a hearing, right to legal counsel, the right to examine records, the right to present evidence and to cross-examine, and the right to independent evaluation.

New York State Association for Retarded Children v. Rockefeller (1973). The plaintiffs were residents of Willowbrook State School, who alleged that, since confinement, their physical, mental, and emotional condition had deteriorated. The consent decree, signed by both sides in 1975, stipulated no seclusion, corporal punishment, degradation, medical experimentation, or routine use of restraints. Furthermore, residents were to be prepared for return to the community. To attain normalization, both litigants consented to the formation of individual plans for the education, therapy, care, and development of each resident. The decree also created a seven-member consumer advisory board to hear complaints of illegal practices.

Halderman v. Pennhurst (1977). The court ruled that institutions for mentally retarded persons are too restrictive. It was further stated that mentally retarded persons have a federal statutory right to individualized programming and habilitation, and that such services be provided preferably outside of an institutional setting. In a review of this decision in 1979, the court sustained its earlier ruling and reiterated its stand that institutions are too restrictive, but acknowledged that some programming for some clients may have to take place within an institutional setting.[1]

Although many of the legal decisions have involved mentally retarded persons, the implications are obvious regarding the use of behavior modification procedures with other exceptional persons in a residential, educational, clinic, or home setting. One clear implication is that behavior modification should be used in the least restrictive alternative setting *and* that least restrictive procedures—that is, reinforcement procedures—should first be used before proceeding to more restrictive procedures, that is, behavior reduction methods (Ollendick & Cerny 1981; Morris, Barber, Hoschouer, Karrels, & Bijou 1979; Morris & Brown 1983).

SUGGESTED GUIDELINES FOR BEHAVIOR MODIFICATION PROCEDURES[2]

Because behavior modification emphasizes the control of behavior, and because it has been found to be effective in modifying a variety of behaviors in exceptional children, its possible misuse and abuse have been the subject of many discussions over the past twenty years. Few professionals who work in the area of behavior modification would deny that the possibility exists that these procedures could be abused. The fruits of any scientific research can be used for many purposes—whether we are talking about the misuse or abuse of the psychological principles underlying behavior control or of the principles underlying nuclear energy or laser technology. As Ross (1980) states,

> *"Knowledge is a tool and like other tools, whether knives or nuclear energy, it can be used for good as well as for evil. . . . Psychology [and the principles underlying the control of behavior] can tell us how to get to a goal; it cannot help us decide what the goal should be. That decision depends on our values."* (p. 73)

As a result of increased public and professional awareness of and sensitivity to human rights, professional ethics, and the law *vis-à-vis* exceptional persons, various national associations, institutions, school districts, and states began writing guidelines and position statements about the use of behavior modification procedures (e.g., Association for Advancement of Behavior Therapy 1977; National Association for Retarded Persons 1975; National Society for Autistic Children 1975; State of

Arizona 1979; State of California 1977; State of Wisconsin 1977). Two of these sets of guidelines, one from the Association for the Advancement of Behavior Therapy and the second abstracted from the Accreditation Council for Services for Mentally Retarded and Other Developmentally Disabled Persons, have already been presented in this chapter.

One of the earliest sets of guidelines, and certainly the most detailed, was developed in 1975 by May, Risley, Twardosz, Bijou, and Wexler, under the sponsorship of the Florida State Division of Retardation and the Florida State University (see National Association for Retarded Persons, 1975). Although these guidelines were specifically written in regard to those services provided retarded persons, their overall content, organization, and structure can be easily adapted and applied to virtually every category of exceptionality in a variety of settings.

Based on these earlier sets of guidelines and previous publications on this topic, Morris and Brown (1983) proposed the following checklist for service providers, which should be reviewed before implementing a behavioral program. The service provider should make sure that

1. The program is consistent with the available treatment literature and does not represent any novel intervention approaches (if a new treatment method is being proposed where there are no data to support its relative effectiveness, the person may want to propose the treatment program as an experimental procedure)

2. The program is consistent with the overall treatment objectives for the client [child] and is in the client's best interests

3. The program involves the least restrictive alternative program for the client

4. The program can be carried out easily given the number of staff available and the level of staff training and competence

5. The client's progress will be monitored using a specific procedure and the client will be observed closely for possible adverse side effects of the program

6. The staff have been trained to a criterion level to ensure the provision of quality treatment

7. Informed consent has been obtained from the client or, in the case of incompetent clients, from the client's advocate(s) and guardian (Morris & Brown, 1983, pp. 79–81)

These considerations were written specifically for those services provided mentally retarded children and adults in either an educational, institutional, or community living setting. The statements on this checklist, however, are also appropriate—with slight changes in wording—

for the use of behavioral procedures with any other group of exceptional children.

One of the considerations listed above may pose some difficulty for behavior modifiers, namely, "the program involves the least restrictive alternative program." By providing children with the least restrictive alternative program plan, the behavior modifier is providing them with the opportunity to change under minimally restrictive or intrusive conditions. Since there are few comparative studies in which the same set of procedures is compared across exceptionalities using the same target behavior, we are not in a strong position to advocate using more restrictive or intrusive procedures (i.e., behavior reduction methods) before exhausting less restrictive or intrusive methods (i.e., reinforcement procedures). The terms *restrictive* and *intrusive* are certainly somewhat ambiguous. If, however, we define *restrictive* in terms of a loss of liberty or freedom, and *instrusive* in terms of placing a person at risk, using force to modify the person's behavior, and invading or touching someone's body (e.g., Friedman 1975), then we come closer to what is meant by these terms in this chapter.

Table 8.3 represents a modification of a level system proposed by Morris and Brown (1983). It varies along the dimensions of (1) restrictiveness and intrusiveness, and (2) aversiveness, which is defined in terms of the intensity of the aversive stimulus being used. Table 8.3 includes the procedures discussed in this book. As a general rule, behavior modifiers should document with charts that the Level I procedures have been ineffective in controlling a target behavior before proceeding to the use of Level II procedures. Similarly, before Level III procedures are used, the behavior modifier must document that Level II procedures have been ineffective. The view implicit here is that a behavior modifier is justified in introducing behavior reduction programs (with the exception of an extinction procedure) only after more positive procedures have been found unsuccessful in achieving the criterion for success. As mentioned earlier, whichever procedure is used should be accompanied by the informed consent of the child and his or her parent or guardian.

In addition, whenever behavior programs are proposed, the behavior modifier should obtain approval from the school's, institution's, or clinic's Program Review (PR) board and Human Rights and Ethics (HRE) board. The purpose of the program review board is to ensure the appropriateness and technical feasibility of the intervention procedure, whereas the human rights and ethics board ensures that the rights of the child will be maintained during the implementation of the program.[3]

Program Review (PR) Committee. The PR Committee reviews all behavioral programs planned for a particular child or student, whether these programs involve Level I, II, or III intervention strategies (see

TABLE 8.3

Proposed levels of restrictiveness/intrusiveness and aversiveness of behavior modification procedures

Level I Procedures
Reinforcement (including DRO, DRL, DRH procedures)
Group reinforcement
Shaping
Behavioral chaining
Modeling
Token economy system
Contingency contracting
Self-control
Reinforcement of incompatible behaviors
Relaxation training
Extinction
Situation Control
Level II Procedures
Contingent observation
Exclusion time-out
Response cost system
Contact desensitization
Level III Procedures
Overcorrection
Seclusion time-out
Physical punishment

Table 8.3). This committee does *not* function as an adversary group to the behavior modifier, but as a "helping" or advocacy committee in which the goal is to provide people with the best available advice about the adequacy and appropriateness of the proposed program plan. As such, the committee would base its approval or disapproval of a program plan on: (1) the available literature supporting the treatment procedure; (2) the clarity with which the procedure is described and whether the program is consistent with the overall treatment or educational objectives for the child or student; (3) whether the procedure involves the least restrictive or intrusive and least aversive level of programming possible; (4) whether, in those cases where more restrictive and/or aversive procedures are being proposed, there are data available to show that less restrictive and aversive procedures were not effective; (5) whether the staff involved is/are sufficiently trained to implement the program and if there are sufficient staff to maintain program consistency; (6) what data will be collected and how often the child will be monitored for possible side effects of the program; and, (7)

the committee's best judgment as to whether the program is in the best interests of the child and will, in fact, change his or her behavior. If the PR Committee does not approve a particular procedure, its next function is to offer suggestions or advice on how the procedure could be improved, and to ask the behavior modifier to resubmit the program plan at a later date.

The membership of the PR Committee is very important. In addition to the area principals or directors of clinical and/or educational services, the committee should consist of at least one parent of an exceptional child, recognized experts from the health and human services community (such as psychologists, pediatricians, psychiatrists, psychiatric nurses, and social workers), and a number of the particular behavior modifier's peers (e.g., other teachers and school administrators).

Human Rights and Ethics (HRE) Committee. The HRE Committee provides independent and external monitoring of the maintenance of the rights of all children receiving behavior program plans. The committee also reviews allegations by any child, staff member, peer, parent, guardian, or community group of violation of the rights of a child receiving these services. Whereas the PR committee's major purpose is the review of behavior program plans regarding their technical feasibility and appropriateness, the HRE Committee's primary function is to serve as an external and independent group to assure that the rights of children are protected.

Since members of the HRE Committee are essentially external to the school, clinic, community residence, or institution, and have not had responsibility for approving or disapproving a particular program, they are less likely to support it if a rights or ethics question is raised. The membership of the HRE Committee should be quite diverse, consisting of lawyers knowledgeable in the area of law and the handicapped, parents of an exceptional child, people from the local or state child protection and advocacy agency, and psychologists, special educators, physicians, counselors, or social workers. Thus, by being concerned with issues that are separate from the PR Committee, the HRE Committee can more objectively determine which human rights issues, if any, are raised by a particular program plan and whether any action is indicated.

Two of the major concerns often voiced about this review system have to do with (1) the amount of time it takes to obtain the approval of each committee, (2) the costs associated with maintaining such a committee structure, which are very high, both in terms of staff time as well as the time of the paid consultants who sit on each committee, and (3) the overall challenge to, for example, a teacher's decision making about instruction. There is little doubt that these concerns are well founded—it will take longer for a behavior modifier to have the opportunity to implement a behavior program, the system will cost money to operate, and the teacher will not have sole decision-making power regarding instruction. Although operating the committees may not be cost-efficient, it is believed that through their independent functioning we will be able to ensure that ethical practices will be followed in the conduct of behavior modification. The potential benefits of knowing that such practices are taking place, and that accountability is integrated into the entire system of program planning, seem to outweigh the potential delays in implementing a particular program plan.

We are emphasizing here the monitoring of behavior modification programs because of the potential of abuse. Indirectly, however, we are giving tacit support for other child intervention procedures with exceptional children—such as psychoanalytic, client-centered, psychopharmacological, relationship, and Adlerian approaches. Each of these intervention approaches should be scrutinized in the same way as behavior modification. If the ultimate goal of our work with exceptional children is to provide them with the most effective intervention approaches while minimizing the use of unsafe, ineffective, and potentially dangerous behavior change practices, then we should make sure that all intervention approaches receive the same two-committee detailed review process as that being proposed here for behavior modification. In this way we can assure the public that we are offering the best possible services to the exceptional children that we serve.

STUDY QUESTIONS

1. Which two issues often arise during discussions of using behavior modification procedures with exceptional children? (Review p. 186 to check your answer.)

2. What is meant by the term *behavioral control?* (Review pp. 186-87 to check your answer.)

3. What is meant by the term *ethical practices* as it is used in behavior modification? (Review pp. 187-88.)

4. Review Tables 8.1 and 8.2. What additional questions can you think of for the use of behavior modification with exceptional children? (Review pp. 188-192 to assist you.)

5. List three legal decisions that have had a direct impact on the use of behavior modification procedures with exceptional children? (Review pp. 192-94 to check your answer.)

6. What is meant by the *level system* in behavior modification? How does one apply this system within a school district? (Review pp. 196-97 to check your answer.)

7. What is meant by a *Program Review Board* and a *Human Rights and Ethics Board?* What are some of the problems associated with the establishment of these two boards within a school system? (Review pp. 196-99 to check your answer.)

NOTES

1. In an opinion regarding this case in January 1984, the U.S. Supreme Court overturned a federal appeals court ruling and found that "federal courts cannot order injunctions against state officials under state law, even if the officials are violating the law. [The court stated that] 'a federal suit against state officials on the basis of state law contravenes the 11th Amendment when—as here—the relief sought and ordered has an impact directly on the State itself'" (Cunningham 1984). This ruling was specifically related to the Pennsylvania state statute having to do with guarantees associated with "minimally adequate habilitation" (Cunningham 1984).

2. Appreciation is due Mr. Ronald S. Barber, Program Manager, Arizona Division of Developmental Disabilities—District II, and his staff for their stimulating discussions on this topic. Their many insightful comments over a six-year period have been invaluable in the formulation of the position statements made in this section.

3. This discussion is based on a program review and human rights and ethics committee system established at Arizona Division of Developmental Disabilities—District II, Tucson, Arizona (see Morris, Barber, Hoschouer, Karrels, & Bijou 1979).

SELF-QUIZ ON KNOWLEDGE OF BEHAVIOR MODIFICATION PROCEDURES

DIRECTIONS

Please Use Pencil

Read each question and each of its four possible answers. Sometimes more than one answer could be correct under certain circumstances; however, you should select the *best* answer or the answer that is most generally true. Completely fill in the square beside that answer with a pencil.

Example:

Probably the most important influence in a young child's life is his . . .

□ Toys
□ Television
□ Parents
□ Friends

Please do not consult others while deciding how to answer the question.

Be sure to fill in only one square for each question.

Be sure to answer every question even if you must guess.

1. Desirable and undesirable behavior are most alike in that they are:
   □ The result of emotions and feelings.
   □ Habits and therefore difficult to change.
   □ Ways the child expresses himself.
   □ The result of learning.

2. Probably the most important idea to keep in mind when first changing behavior is:
   □ To use both reward and punishment.
   □ To reward every time the desired behavior occurs.
   □ To be flexible about whether or not you reward.
   □ To be sure the child understands why you want the behavior to change.

3. Most problem behavior in young children is probably:
   □ A reaction to deeper emotional problems.
   □ Due to lack of communication in the home.
   □ Accidentally taught by the child's family.
   □ Due to a stage which the child will outgrow.

4. A child begins to whine and cry when his parent explains why he can't go outside. How should the parent react?
   □ Ask the child why going outside is so important to him.
   □ Explain that it is a parent's right to make such decisions.
   □ Explain again why he should not go outside.
   □ Ignore the whining and crying.

Reprinted with permission from *Journal of Behavior Therapy, 10,* S. L. O'Dell, L. Tarler-Benlolo, & J. M. Flynn, An instrument to measure knowledge of behavioral principles as applied to children, 1979, Permagon Press, Ltd.

5. Which of the following is most important for parents in controlling their child's behavior?
   □ The rules the parents make about behavior.
   □ The parents' understanding of the child's feelings.
   □ The behaviors to which the parents attend.
   □ Being strict, but also warm and gentle.

6. In changing a child's behavior a parent should try to use:
   □ About one reward for every punishment.
   □ About one reward for every five punishments.
   □ About five rewards for every punishment.
   □ Practically all rewards.

7. Which of the following is the *least* likely way for children to react to the person who punishes them?
   □ The child will try to avoid the punisher.
   □ The child will have admiration and respect for the punisher.
   □ The child may copy the punisher's methods and do similar things to playmates.
   □ The child will associate the punishment with the punisher.

8. Which of the following statements is most true?
   □ People usually fully understand the reasons for their actions.
   □ People are often unaware of the reasons for their actions.
   □ People's actions are mostly based on logic.
   □ It is necessary to understand the reason for a person's behavior before trying to change the behavior.

9. If you are trying to teach a child to talk, you should first:
   □ Reward the child after speaking a sentence.
   □ Reward the child for saying a word.
   □ Reward the child for any vocalization.
   □ Punish the child if he did not speak.

10. If punishment is used for a behavior such as playing football in the house, which type is probably best to use?
    □ Make the child do extra homework.
    □ Clearly express your disapproval.
    □ Remove the child to a boring situation each time.
    □ A reasonable spanking.

11. A child has been rewarded each time he cleans his room. In order to keep the room clean without having to use a reward, the next step should probably be to:
    □ Have a talk about how pleased you are and then stop giving the reward.
    □ Give the reward about one out of five times.
    □ Give the reward almost every time.

□ You must always reward it every time.

12. Parents who use lots of rewards for good behavior and few punishments will probably tend to have children who:

□ Do not understand discipline.

□ Will not cooperate unless they are "paid".

□ Take advantage of their parents.

□ Are well-behaved and cooperative.

13. When should a child who is just learning to dress himself be praised the first time?

□ When he gets his foot through the first hole in his underwear.

□ When he gets his underwear completely on.

□ When he asks to do it himself.

□ When he has completely finished dressing himself.

14. Which of the following is most effective in getting a child to do homework?

□ "When you finish your homework, you can watch T.V."

□ "You can watch this show on T.V. if you promise to do your homework when the show is over."

□ "If you don't do your homework tonight, you can't watch T.V. at all tomorrow."

□ Explain the importance of school work and the dangers of putting things off.

15. Three of the following responses refer to forms of punishment which are mild and effective. Which one is not?

□ Ignoring the undesirable behavior.

□ Sending the child to a dull room for a few minutes.

□ Taking away something the child likes (such as dessert after supper).

□ Scolding.

16. Each time Mother starts to read, Billy begins making a lot of noise which prevents her from enjoying her reading time. The best way for Mother to get Billy to be quiet while she reads is to:

□ Severely reprimand him when this occurs.

□ Pay close attention and praise and hug him when he plays quietly while she is reading and ignore his noisy behavior.

□ Call him to her and carefully explain how important it is for her to have a quiet time for herself each time this occurs.

□ Tell him that he won't get a dessert after dinner if he continues.

17. Which of the following is the most effective form of punishment in the long run for reducing a child's undesirable behavior?

□ Scolding him every time he does it.

□ Occasionally spanking him when he does it.

□ Sending him to his room for five minutes every time he does it.

□ Sending him to his room all afternoon every time he does it.

18. A young child often whines and cries when he is around his mother. In trying to find out why he cries, his mother should probably first consider the possibility that:

□ He is trying to tell her something.

□ He needs more of her attention.

□ She is somehow rewarding his crying.

□ She is not giving him enough attention.

19. A good rule to remember is:

□ Do not reward with money if possible.

□ Catch a child doing something right.

□ Reward good behavior and always punish bad behavior.

□ Punishment is always unnecessary.

20. If a child very gradually receives rewards less and less often for a behavior, what is most likely to happen?

□ He will soon stop the behavior.

□ He will be more likely to behave that way for a long time.

□ He will not trust the person giving the rewards.

□ None of the above.

21. Which of the following is true about punishment?

□ Punishment teaches respect.

□ Punishment should be delayed until it can be carefully determined that it is really necessary.

□ Punishment can teach a child new behaviors.

□ Some punishments can result in a child becoming aggressive.

22. In a reading group, the teacher gives each child candy plus praise for each correct answer. Which of the following statements is most true?

□ The candy is a bribe and doesn't belong in a school setting.

□ At first, the children work to earn the candy and may later work for the praise alone.

□ Children shouldn't be "paid" for doing their school work.

□ It probably doesn't make much difference whether or not candy is used because the children who want to learn to read will do so and the others won't.

23. A boy loves football. What is most likely to happen if, each time he is playing nicely with his sister, his father invites him to play football?

□ He will always be asking his father to play football.

□ He will play nicely with his sister more often.

□ He will be annoyed with

his father for interfering with his activities.
- ☐ He will be encouraged to teach his sister to play football.

24. To record, graph and note the direction of the change of a behavior is:
    - ☐ A minor, optional step in a behavior change program.
    - ☐ An important step in a behavior change program.
    - ☐ A procedure employed only by scientists for research.
    - ☐ Time consuming and complicated. Therefore, these procedures should only be used in special cases.

25. A father is teaching his son to hit a thrown ball with a bat. Which of the following methods will probably most help his son to learn to hit?
    - ☐ Let him try to hit the ball without saying anything, so the child can learn on his own.
    - ☐ Occasionally tell him what he is doing wrong.
    - ☐ Occasionally tell him what he is doing right.
    - ☐ Tell him almost every time he does something right.

26. Which of the following is most true about physical punishment?
    - ☐ It should immediately follow the undesirable behavior and at full intensity.
    - ☐ It should be mild and im-

mediately follow the undesirable behavior.
- ☐ It should begin in a mild form and, if that doesn't work, intensity should gradually be increased.
- ☐ It is ineffective and inappropriate.

27. Punishment, as a way to get rid of an undesirable behavior, is best used when:
    - ☐ You are very upset.
    - ☐ You want to teach the child the right way to behave.
    - ☐ The behavior may be dangerous.
    - ☐ Scolding doesn't seem to be effective.

28. Which of the following is *not* an important step in a behavior change program?
    - ☐ Make certain the child feels ashamed for his misbehavior.
    - ☐ Decide on a particular behavior that you wish to change.
    - ☐ If necessary, break the selected behavior down into smaller steps.
    - ☐ Select a proper time and situation for measuring the behavior.

29. If you want your child to develop proper study habits, you should:
    - ☐ Encourage him to do his homework.
    - ☐ Help him to see school as pleasant.

☐ Reward him whenever he studies.

☐ Give him good reasons why he will need school.

30. Two brothers fight constantly. Their parents decide to praise them when they play together nicely. However, they still continue to fight. Punishment may be necessary. What is probably happening?

☐ They don't want their parents' praise.

☐ The benefits of fighting are stronger to them than their parents' praise.

☐ They have too much anger toward each other to control.

☐ They are at a stage they will grow out of.

31. A child often cries over any small matter that bothers her. How should her parents react to best reduce her crying?

☐ Reward when she reacts without crying.

☐ Use a mild punishment when she cries.

☐ Try to find out what is really troubling the child and deal with that.

☐ Provide her with something interesting so she will stop crying.

32. Mrs. Thomas found out that spanking her seven-year-old son, Bob, did not seem to stop him from using "naughty" words. A friend suggested that rather than spanking him, she should send him to be by himself. The room he is sent to should be:

☐ His own room, so he will still have something to do.

☐ Small and dark.

☐ As uninteresting as possible.

☐ A large room.

33. If you want your child to say "please" and "thank you" at the table, it is probably most important to:

☐ Reprimand him when he forgets to say them.

☐ Explain why good manners are important.

☐ Remember to compliment him when he remembers to say them.

☐ Praise other members of the family when they use these words.

34. Which reward is probably best to help a 12-yr-old child improve his arithmetic skills?

☐ A dollar for each evening he studies.

☐ A dime for each problem he works correctly.

☐ Ten dollars for each A he receives on his report card in arithmetic.

☐ A bicycle for passing arithmetic for the rest of the year.

35. A major problem has been getting Leon to bed in the evening. His mother has decided to change this and

wants to measure the relevant behaviors. Which is the best way for her to do this?

☐ Each evening, record whether or not he goes to bed on time.

☐ Chart his behavior all day long, up to and including bedtime to try to find out what causes his not wanting to go to bed.

☐ Each week, make a note of how easy or difficult it has been to get him to bed.

☐ Ask Leon to keep his own record each week.

36. Mr. Jones agreed to pay his son, Mike, 25¢ each day if he carries out the trash. If Mr. Jones forgets to give Mike the money for a few days, what is most likely to happen?

☐ Mike will continue to take out the trash because he realizes how important this is.

☐ Mike will stop taking out the trash.

☐ Mike will begin to do extra chores, as well as take out the trash, so his father will notice how well he's doing and remember to give Mike the money.

☐ Mike will start to misbehave to take out his anger about not being paid.

37. A father tells a child she cannot go to the store with him because she didn't clean her room like she promised. She reacts by shouting, crying and promising she will clean the room when she gets home. What should the father do?

☐ Ignore her and go to the store.

☐ Take her to the store but make her clean her room when they return.

☐ Calm her down and go help her clean her room together.

☐ Talk to her and find out why she doesn't take responsibility.

38. The first step in changing a problem behavior is to:

☐ Reward the child when he is behaving nicely.

☐ Punish the child for misbehavior.

☐ Carefully observe the behavior.

☐ Seek help from someone who is more objective.

39. In changing a behavior it is most important to use:

☐ Methods which have been tested by others.

☐ Consequences which are rewarding to the child.

☐ Consequences which are punitive to the child.

☐ Rewards which do not bribe the child.

40. Johnny has just torn up a new magazine. Of the following choices, which is the best way for his mother to discipline him?

☐ Tell him he will be spanked by his father when he gets home.

☐ Punish him then and there.

☐ Explain to Johnny about the wrongness of his action.

☐ Angrily scold Johnny so that he will learn that such an act is bad and upsetting to his mother.

41. Stan is doing a number of things that greatly disturb his parents. It would be best for them to:

    ☐ Try to quickly eliminate all of these undesirable behaviors at once.

    ☐ Select just a few behaviors to deal with at first.

    ☐ Select the single behavior they find most disruptive and concentrate on changing that.

    ☐ Wait for 28 to 30 days before beginning to try to change his behaviors to make certain they are stable and persistent.

42. Which would be the best example of an appropriate way to praise Mary?

    ☐ Good girl, Mary.

    ☐ I love you, Mary.

    ☐ I like the way you helped me put the dishes away.

    ☐ I'll tell your father how nice you were when he comes home.

43. Listed below are four methods used to change behavior. Which is usually the best technique to get Frank to stop sucking his thumb?

    ☐ Punish the undesired behavior.

    ☐ Ignore the behavior.

☐ Reward him for desirable behavior in the situation in which he usually misbehaves.

☐ Explain to the child why the behavior is undesirable.

44. Jimmy sometimes says obscene words, but only in front of his mother. She has been shocked and makes her feelings clear to him. How should she react when he uses obscene words?

    ☐ Wash his mouth out with soap.

    ☐ Ignore him when he uses obscene words.

    ☐ Tell him how bad he is and how she doesn't like him when he uses those words.

    ☐ Explain to him the reason such words are not used.

45. If you want to make a behavior a long-lasting habit, you should:

    ☐ Reward it every time.

    ☐ First reward it every time and then reward it occasionally.

    ☐ Promise something the child wants very much.

    ☐ Give several reasons why it is important and remind the child of the reasons often.

46. Punishment will not be effective unless you:

    ☐ Prevent the child from escaping while you punish him.

    ☐ Throw all of your emotions into the punishment so the child will realize how serious you are.

□ Follow it with a careful explanation of your reasons for the punishment.

□ Have tried everything else.

47. The most likely reason a child misbehaves is that:

□ He is expressing angry feelings which he often holds inside.

□ He has learned to misbehave.

□ He was born with a tendency to misbehave.

□ He has not been properly told that his behavior is wrong.

48. Which of the following is probably most important in helping a child behave in desirable ways?

□ To teach him the importance of self-discipline.

□ To help him understand right and wrong.

□ Providing consistent consequences for his behavior.

□ Understanding his moods and feeling as a unique person.

49. A baby often screams for several minutes and gets his parents' attention. Which of the following is probably the best way for his parents to reduce his screaming?

□ If there is nothing physically wrong with the child, ignore his screaming even though the first few times he screams even louder.

□ Distract the child with something he finds interesting whenever he screams.

□ Ignore all noises and sounds the child makes.

□ None of the above. Babies usually have good reasons for screaming.

50. How often a behavior occurs is probably mostly controlled by:

□ The person's attitude about his behavior.

□ What happens to him at the same time the behavior occurs.

□ What happens to him just before the behavior occurs.

□ What happens to him just after the behavior occurs.

KEY:

1. d	11. c	21. d	31. a	41. c
2. b	12. d	22. b	32. c	42. c
3. c	13. a	23. b	33. c	43. c
4. d	14. a	24. b	34. b	44. b
5. c	15. d	25. d	35. a	45. b
6. d	16. b	26. a	36. b	46. a
7. b	17. c	27. c	37. a	47. b
8. b	18. c	28. a	38. c	48. c
9. c	19. b	29. c	39. b	49. a
10. c	20. b	30. b	40. b	50. d

Appendix **B**

BEHAVIOR ASSESSMENT CHECKLISTS

BEHAVIOR EVALUATION CHECKLIST*

Child's name:_____

Child's address:_____ Evaluation date:_____

Name of person performing evaluation:_____

MOTOR SKILLS CHECKLIST

		Always	Sometimes	Never	Comments
A.	Grasps objects				
	Sits unaided				
	Creeps				
	Walks with assistance				
	Toddles				
	Walks without assistance				
	Runs				
	Jumps				
	Climbs stairs with assistance				
	Climbs stairs without assistance				
	Ascends stairs alternating feet				
	Descends stairs alternating feet				
	Marches				
	Hops				
	Bounces ball				
	Throws ball without direction				
	Throws ball with direction				
	Catches ball				
	Kicks ball				
	Rides a bicycle				
	Skips alternating feet				
B.	Touches toes without bending knees				
	Can perform sit-up				
	Performs 5 knee bends or more				
	Performs 3 push-ups				
	Performs 5 sit-ups				
	Performs broad jump of 2' or more				
	Can chin self twice or more				

*This checklist is from an evaluation form used and developed by the Syracuse Developmental Center, Syracuse, New York; reproduced with permission.

SELF-CARE SKILLS CHECKLIST

	Always	Sometimes	Never	Comments
Indicates bathroom need				
Dresses self after toileting				
Uses toilet paper				
Flushes toilet				
Washes hands				
Can blow nose				
Uses tissue or handkerchief				
Can drink from a glass				
Can use a straw				
Can button clothing				
Can zip clothing				
Can snap clothing				
Can undress self				
Can put socks on				
Can tie shoes				
Can put coat or sweater on				
Can put pants or skirt on				
Can put shirt or blouse on				
Can put dress on				
Can use a spoon				
Can use a fork				
Can use a knife				
Can eat a sandwich				
Can drink from soda bottle or can				
Closes mouth when eating				
Is tidy when eating				
Cleans up after eating				

COMMAND-FOLLOWING CHECKLIST

	Always	Sometimes	Never	Comments
Attention Toward Therapist Makes eye contact (for 1–3 sec.) on command with prompt				
Makes eye contact (for more than 3 sec.) on command with prompt				
Makes eye contact (for 1–3 sec.) on command				
Makes eye contact (for more than 3 sec.) on command				
Attention Toward Other Children Looks at other children on command with prompt (for 1–3 sec.)				
Looks at other children on command with prompt (for more than 3 sec.)				
Looks at other children on command (for 1–3 sec.)				
Looks at other children on command (for more than 3 sec.)				
General Command Following Grasps particular object on command				
Gives an object to adult on command				
Gives an object to another child on command				
Picks up object from toy box on command				
Places object in toy box on command				

COMMAND-FOLLOWING CHECKLIST

	Always	Sometimes	Never	Comments
Touches another child on command				
Responds to the command "Come to me"				
Responds to the command "Sit down"				
Responds to the command "Put that down"				
Imitates one simple motor behavior on command				
Imitates two simple motor behaviors on command				
Imitates 3–5 simple motor behaviors on command				
Imitates 5–10 simple motor behaviors on command				
Imitates 10 or more simple motor behaviors on command				
Imitates speech sounds on command				
Imitates words on command				
Imitates simple sentences on command				
Imitates a two-stage motor behavior sequence on command				
Imitates a three-stage motor behavior sequence on command				
Imitates a 4– or 5–stage motor behavior sequence on command				

COMMUNICATION SKILLS CHECKLIST

	Always	Sometimes	Never	Comments
Expresses self by facial gestures				
Expresses self by manual gestures				
Produces undifferentiated sounds				
Produces vowel sounds				
Produces consonant sounds				
Can say single words				
Can say phrases				
Says simple sentences				
Responds to name				
Listens to stories				
Can repeat a story				
Identifies objects by matching				
Identifies objects by pointing				
Identifies objects by name				
Identifies parts of the body by pointing				
Verbally identifies parts of the body				
Greets people				
Delivers message orally				
Traces printed letters				
Copies printed letters				
Copies printed numbers				
Prints unaided				
Produces cursive writing				
Writes first name				
Writes last name				
Writes full name				
Can verbally spell name				
Reads on a primer level				
Reads on first-grade level				
Reads on second-grade level				

MANIPULATIVE SKILLS CHECKLIST

	Always	Sometimes	Never	Comments
Can trace a line				
Can draw a straight line				
Can join a series of dots				
Produces vertical lines				
Produces horizontal lines				
Produces curved lines				
Produces diagonal lines				
Reproduces a square from a model				
Reproduces a circle from a model				
Reproduces a triangle from a model				
Can string large beads				
Can string medium beads				
Can string small beads				
Can fold paper				
Can fold paper in half				
Can fold paper in quarters				
Can roll clay				
Can cut with scissors				
Can cut on a line with scissors				
Smears finger paints				
Creates images with finger paints				
Uses a paint brush				
Uses a peg board				
Can paste				
Handles building blocks				
Holds crayon				
Scribbles				
Colors within a designated area				
Draws face with eyes, mouth, and nose				
Draws face with above features plus hair and ears				
Draws variety of facial expressions				

ACADEMIC SKILLS CHECKLIST

	Always	Sometimes	Never	Comments
Discrimination				
Differentiates between very different objects (e.g., table and chair)				
Differentiates between similar objects (e.g., pants and skirt)				
Differentiates between very different sounds (e.g., talking and object dropping)				
Differentiates between similar sounds (e.g., knocking on wood and metal)				
Number Concepts				
Matches numerals 1–9				
Matches numerals 10–20				
Counts aloud 1–9				
Counts aloud 10–19				
Reads numerals 1–9				
Reads numerals 10–19				
Reads numerals 20–50				
Reads numerals over 100				
Identifies numerals out of sequence				
Time Concept				
Can recognize small and large hands on clock				
States where the hands of clock are (e.g., little hand on 10, big hand on 3)				
Tells time to the hour				
Tells time to the half-hour				
Tells time to the quarter-hour				
Tells time to the minute				
Addition				
Adds 1 to any number under 5				
Adds 1 to any number under 10				
Adds 2 to any number under 5				
Adds 2 to any number under 10				
Adds combination of numbers totaling to 9				
Adds combination of numbers totaling to 20				

Performs addition to 20, mentally without physical aids			
Subtraction Subtracts 1 from any number under 5			
Subtracts 1 from any number under 10			
Subtracts 2 from any number under 5			
Subtracts 2 from any number under 10			
Can subtract any number less than 10 from 10			
Can subtract any number less than 20 from 20			
Money Concepts Recognizes "real" money			
Selects specific coin on request			
Arranges coins in order by value			
Makes change for quarter			
Makes change for dollar			

SOCIAL SKILLS CHECKLIST

Can communicate positive feelings			
Can communicate anger			
Can communicate sadness			
Controls temper			
Is aware of others			
Is courteous			
Does what he is asked			
Is truthful			
Is dependable			
Is accepted by peers			
Accepts help from adults			
Accepts help from peers			
Recognizes ownership of objects			
Respects property of others			
Waits turn			
Shares with others			
Adapts to change in routine			
Displays good sportsmanship			
Shows leadership			
Responds well to kindness			
Shows affection to others			
Offers assistance to peers			
Offers assistance to less able residents			
Can be taken on field trips			

MISCELLANEOUS SKILLS CHECKLIST

	Always	Sometimes	Never	Comments
Likes to watch T.V.				
Likes to listen to music				
Likes to listen to stories				
Likes to be held				
Likes to sing				
Likes to talk				
Likes physical activity				
Likes to be read to				
Likes to read				
Likes to eat meals				
Likes candy snacks				
Likes to be alone				
Likes to be with peers				
Likes to be with staff				
Likes to sleep				
Likes group activities				

TEACHER'S QUESTIONNAIRE*

Name of Child _____   Grade _____

Date of Evaluation _____

Please answer all questions. Beside *each* item, indicate the degree of the problem by a check mark (✔)

	Not at all	Just a little	Pretty much	Very much
1. Restless in the "squirmy" sense.				
2. Makes inappropriate noises when he shouldn't.				
3. Demands must be met immediately.				
4. Acts "smart" (impudent or sassy).				
5. Temper outbursts and unpredictable behavior.				
6. Overly sensitive to criticism.				
7. Distractibility or attention span a problem.				

	Not at all	Just a little	Pretty much	Very much
8. Disturbs other children.				
9. Daydreams.				
10. Pouts and sulks.				
11. Mood changes quickly and drastically.				
12. Quarrelsome.				
13. Submissive attitude toward authority.				
14. Restless, always "up and on the go."				

15. Excitable, impulsive.				
16. Excessive demands for teacher's attention.				
17. Appears to be unaccepted by group.				
18. Appears to be easily led by other children.				
19. No sense of fair play.				
20. Appears to lack leadership.				
21. Fails to finish things that he starts.				

22. Childish and immature.				
23. Denies mistakes or blames others.				
24. Does not get along well with other children.				
25. Uncooperative with classmates.				
26. Easily frustrated in efforts.				
27. Uncooperative with teacher.				
28. Difficulty in learning.				

STUDENT ATTITUDE SURVEY

Name of Child _____ Age _____

Date of Evaluation _____

The things below are things that sometimes make people scared or afraid. Mark the box that tells if they do that to you or not. If you have any questions or don't know some of the words, ask the person who gave you this paper. You should be sure to tell the truth in your answers. What you say will help us know how to help you.

	Doesn't scare me at all	Scares me a little	Scares me very much
1. Being alone.			
2. Being in a strange or funny place			
3. Loud talking			
4. Dead people			
5. People who seem crazy			
6. Cars and trucks on the road			
7. Being teased			
8. Thunder			
9. Failure			
10. Being in a high place and looking down			
11. Imaginary creatures—monsters, animals, etc.			
12. Strangers			
13. Riding in a car or bus			
14. Old people			
15. Bugs, spiders, or worms			
16. Sudden noises			
17. Crowds of people			
18. Large open spaces			
19. Cats or dogs			
20. Somebody hitting or being mean to someone else			
21. Tough-looking people			
22. Being watched when I'm doing something			
23. Guns			
24. Sick people			
25. People telling me I'm wrong			
26. People who are mad			
27. Knives			
28. Being kidnapped			
29. Blood			

	Doesn't scare me at all	Scares me a little	Scares me very much
30. Someone in my family dying			
31. Things that are messy			
32. When people don't like me			
33. When somebody tells me to stop doing something			
34. When people won't listen to me			
35. Being in the dark			
36. Lightning			
37. Doctors			
38. Doing things wrong			
39. When people say I'm silly			
40. Getting sick			
41. Going crazy			
42. Taking tests			
43. Feeling different from other people			
44. Arguing with people			
45. When my heart beats funny			
46. Growing up and getting older			
47. Boys			
48. Girls			
49. Talking to my teacher			
50. Talking in front of the class			
51. Homework			
52. Taking a shower with other kids at school or someplace			
53. Going on dates			
54. People without their clothes on			
55. Going to the bathroom when other people are around			
56. Getting good grades at school			
57. Not being chosen for a team or being chosen near the end			
58. If people don't like me			
59. Dreams or nightmares			
60. Wetting the bed			
61. Finding spots on my underwear			
62. Getting clothes dirty			
63. Spankings			
64. Breaking things			
65. People swearing			
66. Getting married someday			
67. Mornings			
68. Going to bed			

	Doesn't scare me at all	Scares me a little	Scares me very much
69. Being lost			
70. Mom and Dad arguing			
71. Mom or Dad shouting			
72. Hurting myself			
73. Not having any friends			
74. Getting into fights			
75. School			
76. Teachers			
77. The future			
78. Drugs			
79. Drinking			
80. Forgetting things			
81. Being late			
82. People laughing at me			
83. Not doing what I'm told			
84. People who show off			
85. Older kids			
86. Not being invited to parties			
87. Going to parties			
88. Staying overnight with a friend			
89. Riding the school bus			
90. Looking funny in my clothes			
91. Not telling the truth			
92. Getting caught doing something			
93. Water			
94. Not having a home			
95. Losing my breath			
96. Being ugly			
97. Not being smart enough			
98. Not understanding things			
99. Parents getting divorced			
100. Hospitals			
101. Falling			
102. Elevators			
103. Dying			
104. People who are drunk			
105. Being poisoned			
106. End of the world			
107. People from outer space			

Source: Walker, Hedberg, Clement, & Wright, *Clinical procedures for behavior therapy*, 1981, p. 34. Reprinted by permission of Prentice-Hall, Inc., Englewood Cliffs, New Jersey.

Appendix **C**

RECORD SHEETS

*Place additional comments
on backside with date and time*

Child's name _____

Classroom/Residence _____

Person recording information _____

BEHAVIOR ASSESSMENT RECORD SHEET

Date	Time	Situational Cues What happens just *before* the Behavior	Target Behavior	Consequences What happens just *after* the Behavior

Child's name: _____

Child's behavior being worked with: _____

Your name: _____

Date: _____

BEHAVIOR TALLY SHEET

Total number of times behavior
occurred per hour, day, session, etc.

Teacher's name: _____ Week of: _____

Child's name: _____ Child's behavior being worked with: _____

Day of
Week

BEHAVIOR TALLY SHEET

_____

_____

_____

_____

_____

Teacher's name: _____ Week of: _____

Child's name: _____ Child's behavior being worked with: _____

BEHAVIOR TALLY SHEET

Day of Week   min.   Hour

	15							
	30							
	45							
	60							

Average ____ ____ ____ ____ ____ ____ ____ ____

	15							
	30							
	45							
	60							

Average ____ ____ ____ ____ ____ ____ ____ ____

	15							
	30							
	45							
	60							

Average ____ ____ ____ ____ ____ ____ ____ ____

	15							
	30							
	45							
	60							

Average ____ ____ ____ ____ ____ ____ ____ ____

	15							
	30							
	45							
	60							

Average ____ ____ ____ ____ ____ ____ ____ ____

Place Comments on backside

Child's name ————————

Week of ————

Person recording information ————————

POINT SYSTEM SUMMARY CHART

	Sunday	Points	Monday	Points	Tuesday	Points	Wednesday	Points	Thursday	Points	Friday	Points	Saturday	Points
Activities														
Unacceptable Behaviors														

	Week's TOTAL

Rewards

TOTAL

Appendix **D**

BEHAVIOR CHART

Child's name: _____

Target behavior: _____

Date: _____

Person charting behavior: _____

*Use back side for comments
on child's performance*

Number
of times

Percent
of times

Number of
minutes

Number of
steps

(Circle one)

Days, Sessions, Hours, Weeks, or Months *(Circle one)*

0 1 2 3 4 5 6 7 8 9 10 11 12 13 14 15 16 17 18 19 20

POSSIBLE REINFORCERS TO USE IN BEHAVIOR MODIFICATION WITH CHILDREN

A. Edibles

Snacks and sweets (given in small pieces when necessary):
Pretzels
Cookies (e.g., Animal Crackers or other small cookies)
Sugared cereals (e.g., Sugar Loops, Cap'n Krunch)
Candy (e.g., M&Ms, jelly beans, chocolate chips)
Ice cream (spoonful from a cup)
Cake (e.g., Twinkies, cupcakes)
Raisins
Peanuts
Pudding
Gelatin
Marshmallows
French fried potatoes
Potato chips (including corn chips, etc.)
Fruit (including cherries, grapes, oranges, etc.)
Pies
Yogurt

B. Liquids

Drinks typically given in small sips:
Carbonated (e.g., cola)
Noncarbonated (e.g., orange drink, grape drink, Kool-Aid)
Juices
Milk

C. Objects

Relating to personal hygiene:

Hairbrush	Soap	Deodorant
Toothpaste	Mouthwash	Makeup
Toothbrush	Perfume	Hair tonic

Jewelry and clothing:

Bracelet	Football helmet
Watch	Sweatshirt
Ring	Blouse
Necklace	Skirt
Ribbon	Pants
Barrette	Belt
Key chain	Socks
Wallet	Shoes

Based on Larsen, L. A., & Bricker, W. A. *A manual for parents and teachers of severely and profoundly retarded children.* Nashville, Tenn.: IMRID Papers and Reports, vol. V, no. 22, 1968. Reprinted by permission of Dr. Larsen.

Purse   Underwear
Bathing suit   Decals
Hat   Gym shoes (sneakers)

Toys and games:
Speedster cars   GoBots
Dolls   Trucks
Mechanical toys   Waterguns; battery operated "laser" guns
Whistles   Sand and pail and shovel
Balloons   Bubble blower
Tops   Puzzles
Transformers   Video games
                           Remote control cars

Miscellaneous:
Pen (with paper)
Pencil (with paper)
Chalk with slate
Reading material (comic books, children's stories)
Building blocks
Crayons and coloring paper
Clay

D. Activities

Outdoor activities:
Playing catch with therapist/teacher
Playing on swings
Playing on jungle gym
Going on merry-go-round
Bicycle ride
Running
Playing tag or hide-and-go-seek with therapist/teacher
Going for a walk with therapist/teacher
Playing with a pet (dog, kitten, gerbil, etc.)
Playing catch
Going on the teeter-totter
Jumping rope with the therapist/teacher

Indoor activities:
Playing catch, playing with a ball
Watching a cartoon on film, television, or videotape
Watching a television program or movie on videotape
Looking through a book or magazine
Jumping rope with the therapist/teacher
Playing in the gym (unstructured play)

Playing "chase"
Hearing music through stereo headset from radio or tape player
Riding on rocking horse
Running
Finger painting with the therapist/teacher

Special activities:
Home visit
Trip to the museum
Trip to the zoo
Trip to the beach, swimming pool
Automobile ride
Trip to the therapist's or teacher's home
Trip to the circus or carnival
A hike

E. Social Praise

Expressions:
"Good," "Good boy," "Good girl"
"Very good."
"I like that."
"That's good."
"I'm glad you did that."
"I appreciate what you have done."
"That's right."
"That's it . . . very good."
"You did a good job."
"Mmm-hmm."
"Fine."
"You did it. Very good."
"Thank you," "Thank you very much."
"I'm so happy [pleased] with you," "I'm proud of you."

F. Nonverbal Messages and Movements

Facial expressions:
Smiling
Expression of surprise and delight
Nodding head in an approving manner
Laughing
Winking

Proximity to child:
Standing near child
Sitting near child

Physical contact with child:
Hugging
Patting back or head or arm; ruffling hair
Touching arm
Rubbing back
Kissing
Picking child up and holding him or her
Wrestling
Tickling
Bouncing child on knees
Playing patty-cake

SELECTED LISTING OF APPARATUS AND EQUIPMENT USED IN BEHAVIOR MODIFICATION WITH EXCEPTIONAL CHILDREN

The apparatus and equipment listed here are frequently used in behavior modification work with children. Where possible, the address of the distributor or the journal reference (these journals are available at most professional libraries) accompanies each listing. Many of these items can also be purchased commercially or constructed on one's own. This list is provided as a courtesy to the reader and does not constitute either endorsement or approval by the author or publisher.

BUG-IN-THE-EAR SYSTEMS

These systems allow one person (e.g., a teacher, counselor, or therapist) to communicate privately with one or more individuals (e.g., target child and/or parent) during a particular class period or training session. The apparatus is ideal, for example, for giving immediate feedback to a parent, teacher, or aide within the training situation—without distracting the child or interrupting the training process.

Three relatively inexpensive systems have been developed. Each has its own advantages and each uses wires.

Morris, R. J. An inexpensive, easily built "bug-in-the-ear"/intercom system for training therapists in behavior modification techniques. *Behavior Therapy*, 1974, 5, 685–86.

Stumphauzer, J. A low cost "bug-in-the-ear" sound system for modification of therapist, parent, and patient behavior. *Behavior Therapy*, 1971, 2, 249–50.

Weathers, L., & Liberman, R. P. The Porta-Prompter—a new electronic prompting and feedback device: A technical note. *Behavior Therapy*, 1973, 4, 703–5.

Another system is wireless, but is also more expensive. For information, write to: Farrall Instrument Company, Grand Island, Nebraska 68801.

COUNTERS

Counters (often called "digital counters") are very frequently used to count a wide variety of things and children's behaviors. For example, counters are used to count the number of reinforcers given per day, week, or session; the number of times a child performs a desirable or undesirable behavior per day, week, or session; and the number of points or tokens that a child accumulates per day, week or session (which are then exchanged for rewards). Counters come with single or multiple channels. The advantage of multiple channels is that the aide, teacher, clinician, or parent can record the occurrence of more than one behavior or "thing" on the same machine. A counter should be reliable (i.e., register a "count" each time the mechanism is pressed), be error and trouble free, and be easy to operate.

A single channel counter that looks and operates like commercially available golf counters can be purchased from:

Behavior Research Company
Box 3351
Kansas City, Kansas 66103

A multiple-channel (5 channels) counter is available from:

Lafayette Radio and Electronics
111 Jericho Turnpike
Syosset, L.I., New York 11791

Also, a variety of multifunction digital watches are available commercially, each of which could be used in the "time-set" mode to record up to 99 responses.

CHARTING EQUIPMENT

Charts are most often used to present graphically the occurrence of a particular behavior, providing the change agent with a graphic description of the progress of a child's program. Charts are also used, for example, to record the number of reinforcers per session a child receives.

Besides graph paper (like that presented in Appendix D), most charting equipment is electrically operated. The chart paper moves at a fixed speed. Connected to the paper is an ink pen which records a straight line as time progresses. When the pen is electrically activated by a switch held by the behavior modifier, a small mark is recorded at a right angle to the line. Some equipment record each mark in a cumulative fashion (called a *cumulative recorder*), a second pen moving higher and higher each time a response is recorded. Once the pen reaches the top of the chart, it automatically resets and returns to the bottom of the chart—moving up again each time it is activated.

Other equipment records each response on only one pen (called an *event recorder*). Here, the pen also records on a straight line as time progresses. When a response is recorded, the pen moves a very short distance away from the line and then back. More complex charting equipment, such as multipurpose polygraph machines like those used for recording electroencephalograms and electrocardiograms, are also available. For more information on charting equipment, write:

Lafayette Instrument Company
Box 5729
Lafayette, Indiana 47903

or

Esterline Angus
Box 24000
Indianapolis, Indiana 46224

LIQUID DISPENSERS

At times in behavior modification work, it is necessary to reinforce a child with a liquid refreshment. The question which then arises is, "How should I dispense this liquid?" Some behavior modifiers use a plastic straw in a juice glass or soda glass. Others pour the child's refreshment portion in a small glass and have the child drink from the glass each time. Still others use a plastic dispenser for liquids which has a long spout. The liquid comes out of the spout each time the container is squeezed. In this way, the child receives his or her refreshment directly from the behavior modifier and the behavior modifier has better control over how much goes into the child's mouth. This type of container, as well as others, is available commercially.

PORTABLE TIMERS

Timers are often very important in behavior modification work. Timing the length of a particular training session, timing the length of time between observation periods, knowing how much time has elapsed since the last reinforcer was delivered, timing how long a child is in a time out situation, and knowing how much time has passed since one last gave the child an instruction or fed or "checked up" on him or her are some very important ways that a timer is used in behavior modification work. Timers can also be used to help children understand the concept of time—for example, elapsed time, how long a minute is versus 15 minutes, 30 minutes, and one hour.

One such timer is the Memo-Timer, distributed by:

> Charles Alshuler Company
> Box 3720
> Milwaukee, Wisconsin 53217

Others (such as kitchen timers and parking meter timers) are available commercially in hardware and department stores. Another useful timer is a commercially available stopwatch with either a 30-minute or a 60-minute cycle.

The obvious limitation of each of these timers is the length of time that they record, namely, 5 to 60 minutes. Few will record longer than 60 minutes. Another limitation is their loudness. When in operation, they are often noisy, and such noise can provide the child with potential cues about, for example, forthcoming rewards.

More expensive electromechanical and electronic timers are also available. For further information on these timers write:

BRS/LVE, Inc.
9381-D Davis Avenue
Laurel, Maryland 20707

or

Lafayette Instrument Company
Box 1279
Lafayette, Indiana 47902

In addition, a variety of multifunction digital watches are available commercially, many of which have a stopwatch and/or lap mode. The stopwatch mode can often record up to 99 minutes, and some can record even seconds, minutes, and hours of elapsed time. On some watches the alarm mode can also be used to indicate time intervals that have elapsed.

TIME OUT AREAS

Often, it is difficult to establish a suitable time out room or area for a child. The room is occasionally too big or too small, too cluttered with distracting toys and objects, or too far away to be used promptly. The commercially available (Sears, Roebuck) three-panelled screen discussed in the following reference can be used as a suitable time out room: Harris, S., Ersner Hershfield, R., Carr Kaffashan, L., and Romanczyk, R. G. The portable time-out room. *Behavior Therapy*, 1974, *5*, 687-688. Its advantage is that it is both small and portable. Modified "do-it-yourself" versions can also be easily constructed.

TOILET-TRAINING DEVICES

One behavior problem which parents, teachers, aides, and clinicians often have difficulty solving is a child's lack of bladder and bowel control. Often, attempts at modifying the child's behavior are filled with anxiety, confusion, ignorance, and inconsistency—leading in many cases to the child not being trained and the behavior modifier giving up for at least a while.

A number of devices have been discussed.

One apparatus which can be used for urine training children on the toilet (called "Potty Alert") as well as detecting when the children are wet away from the toilet (called "Pants Alert") is available from:

BRS/LVE, Inc.
9381-D Davis Avenue
Laurel, Maryland 20707

See also: Kahinsky, W. Two low cost micturation alarms. *Behavior Therapy*, 1974, 5, 698–700.

A second toilet-training device (called the Mark II Toilet Trainer) for alerting behavior modifiers when the child has wet his or her pants is distributed by:

Psytec
P.O. Box 26006
Tempe, Arizona 85281

A third device can be used at night for detecting if the child has wet his or her bed and for training him/her in bladder control. This apparatus is distributed commercially through Sears, Roebuck and Company and Montgomery Ward, Inc.

Other devices for enuresis control have been described in: Fried, R. A device for enuresis control. *Behavior Therapy*, 1974, 5, 682–84; Yonovitz, A., & Michaels, R. (1977). Durable, efficient and economical electronic toilet training devices for use with retarded children. *Behavior Research Methods and Instrumentation*, 9, 356–58; and Hanson, R. H., Myers, C. J., & Schwarzko, K. H. (1977). A Durable enuresis alarm. *Behavioral Engineering*, 4, 51–54. They are small, inexpensive to build, and can be used, as can the previous devices, within a behavior modification program.

One procedure for bowel training children (in particular, retarded children) has been outlined in a book by Richard M. Foxx and Nathan H. Azrin called *Toilet training the retarded* (Champaign, Illinois: Research Press, 1973).

An article on the acceptability of these toilet training devices can be found in Finchman, F. D., and Spettell, C. (1984). The Acceptability of dry bed training and urine alarm training as treatments of nocturnal enuresis. *Behavior Therapy*, 15, 388–94.

OTHER EQUIPMENT

Other equipment which has been used in behavior modification work—mainly in conjunction with training behavior modifiers (or giving feedback) are the following:

1. *Audio tape recorders*: either reel-to-reel or cassette tape recorders.

2. *Video tape recorders and cameras*: either portable battery operated or stationary video recorders; both color and black-and-white systems are available; lenses of varying sizes and F-stops are available.

3. *Movie cameras*: available in 8mm., Super 8, or 16mm. Sound can be recorded on some Super 8 and most 16mm. movie cameras; film is available for both color and black-and-white movies; lenses of varying sizes available.

4. *Electromyography (EMG) and related biofeedback machines*: either portable battery operated or stationary biofeedback machines are available for teaching or controlling a variety of behaviors (including relaxation and calmness, athetoid movement in the extremities, and so forth).

5. *Computers*: with or without voice synthesizer; have been used for teaching a variety of behaviors—including reading, discrimination tasks, math concepts, language activities in nonverbal autistic children, and so forth.

Further information about this equipment is available from most commercial instrumentation, photography, and computer companies.

Additional information about equipment used in behavior modification is available from the following sources:

> BRS/LVE
> 9381-D Davis Avenue
> Laurel, Maryland 20707

> Lafayette Instrument Company
> Box 5729
> Lafayette, Indiana 47903

> Farrall Instruments Company
> P.O. Box 1037
> Grand Island, Nebraska 68802

SELECTED FILMS AND VIDEOTAPES ON BEHAVIOR MODIFICATION WITH CHILDREN

Each of the films listed may be rented or purchased from the distributor named in each listing. The rental fees vary. Many of the films are free. Most of the films can be kept from one to three days. This list is provided as a courtesy to the reader. The films listed are not approved or endorsed by the author or publisher. The address of each film distributor appears at the end of this list.

THE ABC'S of Behavioral Education
(C, 16mm, 20 min.) Illustrates the design and use of a contingency management system in public educational setting designed for teenagers ejected from public schools due to severe social and academic deficiencies. Demonstrates and emphasizes the use of tokens and contingency contracting with parents.
Hallmark Films

The ABC's of Behavior Modification
(C, 16mm, 20 min.) This film emphasizes the relationships between antecedents, behaviors, and consequences and describes how antecedents and consequences can be programmed in a school environment to influence staff and students. The students in this film are from twelve to seventeen years old and are being taught in the Anne Arundel County (Maryland) Learning Center. The students have a variety of academic and social deficits. Motivation is built through the use of positive reinforcement.
Hallmark Films

The ABC's of Child Management
Training program utilizing four films and written materials:

1. Reward Procedures for Behavior Management (B/W, 16mm, 25 min.)
This film demonstrates how to describe, analyze, select, and change child behaviors using reinforcement procedures. The management techniques are demonstrated with actual families showing a diversity of behavioral problems.

2. Reward Procedures for Classroom Management (B/W, 16mm, 25 min.)
This film instructs teachers how to use a variety of reinforcement techniques in the classroom. Both regular and special education

The author wishes to express his gratitude to those distributors who provided descriptive material and information regarding their films, and to the Association for Advancement of Behavior Therapy for their permission to reprint summaries of films from *Audio-visual directory—A filmography on behavior modification, behavior therapy, biofeedback, programmed instruction, learning and conditioning.* AABT, Mimeo, 1979 (Samuel Berkowitz, Rosemary O. Nelson, & Steven C. Hayes).

teachers demonstrate step-by-step procedures for modifying student's academic and social behavior.

3. **Time Out: A Way to Help Children Behave (B/W, 16mm, 25 min.)**
   This film demonstrates what *time out* is, when to use it, and how to use the procedure to reduce unwanted child behavior. Parents and teachers demonstrate how to use the time-out technique to modify a variety of behavioral problems.

4. **Teaching Children New Behavior (B/W, 26mm, 25 min.)**
   This film shows how parents and professionals can use modeling, shaping, demonstration, and related instructional procedures to teach children. The film stresses the adult's role and suggests simple but effective learning techniques.
   Informatics

Achievement Place
(B/W, 16mm, 30 minutes) This is a documentary on the day-to-day activities at Achievement Place, a foster home for predelinquent boys. The home is located in Lawrence, Kansas, and is operated within an operant conditioning framework.
Bureau of Visual Instruction

Achievement Place
(B/W, 16mm, 9 min.) This film shows a token reinforcement system in a foster home for 6–8 court committed predelinquent boys. The boys attend their regular schools while being reinforced at home for appropriate behaviors. Tokens are exchanged for privileges.
Bureau of Visual Instruction

Acquisition of Social Behavior Through Modeling
(B/W, 1-inch videotape/ampex, 52 min.) This tape discusses operant conditioning particularly as it pertains to imitation. It is designed especially for use with the retarded, but principles are also applicable for use with children or regressed mentally ill patients.
Camarillo State Hospital

" . . . and so they learn:
(C, 16mm, 35 min.) Four approaches to early childhood education observed in four Pennsylvania schools: a modified Bereiter-Engleman approach, a team-teaching kindergarten, a Montessori school, and a one-teacher public school classroom. It is pointed out that each method can be effective, depending on the pupils and the learning situation, and that the methods are basically similar.
University of Southern California

And Then Ice Cream

(B/W, 16mm, 11 min.) Two children don't like their meal. Ice cream is placed on the table, but they are not allowed to touch it until they have eaten portions designated by teacher. In another school, two children are invited to taste everything, but the teacher accepts the child's decision and ice cream is considered by the children and teachers as part of the meal. Designed for discussion and for practice in observing behavior.

University of Southern California

Applied Behavior Analysis Research Designs

(C, 16mm, 40 min.) Drs. Don Baer, Montrose Wolf, and Todd Risley, who wrote a definitive article on applied behavior analysis, talk with Dr. R. Vance Hall about why it was necessary to develop applied behavior analysis, what makes it work, what has resulted from the technique, and some implications of applied behavior analysis in our changing social system.

Audio-Visual Center

The Art of Parenting: A Complete Training Kit

(5 filmstrips, cassette tapes, workbook.) A multimedia package for training parents in effective childrearing techniques. Designed as a five session workshop, the sessions are *Communication, Assertion Training, Behavior Management: Motivation, Behavior Management: Methods,* and *Behavior Management: Discipline.*

Research Press

Ask Just for Little Things

(C, 16mm, 20 min.) The second film in *The Step Behind Series*, it is a sequel to *Genesis*, showing a graduation from self-help skills to life skills, providing the retarded child with a larger repertoire of behaviors that enable him or her to function more fully in society. Three life skills, ambulation, personal hygiene, and attending are taught. The film attempts to teach the parent or nonprofessional how to train the child in a home or other setting.

Hallmark

Asset: A Social Skills Program for Adolescents

(16mm, 64 min.) *ASSET* is a complete systematic behavior modeling program designed specifically for skill deficient adolescents. This video series offers modeling displays that show kids interacting with peers, parents, teachers, and other adults. ASSET provides everything necessary to conduct skill-building programs for early intervention. The program consists of eight 16mm films or eight videotapes, a Leader's guide, and program materials.

Research Press

Autism's Lonely Children

(B/W, 16mm, 20 min.) Work with autistic children being conducted by Dr. Frank Hewett of the Neuropsychiatric School at UCLA. With a device called the *learning box*, Dr. Hewett is shown attempting to teach individual children to talk and to identify objects for the first time. Produced by NET.
Psychological Cinema Register

Behavior Analysis Classroom

(C, 16mm, 20 min.) Film demonstrates several follow-through classrooms. Briefly explains behavior analysis principles and procedures, showing how parents supplement the teaching force to give more individual attention to specific problems. Shows how tokens are used in public school classes.
Bureau of Visual Instruction

Behavior Contracting Systems

(Overhead transparencies and cassette tapes) This training kit describes how various types of verbal and written contracts can help educators and parents manage social and academic behavior problems. The presentation begins with a description of the basic principles and rules of contracting. Simulation exercises are included. This kit contains duplication masters of contract forms that can be immediately implemented. Presents the use of contracting procedures in the classroom and the use of contracts to enhance school-home communication.
Behavioral Products

Behavior Control: From Cure to Prevention

(B/W, 16mm, 30 min.) Describes classroom usage of behavioral techniques, demonstrating actual work with children including imitation training with a young girl and several others.
Behavior Development Corporation

Behavior Management in the Classroom

(Overhead transparencies and cassette tapes) The presentation covers four basic areas: introduction to the behavioral approach, basic principles of learning, specific techniques for strengthening desired behaviors, and specific techniques for weakening undesired behaviors. Basic behavior change principles are presented and participants are shown ten practical behavior management techniques.
Behavioral Products

Behavior Management in the Home

(Overhead transparencies and cassette tapes) This kit is designed to aid in teaching parents to manage more effectively the behaviors of

their children. The program is designed to be used over a series of four weekly sessions so that participants can become actively involved in implementing the procedures. Simulated problem situations are built into the audio-visual presentation to enable participants to work as a group in generating problem-solving strategies. Parents are provided with suggestions for changing behaviors.
Behavioral Products

Behavior Modification
(B/W, 16mm, 15 min.) This film explains a behavior modification program and shows how this program is used to individualize learning for elementary students.
Educational Coordinates

Behavior Modification: An Approach to Language Learning
(C, 16mm, 10 min.) A photographic demonstration of some key concepts involved in behavior modification.
National Audiovisual Center

Behavior Modification in the Classroom
(C, 16mm, 24 min.) This film presents behavior management in three classrooms, demonstrating how to train teachers in the implementation of behavioral procedures. It demonstrates positive reinforcement and modeling techniques to modify the behavior of students whose performances suffer because of their distracting behavior of daydreaming, and specifies the need for determining appropriate rewards and generalizing rewards from specific tangible objects to verbal and nonverbal reinforcement.
University of California

Behavior Modification in the Classroom: Excessive Talking
(35mm slides, 27 min.) The hero of this lively Old West presentation is Tex Nology, who implements a token economy program in an elementary school classroom. By using tokens to reward the student's appropriate behaviors, a pleasant and productive classroom situation is created, in which the students and teacher reap the benefits of this innovative behavioral procedure. One specific problem dealt with is that of talking out behavior, which often plagues teachers working with young children. Created in cartoon format with figures from the Old West.
Behaviordelia

Behavior Modification in the Classroom: Underachievement
(35mm slides, 24 min.) Rocky, like many junior high school students, lacks the reading skills necessary to adapt successfully to school and modern society. The slides describe how the implemen-

tation of a systematic program of behavior procedures allowed one student to acquire the skills involved in reading. The emphasis is on moving away from the traditional classroom structure and toward more innovative procedures—such as using other students as tutors to set up an intensive reading program.
Behaviordelia

Behavior Modification: Teaching Language to Psychotic Children

(C, 16mm, 42 min.) Based on the work of Ivar Lovaas, this film describes the use of reinforcement and stimulus fading techniques in the teaching of speech to psychotic children. Initially depicted is the nature of psychotic behavior in autistic and schizophrenic children, such as bizarre echolatic speech, self-destruction, and pervasive failures in acquisition of social and intellectual behaviors. Imitative verbal behavior is next established. Examples are given of the acquisition and use of speech for spontaneous conversation. Procedures and learning rates are graphically presented.
Audio-Visual Center

Behavior Therapy with an Autistic Child

(B/W, 16mm, 42 min.) Demonstrates a technique for producing noticeable behavior changes in a five-year-old autistic child during one therapeutic session through the systematic application of reinforcement in the form of candy for obedience and responsive behavior. Participants: Drs. Gerald C. Davison and Leonard Krasner.
Public Health Service

Behavioral Counseling

(16mm.) Ophidiophobia—fear of snakes—stands out as just one of the counseling problems resolved in Dr. Ray Hosford's *Behavioral Counseling*. This film package consists of eight films and shows counselors how to use behavioral techniques to explore and resolve client problems, whatever their nature.

1. Identifying the Problem

(21 min.) Demonstrates how a behavioral counselor translates a problem into behavioral terms and helps a client express his feelings.

2. Formulating the Counseling Goal

(19 min.) How a behavioral counselor helps a client consider a variety of counseling goals before selecting the specific behavioral goal that the client wants to learn.

3. **Observing and Recording Behavior**
   (17 min.) The counselor helps a teacher learn how to observe and record so that she can tell if a student is changing his behavior in response to her efforts.

4. **Counseling Techniques: Reinforcement Procedures**
   (13 min.) Counselor shows how to use verbal and nonverbal reinforcement techniques with client and shows client how to use several self-modification techniques.

5. **Counseling Techniques: Social Modeling**
   (15 min.) The counselor models the behavior that the client must learn while the client observes closely, noting specific cues that he can use.

6. **Counseling Techniques: Assertive Training**
   (14 min.) Behavioral counselor helps a client learn to be more assertive with his boss.

7. **Counseling Techniques: Desensitization**
   (Part 1, 25 min.; Part 2, 16 min.) A client's fear of snakes and how the counselor helps to dispel the phobia make a lucid model for desensitization techniques.

8. **Counseling Techniques: Self-as-a-Model**
   (12 min.) Demonstrates a new approach to counseling being employed at the University of California, Santa Barbara.
   APGA

Behavioral Group Counseling
(C, 16mm, 28 min.) In the film Dr. Carl E. Thoresen of Stanford University demonstrates the use of behavioral counseling techniques with a group of high school students. Before beginning the counseling group, Dr. Thoresen first moves out into the environment to assess student needs and to enlist the cooperation of parents and faculty members. During the first group session, the developing of individualized goals and objectives and the establishing of a baseline on behavior to be changed is shown. Additional sequences emphasize the use of the group as a safe and positive environment for students.

Behavioral Principles for Parents
(C, 16mm, 12 min.) This training program consists of 35 short vignettes of parent-child interactions. The vignettes include examples of positive reinforcement of both appropriate and inappropri-

ate behaviors, time-out procedures and extinction. Some vignettes show incomplete interactions and viewers are encouraged to form their own responses in order to complete each interaction. The accompanying leader's guide contains the script and discussion questions for each scene. Content consultant, Dr. Rex Forehand.
Research Press

Born to Succeed: Behavior Procedures for Education
(C, 16mm, 2 parts, each 30 min., outline and study guide available.)

Part 1:   The Concept of Number   Basic behavioral procedures are described within the framework of a program for teaching number concepts to retarded children.

Part 2:   Arithmetic   This reel illustrates teaching retarded children arithmetic starting with the concepts of more and less, order, equality, and addition.
Hanover Communications Film Library

The Broken Bridge
(c, 16mm, 35 minutes) Therapy sessions with autistic children are shown. The therapist is Irene Kassorla, and she demonstrates how to establish communication skills in autistic children. Three steps are shown: imitation learning, responses to questions, and initiative question asking.
Time-Life Films

Building Social Skills in the Preschool Child
(16mm, 25 min.) This film deals with the systematic application of behavior modification principles in increasing socially desirable responses in young children. The first part of the film is directed toward general application to a preschool class as a whole, regardless of curriculum content while the latter part focuses on specific application.

Changing Kip
(16mm, 30 min.) This film is designed to teach parents how to alter their children's behavior. Instruction in the basic principles of behavior modification and their application is presented within the framework of the actual treatment program for a five year old boy with autistic behaviors. The film emphasizes that these principles are applicable for all children.
Media Services

Charting Behavior Series

1. Charting Behavior
(Newscast 1970—C, 16mm, 11 min.) An interview with Dr. Ogden R. Lindsley, creator of Precision Teaching, stressing the importance and various applications of the behavior chart—from fetal movement to Chicago Police control. Five-year-old Stephanie Bates tells how she used the behavior chart to teach her two year old brother to read.

2. Charting Rates with Stephanie Bates
(C, 35mm slides, cassette tape, 30 min.) Introduces charting applications stressing charting ease and importance. Stephanie Bates, a five-year-old kindergarten student, will teach audience how to use the behavior chart. Stephanie covers all necessary details in the "tried and proven presentation."
Film Fund

Child Behavior = You
(C, 16mm, 15 min.) To modify child behavior from infancy through adolescence, the simple principle is to reward and reinforce the desired behavior—whereas in practice it is often the undesirable actions that receive attention. Uses humorous animation to show parent-child relations during those years.
Benchmark Films

Childhood Aggression: A Social Learning Approach to Family Therapy
(C, 16mm, 30 min.) This film shows the social learning based family intervention procedures developed by Drs. Patterson and Reid at the Oregon Research Institute, especially with aggressive behavior problems. The film depicts the environment in which a preteen boy confronts his family. It demonstrates the impact of his problem behaviors on other family members and allows the viewer to see the treatment techniques in action. Contracting, point system, time out, and behavioral rehearsal are demonstrated.
Research Press

Children Are Not Problems; They Are People
(C, 16mm, 27 min.) This film depicts a preschool at the University of Kansas, which trains teachers and serves as a model for teaching severely handicapped children in a normal, integrated classroom. The film shows how normal children serve as behavior models and

how several professional disciplines help meet special needs of each child. Includes discussions of goals, problems, achievements, and the practicality of the model.
Audio-Visual Center

Classroom Management

(C, 16mm, 18 min.) The film portrays the techniques teachers use to manage children's behavior, focusing on the kinds of problems that naturally arise in any elementary classroom. It specifies concrete teacher behavior that correlates with work involvement and freedom from misbehavior in classroom activities.
New York University

Classroom Management Techniques

(C, videotape and cassette, 30 min.) This film demonstrates a series of management techniques to control and prevent behavior problems in the classroom. Faced with disruptive behavior, the teacher has several alternatives. The film provides a series of twelve techniques.

Counting Movement Cycles

(16mm, 15 min.) The choice of recording devices may ultimately determine the amount of data one can collect during the day in the classroom, the ease with which one can collect this data, and the amount of pupil involvement that will be possible in the data collection process. This film was designed to present some of the possible alternatives for those interested in collecting data in their classrooms. The suggestions offered are based upon experience with different data collection devices. Suggestions are included for inexpensive devices which the teacher may make.
Media Services

Dare to Do

(B/W, 16mm, 28 min.) Shows the use of a token economy in an elementary school classroom. It changes a semi-chaotic class into one of improved academic performance with disruptive behaviors eliminated.
Synchro Films

Developing Auditory Stimulus-Response Control with Young Children

(C, 16mm, 16 min.) Auditory stimulus-response control is a critical dimension in the auditory testing of children two years of age. Children may have suspected hearing losses, but they may be too

young to respond to spoken instructions. Their behavior may be directed toward attempts to escape from the testing environment rather than toward cooperating with the audiologist. If the child can be placed under stimulus-response control, the auditory measurement becomes rather routine. This film demonstrates behavioral techniques used to obtain reliable bilateral auditory data from children as young as nine months.
Audio-Visual Center

Developing Observational Techniques

(C, 16mm, 13 min.) In a learning disabilities class of eight six- to eight-year-old pupils with low I.Q. and achievement levels, a teacher and aide demonstrate instructional control and organization techniques and strategies for preventing or coping with children's inappropriate behavior. Also included are the cues by which such behaviors are observed.
University of Wisconsin

Developing Study Habits

(C, 16mm, 13 min.) In an experimental classroom suite, there are twelve children of a broad range of ability, but with both learning disabilities and emotional-behavioral problems. Two teachers and an aide teach study habits through individual and group learning activities: selection of individual learning tasks, consistent praise, individual progress charts, and a reward system granting free time or toys for accurate work.
University of Wisconsin

Diapers Away: Toilet Training the Mentally Retarded Child at Home

(C, 35mm filmstrip, 55 frs.) Filmstrip demonstrates technique for teaching toilet use to a child at home.
National Audiovisual Center

Diapers Away: Toilet Training Mentally Retarded Children in Groups

(C, 35mm filmstrip, 49 frs.) This filmstrip demonstrates technique for teaching toilet use to groups of children in institutions and day-care centers.
National Audiovisual Center

Do It

(16mm, 20 min.) The development of role play for mentally handicapped persons is broken down into simple steps. Each step is an exercise or game designed to lead the handicapped individual to-

ward discoveries. The film is aimed primarily toward practicing and potential teachers, counselors, aides, and administrators of mentally handicapped persons.
Hallmark

Don't Be Afraid
(16mm, 11 min.) Tells the story of how a young boy is helped by his mother to overcome his fear of the dark. Points out that many fears have a useful purpose by serving as a warning of danger. Explains how to determine whether a fear is a useful one or not and how to go about overcoming undesirable fears, such as fear of dogs, fear of water, and fear of what others might think.
Audio-Visual Center

Educational Technology
(C, 16mm, 12 min.) This film is a presentation of how teaching machines, auditory aids, recording devices, and visual displays are used in educational programs for the development of speech with the hearing impaired.
National Audiovisual Center

Effective Behavioral Programming: Procedure for Educating & Training Retarded Persons
(Videotape, 5 hours) The eight-tape series trains staff to implement a behavioral program with severely and profoundly retarded persons. This program emphasizes the application of behavioral procedures. Dr. Foxx details the use of these procedures as well as their advantages and disadvantages. Examples of how behavioral procedures work in everyday situations are included.
Research Press

Albert Ellis: A Demonstration with an Elementary School Age Child
(C, 16mm, 30 min.) The response of a nine-year-old boy to rational emotive psychotherapy is shown. After a lively exchange between Albert Ellis and the child, Ellis describes how he conceptualizes a problem, what he is accomplishing, and how rational emotive psychotherapy may be applied to children.

Freeplay
(B/W, 16mm, 30 min.) Describes the behavioral-educational settings called Learning Villages, located in Kalamazoo, Michigan, where 80 children, ranging in age from two months to eleven years, attend sessions.
Behavior Development Corporation

From Care to Prevention

(B/W, 16mm, 30 min.) Presentation of classroom applications of behavioral techniques emphasizing preventative measures. Scenes include imitation training and concentration training among others.
Behavior Development Corporation

The Gentle Chain

(B/W, 15 min.) Behavior modification of eating skills of retarded children is discussed. The instructors break down the eating process into a series of steps in order to aid the children in learning. As a child successfully completes each step, his behavior is reinforced with a treat and approval from the staff member.
National Children's Center

Genesis

(16mm, 25 min.) *Genesis*, film one in *Step Behind Series*, teaches how to train the mentally retarded in basic self-help skills: dressing, eating, and toileting. The techniques demonstrated in this film are based on principles of learning.
Hallmark

Harry: Behavioral Treatment of Self-Abuse

(16mm Film, 38 min.) This film shows how a self-abusive mildly retarded young man is taught to live without physical restraints by means of behavior modification techniques. A unique documentary record of the entire period of treatment by Dr. Richard M. Foxx.
Research Press

The Headbangers

(B/W, 16mm, 30 min.) Describes a treatment program for retarded, severely self-destructive children. Pictures several institutionalized children who engage in headbanging behavior. One child blinded herself and was subsequently placed in a special study unit. Emphasizes the persistent, cooperative effort of the staff and therapist as the primary mode of treatment.
National Audiovisual Center

Help for Mark

(C, 16mm, 17 min.) This film is directed toward parents and teachers of trainable retarded children, as well as students in special education, educational psychology, child development, clinical child psychology, and behavior modification. Application of behavior modification principles and techniques which can be applied in the home environment receive the most attention. Comparison of

behavior exhibited before, during, and after training reveals the need for keeping accurate records of the child's progress. Problems, such as those arising from reinforcement of undesirable behavior, are discussed. Produced by Baldwin and Fredericks of Teaching Research, Monmouth, Oregon.
Prentice-Hall

Helping Families Learn
(B/W, Super 8mm, 30 min.) The film shows how a short-term residential program for disturbed, retarded children returns the children to the community. This is accomplished both by retraining the children, and by training parents and teachers in the behavioral approach. The basics of behavior modification are demonstrated through the changes in one hyperactive child and her mother in only an eight-week period. The film shows how the behavioral approach is applied in the residential program, the home, and in the community school to which the child returns.
Madden Zone Center

Home Management Procedures
(videotape, 35 min.) This film is designed for training students in behavior management procedures in a home setting. The tape is composed of four parts:
1. Initial interview: Identifying the problem
2. Design and implementation of home program
3. Evaluation of home program
4. Terminating the case
Media Services

Horizon of Hope
(C, 16mm, 15 min.) Reinforcement is demonstrated with learning disabled children at a special school at the UCLA Neuropsychiatric Institute. Although the disabilities have various causes, reinforcement is shown to be useful in teaching appropriate behaviors. Children's problems range from mental retardation, brain damage, psychological impairment, to cultural deprivation.
University of California

How to Use Tokens in Teaching
(C, 16mm, 8 min.) Shows a teacher, a mother from the community, demonstrating the proper way to use tokens in preschool education. Shows how tokens are delivered, explains when tokens are taken back, and gives several specific points to remember when using tokens as reinforcers in an educational setting.
Audio-Visual Center

Impact of a Teacher's Behaviors on Learners and Learning

(B/W, 16mm, 71 min.) Unrehearsed teaching demonstration for inservice and preservice teachers. Two instructional modes are used to emphasize impact of verbal and nonverbal behaviors on learners. Veteran and neophyte teachers are alerted to the influence their behaviors have on learners. Guidelines for systematic analysis of any type of teaching behaviors are presented. Teachers' self-evaluations and discussion are stimulated.
Psychological Cinema Register

I'll Promise You a Tomorrow

(16mm, 20 min.) This is the final film in the Step Behind Series (the others are *Genesis* and *Ask just for little things*). After the child is taught self-help skills and life skills, the next area of concern is teaching him more advanced skills to prepare him for a special education setting. In particular, communication, direction following, and group participation are illustrated in this film.
Hallmark Films

An Individual Behavior Modification Program

(C, 16mm, 14 min.) This film introduces behavior modification procedures on a basic level of understanding. Steps in the development of a behavior modification program are detailed, illustrating the importance of specifying the behavior to be changed, taking baselines, charting, and implementing a consistent treatment program.
Camarillo State Hospital

An Introduction to Behavioral Counseling

(C, 16mm, 26 min.) This film demonstrates through the use of a case study how a behavioral counselor works with the client, parents, and teachers in helping the client solve the problem for which he sought counseling. The counselor, Dr. Ray E. Hosford, University of California—Santa Barbara, uses such behavioral counseling techniques as reinforcement, social modeling, role playing, and environmental modification to help Mike, a fourteen-year-old, modify his maladaptive behavior. Dr. John D. Krumboltz, Stanford University, reviews the techniques used by the counselor at crucial points throughout the film.
Counseling Films

Jennifer Is a Lady

(C, 16mm, 25 min.) Jennifer is a five-year-old autistic child attending the Pre-Schoolers' Workshop. The film illustrates an attempt to develop language skills in Jennifer, using her fascination with

makeup and other "lady-like" paraphernalia as a motivation.
New York University

Kids Are People Too, You Know

(C, 16mm, and videotape, 35 min.) The film begins with a father
describing his frustrations with child management, and then allud-
ing to a Parents' Workshop, which imparted some very helpful
parenting skills. The father annotates a series of twelve parent-child
vignettes, which demonstrates the difference between correct and
incorrect child management techniques. Immediate and contingent
social reinforcement of desirable child behavior is emphasized.
Camarillo State Hospital

Language

(Videotape and 16mm, 60 min.) Summarizes a program for teaching
receptive language and speech. Demonstrates the use of reinforcement, shaping, chaining, and fading.
Behavior Modification Technology

Managing Behavior: A Program for Parent Involvement

(3 filmstrips, 3 cassette tapes) An introductory program in behavior
change methods, focusing on positive reinforcement and simple
behavior charting. It uses filmstrips and audio cassettes plus parent
log books to provide practice exercises to support learned material.
Research Press

Mommy, Daddy and Us Kids

(C, 16mm, video cassette, or Super 8mm, 31 min./short version;
50 min./long version) This film demonstrates behavioral principles
which parents can use to more effectively raise their children. Although the interaction between biological and environmental factors is recognized, parents are encouraged to maximize the latter.
As alternatives to permissiveness and to excessive punitive control,
reinforcement of desirable behaviors and extinction of undesirable
behaviors are demonstrated.
Cine VIP Company

No Gun Towers, No Fences

(C, 16mm, 30 min.) A description is presented of the Robert F.
Kennedy Youth Center in Morgantown, West Virginia, a minimum
security federal institution that seeks to change its students' behavior by stressing freedom and responsibility. Glass walls replace iron
bars and mountains substitute for fences. Demonstrates how responsibility is rewarded with bonus points—the center's cur-
rency—and how students with similar behavioral problems are

classified and grouped in living quarters or cottages. (The program was originally developed at the National Training School for Boys in Washington by Harold Cohen. See Case II and Case II—Model in this listing.)
University of California

No Time

(C, 16mm, 10 min.) Educators utilizing behavioral principles in the classroom are faced with the problems of how to record behavior in an unobtrusive and efficient manner. This film demonstrates how to obtain accurate data by adapting presently used low-cost classroom materials. Methods currently used by teachers for keeping daily records are shown to be analogous to behavioral recording techniques. Other examples of recording instruments and procedures emphasize economy, teacher mobility, and flexibility. This film is designed for in-service or other training formats.
Behavioral Paraphernalia

Nobody Took the Time

(16mm, 26 min.) This film produced by the Dubnoff School for Educational Therapy is directed toward the ghetto child handicapped with learning disabilities, the one most labeled MR. The teachers demonstrate that basic trust in himself or herself and others is the first need of these children. This is accomplished through treating each child as a unique individual. A variety of highly structured classroom and playground techniques help these children learn there is order to everything, develop language, and an awareness of their surroundings.
AIMS

Non-Slip

(C, 16mm, 25 min.) Non-Slip (non-*S*peech *L*anguage *I*nitiation *Pro*gram) is a set of procedures for nonverbal persons through the process of learning communications skills. Plastic symbols that represent words are used to teach language rules to the child. The symbols are unique geometric forms that the child picks up and places on a tray to construct symbolic sentences. These procedures are demonstrated, and a background is provided in symbolic language research.
Audio-Visual Center

One Hour a Week

(C, 16mm, 18 min.) Shows the League School for Seriously Disturbed Children's Home Training Program for parents with children on the school waiting list. To help parents cope with their

child's emotional disturbance this program demonstrates behavior modification techniques parents can use at home.
National Audiovisual Center

One Step at a Time: An Introduction to Behavior Modification

(C, 16mm, 30 min.) This film is set in an elementary classroom, a preschool, and a state hospital where teachers work to develop learning experiences by praising good efforts. Among the segments of the film is one that describes a behavioral technique by which older students become teachers for younger ones. In this way, the distinctions between students and teachers begin to break down, and the school begins to become a center for an exchange of ideas, rather than a one-directional flow from teachers to student. Many techniques are demonstrated, including charting, tokens, and praise. Narrated by Roger Ulrich.
Behavior Development Corporation

Operant Conditioning—Token Economy

(C, 16mm, 40 min.) This film demonstrates the use of operant conditioning procedures, particularly positive reinforcement and token economy systems. The film depicts a day in the life of a mentally retarded resident on a token economy system.
Camarillo State Hospital

Out of the Shadows

(C, 16mm, 17 min.) This film demonstrates the use of behavior modification procedures to help retarded children learn basic self-help and social skills (e.g., feeding, motor skills, speech, toileting). Emphasis is placed on the use of reinforcement methods.
Audio-Visual Center

PACA: Paraprofessionals as Change Agents

(C, 16mm, 27 min.) PACA is a community based behavior management program in which parents learn how to measure and change specific behaviors in children. The program involves learning how to use materials, how to give demonstrations, how to work with parents and children in the home. Trainees in the program learn to be skilled paraprofessionals who can work both in the home and in the classrooms to help teachers and parents become positive influences in remediating problem behaviors that are keeping children from making the most of their school experiences.
Bureau of Visual Instruction

Parents and Children: A Positive Approach to Child Management

(C, 16mm, 24 min.) This film presents an overview of reinforcement principles in easily understood, nontechnical language. It examines the parent-child relationship as a special learning experience in which the use of rewards can play a crucial role. This film shows how to use positive reinforcement to teach children and improve their behavior.

The concepts covered include: the learning experience between parent and child, how and when to use rewards effectively, attention rewards, activity rewards, material rewards, strengthening or maintaining good behavior, teaching new or complex behavior, and eliminating undesirable behavior. This film offers a positive approach to parents who are interested in motivating and teaching their children.

Research Press

Pinpoint, Record and Consequate

(C, 16mm, 14 min.) Precision teaching—adapting operant conditioning, principles to home behavior management is described. The three steps: Pinpoint, Record, and Consequate are explained. Graphs showing how parents use contingent access to commercial television programs to accelerate new words learned and eliminate bed wetting are analyzed.

Film Fund

Pinpointing Classroom Behavior

(16mm, 12 min.) Pinpointing is a skill for teachers regardless of the classroom situation in which they may find themselves. Pinpointing is also an important first step toward effective measurement of classroom performance, for without accurate and precise pinpoints, data have little value. Through examples of social and academic behavior, the viewer is introduced to pinpointing and given opportunities to practice this skill in a variety of classroom situations, in order to accurately specify the target behavior to be changed.

Media Services

Placement, Programming, and Pool

(35mm slides, 8 min.) A brief overview of initial assessment, classroom behavior management, and specific academic programs (reading, spelling, writing, math) developed for use with mild to moderate learning disabled pupils in one Experimental Education Unit classroom.

Media Services

Peer Conducted Behavior Modification

(C, 16mm, 24 min.) Through the work of a trained psychologist, the child's parents are taught the principles and techniques of behavior modification. The viewer sees how the child's parents learn to recognize maladaptive behaviors and to deal with them. The film

illustrates the way in which the child's schoolmates and their parents are mobilized in a neighborhood effort to modify the aggressive behavior problems causing the most difficulty. The film highlights the ways and means in which positive and negative reinforcements and a token economy are applied in several situations, showing examples of the ultimately positive outcome. Commentary is provided by Dr. Gerald Patterson, whose original research provided impetus for the work depicted in the film.
Neuropsychiatric Institute

Precision Teaching

(Sound filmstrip, 20 min.) Demonstrates how a teacher in an elementary classroom makes specific curriculum selections and decisions for each individual child. Students are shown charting and observing improvement of their own behavior.
Council for Exceptional Children

PREP (Preparation through Responsive Educational Programs)

(C, 16mm, 27 min.) Remedial educational procedures are shown with adolescent youth who have social and/or academic problems. Emphasis is on the use of an elaborate reinforcement system. Interpersonal skills training is also shown, as well as parent training and follow-up evaluation.
Institute for Behavioral Research

Randy's Up—Randy's Down

(16mm, 22 min.) This film shows the progress and the regressions associated with an attempt to use contingent shock therapy to control self-abusive behavior in an institutional environment. The film shows not only the behavior of the child, it also examines the moods and attitudes of the child care workers and the psychologists who worked with the child day to day, as they faced both success and failure in their attempts to eliminate Randy's self abuse.
Bureau of Visual Instruction

Reinforcement Therapy

(B/W, 16mm, 45 min.) Documents three behavioral programs with: autistic children, retardates, and chronic institutionalized adult schizophrenics. Demonstrates shaping, fading, and use of punishment and tokens. Drs. O. Ivar Lovaas and Jay Birnbrauer discuss their programs. Study guide available.
National Library of Medicine

Reward and Punishment

(C, 16mm, 15 min.) Dr. James Gardner outlines the principles underlying both reward and punishment and provides some

guidelines for using these principles effectively to develop new behaviors or change existing behaviors of young children. The uses and abuses of punishment are discussed, using everyday examples, with particular regard to their negative side effects, and their positive applications. The film points out that attention and affection are the most universal reinforcers, and that when closely queried, teachers and parents are often shocked to discover how frequently they withhold them.
McGraw-Hill Films

Reward Procedures for Behavior Management
(B/W, 16mm, 25 min.) This film offers the observer a basic introduction to the topic of child management through reinforcement methods. It presents three simple reinforcement procedures that adults can use to influence child behavior.
Behavior Technics, Inc.

Rewards and Reinforcements in Learning
(B/W, 16mm, 26 min.) Demonstrates four behavioral projects: retarded child learning to walk, child learning to tie shoes, child with speech problem, and behavior modification procedures in several classroom settings with underprivileged children. The film demonstrates shaping, fading, token systems and other behavioral techniques. Study guide available.
Behavior Modification Productions

Self-Help Skills
(Videotape or 16mm, 40 min.) Demonstrates in detail a behavior modification program for teaching self-help skills. Can be used as an introduction to behavior modification.
Behavior Modification Technology

Self-Management of Behavior
(C, 16mm, 33 min.) With commentary by B. F. Skinner, the film follows the evaluation of two behavior-problem children and the ensuing development of self-intervention behavior modification programs. An eleven-year-old child, living in a residential treatment program, is discussed by the ward staff, including nurses, psychiatric technicians, social workers, the pediatrician, and psychiatrist. The viewer witnesses the severity of the child's maladaptive behavior, and watches the interdisciplinary development and implementation of a behavioral program administered by the child himself. Parental attitudes are discussed with the staff during the course of treatment. A second child, seven years of age, is evaluated and treated in an outpatient setting. The viewer is shown the complex interaction between parent, child and therapist, as a self-

regulatory behavioral program is developed and implemented.
Neuropsychiatric Institute

Shaping Independent Living Skills Using Graduated Guidance
(16mm) This film shows the use of the technique of "graduated guidance." Developed by Drs. Richard Foxx and Luke Watson.
Behavior Modification Technology

Siblings as Behavior Modifiers
(C, 16mm, 25 min.) Cary, a mentally retarded youngster, represents a challenge to his brothers and sisters, as well as to his parents. Through the counseling of a psychiatric social worker, the family is taught new management techniques which use behavior modification in the home, rather than the institution; techniques which involve the entire family. The film leaves little doubt that institutionalization is not the only alternative when siblings act as behavior modifiers, teaching new skills, and reinforcing positive behavior.
Neuropsychiatric Institute

Skills Training for the Special Child
(C, 16mm, 30 min.) This film demonstrates the application of behavioral techniques used in the classroom management of problem children. The behavioral procedures featured here are used to teach number concepts and arithmetic to retarded and developmentally disabled children. These methods can be readily adaptable to all teaching situations, making this film a resource not only for those involved in accelerating learning in special children, but also for students and professionals in psychology and mainstream education. Developed by Dr. Ellen Reese.
Harper & Row

Spearhead at Juniper Gardens
(B/W, 16mm, 40 min.) Demonstrates a preschool and remedial education research project in a deprived community of Kansas City, Kansas. Reinforcement principles are used to develop the language of preschoolers and to motivate slow-learning grade school children. Mothers of children are trained as teachers.
Bureau of Visual Instruction

Specific Learning Disabilities: Remedial Programming
(C, 28 min.) This film describes how information gained through evaluation and observation can be translated into appropriate individualized remedial planning; follows one child into the classroom

and through remediation; presents and discusses techniques and procedures which teachers can use in the classroom.
University of Southern California

Systems for Precise Observations for Teachers: Project S.P.O.T.
(C, 16mm)

1. **Problems in Academic Task Performance**
   (7 min.) Presents portions of one student's verbal and written response to alphabet symbols presented orally or visually. These skills, seen as being basic to reading and spelling achievements, are only representative of academic skills for which precise observation is helpful. The accompanying observation guide is designed to help the viewer to record precisely the relevant elements of the academic materials and instructions presented to the students by the teacher, and to record precisely the student's performance.

2. **Problems in Self-Help Task Performance**
   (6 min.) Shows handicapped children attempting to perform certain self-help tasks. The observation guide presents a system of observing and analyzing which parts of the tasks were performed successfully by the student and which were not. Once the incomplete parts of a task are described, the viewer can decide upon an appropriate teaching strategy. The choice of teaching strategies might involve (1) teaching the student to perform the parts of the task which are not performed, (2) inventing another way for the student to accomplish the task without the use of assistive devices, or (3) using devices or aids to facilitate the student's performance of the task.

3. **Devices for Self-Help Task Performance**
   (12 min.) Illustrates some examples of procedures, equipment, and material used to facilitate performance of self-help tasks by crippled children who have rather severe physical limitations. The accompanying observation guide for this part directs attention to pictures which can be kept as a permanent record of ideas presented on the film. This part provides open-ended sections to stimulate discussion and the sharing of additional ideas.
   National Audiovisual Center

Teacher Training Videotape Series
(Videotape) This video tape series was designed to provide an individualized course concerning the topic of precision teaching. Each tape presents one major procedure vital to precision teaching and contains examples taken from classrooms at the Experimental

Education Unit. Each tape concerns a different aspect of precision teaching. (This series is available on both ½" EIAF format and ¾" U-Matic videocassette format. The lengths vary and are listed below with the individual program titles.)

2   Precision Teaching Today (61 min.)
3   Pinpointing Social Movement Cycles (29 min.)
4   Pinpointing Academic Movement Cycles (61 min.)
5   Counting and Timing Devices (59 min.)
6PA Rate as a Measure, Part A (45 min.)
6PB Rate as a Measure, Part B (39 min.)
6A   Measurement Systems for the Classroom—Panel Discussion (59 min.)
7   The Standard Behavior Chart (51 min.)
8   Charting Conventions (59 min.)
9   Self-Management Techniques (57 min.)
11A Establishing Educational Objectives, Part A (57 min.)
11B Establishing Educational Objectives, Part B (58 min.)
12   Probes: What, When, Why, How (56 min.)
12A Probes: Examples (59 min.)

Teaching/Discipline: A Positive Approach for Educational Development

(C, 16mm) Based on material developed by Drs. Charles and Clifford Madsen. The six (of a proposed eight) films are meant to be used as a set. Each presents concepts built upon the next films in the series, and are not produced to be used separately or interspersed with other films.

1. **Desire vs. Behavior**
   (30 min.) Explains the disparity between the positive behavior one desires to display and the way one actually behaves.
2. **Values vs. Techniques**
   (40 min.) Identifies the role of one's value choices on behavior and explains the relationship between value choice and behavioral techniques.
3. **Consequences of Behavior**
   (60 min.) This film demonstrates the postitive and negative social and academic consequences which modify behavior in typical school scenes. Methods for establishing contingent relationships with students are explained and illustrated.
4. **Recording Student Behavior**
   (30 min.) Teaches a systematic method of observing and an individual student's on-task/off-task behavior.
5. **Recording Teacher Behavior**
   (40 min.) Teaches a systematic method (the Madsen Observation

Form) of observing and recording teacher approvals and disapprovals.

6. **Observing Student/Teacher Interaction**

(40 min.) Teaches a systematic method of observing and recording teacher approvals and disapprovals, as well as either an
individual student's or entire group's on-task/off-task behavior.
P.I.T.

Teaching Language Skills to Children with Behavioral Disorders

(B/W, 16mm videotape, 40 min.) This film demonstrates a program
for teaching receptive language and speech. The use of reinforcement, fading, shaping, prompting, and chaining is shown. It is
designed to be used in conjunction with teaching self-help skills to
children with behavioral disorders.
Behavior Modification Technology

Teaching Self-Help Skills to Children with Behavioral Disorders

(B/W, 16mm videotape, 40 min.) Behavior modification programs
are detailed for teaching various self-help skills to retarded children
and other children with behavior disorders. The film shows the use
of reinforcement, shaping, stimulus control, prompting and other
behavior modification procedures.
Behavior Modification Technology

**Teaching Social Recreational Skills to Children with Behavioral
Disorders**

(B/W, 16mm videotape, 40 min.) One of three films distributed by
Behavior Modification Technology, this film shows how behavior
modification procedures can be used to teach retarded children, as
well as psychotic children, to play games and socially interact.
Behavior Modification Technology

Teaching the Mentally Retarded—A Positive Approach

(B/W, 16mm, 22 min.) Step-by-step description and explanation of
operant procedures used in an institutional setting. Informative and
appropriate for ward personnel. Training toileting, dressing, self-
feeding, and manners with four profoundly retarded children.
Demonstrates reinforcement, time-out, shaping, and fading techniques applied by ward personnel. Booklet available.
National Library of Medicine

Teaching Verbalization by Contingency Management

(C, 16mm, 15 min.) Follows the development of a language training
program for a five-year-old mentally retarded girl, from a vocabu-
lary of five words to 200 words.
Independent Learning Systems

That's What It's All About

(C, 16mm, 29 min.) Shows all aspects of the Regional Intervention Program of Nashville, Tennessee. This program trains mothers to use behavior modification modules to alter and cope with their unacceptable parent-child relationships. There is a minimum staff of three professional educators, but all daily remediations and therapies are conducted by the mothers themselves. It is essentially a free service as the mothers pay back their obligated time by participating in the program.
National Audiovisual Center

Time Out: A Way to Help Children Behave Better

(B/W, 16mm, 25 min.) This film teaches rules for using time-out procedures to reduce unwanted behavior. Illustrations include a wide range of ages and situations: rule breaking in school and home, sibling quarrels, and classroom tantrums. The emphasis is on reinforcement, not punishment, as preferred strategy.
Behavior Technics

Time's Lost Children

(C, 16mm, 25 min.) Presents behavioral program developed for autistic children at the Los Ninos School in San Diego. Demonstrates development of attention, imitation, eye contact, following directions, and language. Also illustrates a parent training program.
Indiana University

Toilet Training: A Program for Retarded Students & Residents

(Videotape, 52 min.) This videocassette presents the prerequisites for toilet training the retarded and then presents the basic procedures used in the program. Dr. Foxx discusses the process from helping the student adapt to the training environment to establishing self-initiated toileting.
Research Press

A Token System for Behavior Modification

(C, 16mm, 8 min.) The film demonstrates how behavior modification and a token economy contribute to the education of severely retarded and moderately retarded girls in an institutional setting. Tokens are applied to increasingly more complex behaviors.
Audio-Visual Center

Try Another Way

(C, 16mm, 27 min.) Approach to teaching complex assembly tasks to the mentally retarded, developed by Dr. Marc Gold at the Chil-

dren's Research Center, University of Illinois. Introduction to the Marc Gold Training series.
Pennsylvania Cinema Register

Using Teacher Attention to Reinforce Behavior or . . . "Clay Sticks to Your Fingers"

(Videotape, 20 min.) This tape illustrates a variety of ways in which teachers can use their attention to reinforce children. It is based on teacher attention to encourage desirable behaviors. Illustrations are from candid video tape recordings in a preschool classroom. (Also available on a 5" reel for the battery-operated Sony VideoRover, if specifically requested.)
Media Services

What's the Difference Being Different?

(16mm, 19 min.) This film demonstrates how a multicultural program can be implemented to a school system. It shows students and teachers participating in activities which increase feeling of self-worth and understanding of others. Ideal for teacher training courses and for teachers and school administrators.
Research Press

Winning with Warmth: Helping the Problem Child in the Classroom

(C, 16mm, 30 min.) Using real-life situations, psychologists K. Daniel O'Leary and Marlene Schneider demonstrate the uses of behavior modification techniques so teachers and their aides can better cope with behavioral and learning-problem children in the regular classroom.
Prentice-Hall

Who Did What to Whom?

(C, 16mm, 16½ min.) The film comes with a leader guide and consists of 40 short scenes representing typical events which take place in the home, school, and office. Some scenes show children, some depict only adults, and others utilize both children and adults. The film helps the observer learn to recognize four principles of learning: positive reinforcement, negative reinforcement, extinction, and punishment. Although the film is short, with the discussion time that is alloted between each scene there is enough material for a two-hour session. Upon request, the distributor will send a free preview brochure.
Research Press

Addresses of film distributors

AIMS Instructional Media
Services
P.O. Box 1010
Hollywood, California 90028

APGA Film Department
1607 New Hampshire Avenue,
N.W.
Washington, D.C. 20009

Audio-Visual Center
University of Kansas
746 Massachusetts Street
Lawrence, Kansas 66044

Behavior Modification
Productions
P.O. Box 3207
Scottsdale, Arizona 85257

Behavior Modification
Technology
Dr. Luke Watson
P.O. Box 1730
Tuscaloosa, Alabama 35401

Behavior Technics, Inc.
Box 116
Lemont, Pennsylvania 16851

Behavioral Development
Corporation
7943 South 25th Street
Kalamazoo, Michigan 49002

Behavioral Paraphernalia
4313 Hamilton Street
Hyattsville, Maryland 20781

Behavioral Products
219 Farrer Boulevard
Department A
Dayton, Ohio 45419

Behaviordelia, Inc.
P.O. Box 1044
Kalamazoo, Michigan 49005

Benchmark Films, Inc.
145 Scarborough Road
Briarcliff Manor, New York
10510

Bureau of Visual Instruction
6 Bailey Hall
University of Kansas
Lawrence, Kansas 66044

Camarillo State Hospital
Box A
Camarillo, California 93010

Cine VIP Company
P.O. Box 2278
Orange, California 92669

Council for Exceptional Children
1411 S. Jefferson Davis Highway
Suite 900
Arlington, Virginia 22202

Counseling Films, Inc.
P.O. Box 1047
Madison, Wisconsin 53701

Educational Coordinates
432 S. Pastoria Avenue
Sunnyvale, California 94086

Film Fund
Box 3026
Kansas City, Kansas 66103

Hallmark Films, Inc.
51–53 New Plant Court
Owings Mills, Maryland 21117

Hanover Communications Film
Library
P.O. Box C
Northhampton, Massachusetts
01060

Harper & Row Media
2350 Virginia Avenue
Hagerstown, Maryland 21740

Independent Learning Systems
18 Professional Center Parkway
San Rafael, California 94903

Indiana University
Audio Visual Center
Bloomington, Indiana 47401

Informatics
Department C
8531 Schaefer Highway
Detroit, Michigan 48222

Institute for Behavioral Research
2429 Linden Lane
Silver Spring, Maryland 20910

Institute for Rational Living
45 East 65th Street
New York, New York 10021

Madden Zone Center
Pavilion 11
1200 South First Avenue
Hines, Illinois 60141

McGraw-Hill Films
1211 Avenue of the Americas
New York, New York 10020

Media Services
Child Development and Mental
  Retardation Center
University of Washington
Seattle, Washington 90195

National Audiovisual Center
  (GSA)
National Archives and Records
  Service
Washington, D.C. 20409

National Children's Center
6200 2nd Street, N.W.
Washington, D.C. 20011

National Library of Medicine
U.S. Department of H.E.W.
National Medical Audio
  Visual Center (annex)
Chamblee, Georgia 30005

NETCHE Videotape Library
P.O. Box 8311
Lincoln, Nebraska 68501

Neuropsychiatric Institute
MRCPP Media Unit
760 Westwood Plaza
Los Angeles, California 90024

New York University Film
  Library
26 Washington Place
New York, New York 10036

P.I.T.
Box 45
Hiawatha, Iowa 52233

Prentice-Hall
Film Library
Englewood Cliffs, New Jersey
  07632

Psychological Cinema Register
Audio Visual Services
Pennsylvania State University
University Park, Pennsylvania
  16802

Research Press
2612 North Mattis Avenue
Champaign, Illinois 61820

Synchro Films
43 Bay Drive West
Huntington, New York 11743

Time-Life Films
Multi-Media Division
43 West 16th Street
New York, New York 10011

U.S. Public Health Service
Audio Visual Facility
Atlanta, Georgia 30333

University of California
Media Center
2223 Fulton Street
Berkeley, California 94720

University of Southern
California
Film Distribution Section
University Park
Los Angeles, California 90007

University of Wisconsin
Bureau of Audio-Visual
  Instruction
1327 University Avenue
P.O. Box 2093
Madison, Wisconsin 53701

SUGGESTED READINGS

Books

Bandura, A. (1969). *Principles of behavior modification.* New York: Holt, Rinehart & Winston.

Bandura, A., & Walters, R. H. (1963). *Social learning and personality development.* New York: Holt, Rinehart & Winston.

Barkley, R. (1981). *Hyperactive children: A handbook for diagnosis and treatment.* New York: Guilford.

Cautela, J. R., & Groden, J. (1978). *Relaxation.* A comprehensive manual for adults, children, and children with special needs. Champaign, Illinois: Research Press.

Ellis, A., & Bernard, M. E. (Eds.) (1983). *Rational-emotive approaches to the problems of childhood.* New York: Plenum.

Forehand, R., & McMahon, R. (1981). *Helping the non-compliant child.* New York: Guilford.

Foxx, R. M., & Azrin, N. Y. (1973). *Toilet training the retarded.* Champaign, Illinois: Research Press.

Gardner, W. I. (1971). *Behavior modification: Applications in mental retardation.* Chicago: Aldine.

Gelfand, D. M., & Hartmann, D. P. (1984). *Child behavior analysis and therapy.* New York: Pergamon.

Goldstein, A. P. (1974). *Structured learning therapy: Toward a psychotherapy for the poor.* New York: Academic Press.

Goldstein, A. P. (1978). *Prescriptions for child mental health and education.* New York: Pergamon.

Goldstein, A. P., Apter, S. J., & Harootunian, B. (1984). *School violence.* Englewood Cliffs, New Jersey: Prentice-Hall.

Goldstein, A. P., & Kanfer, F. H. (Eds.) (1979). *Maximizing treatment gains.* New York: Academic Press.

Goldstein, A. P., Sprafkin, R. P., Gershaw, N. J., & Klein, P. (1980). *Skillstreaming the adolescent.* Champaign, Illinois: Research Press.

Graziano, A. M. (Ed.) (1975). *Behavior therapy with children.* Chicago: Aldine.

Hammill, D. D., & Bartel, N. R. (1982). *Teaching children with learning and behavior problems* (3d edition). Boston: Allyn & Bacon.

Harris, S. B. (1977). *Teaching speech to the nonverbal child.* Lawrence, Kansas: H. & H. Enterprises

Haynes, S. N. (1978). *Principles of behavioral assessment.* New York: Gardner Press.

Hersen, M., & Bellack, A. S. (1981). *Behavioral Assessment: A practical handbook.* (2d. ed.) New York: Pergamon.

Kanfer, F. H., & Phillips, J. S. (1970). *Learning foundations of behavior therapy.* New York: Wiley.

Karoly, P., & Kanfer, F. H. (Eds.) (1982). *Self-management and behavior change: From theory to practice.* New York: Pergamon.

Kazdin, A. E. (1980). *Behavior modification in applied settings.* (Rev. ed.) Homewood, Illinois: Dorsey.

Kendall, P. C., & Hollon S. D. (1979). *Cognitive-behavioral interventions: Theory, research and procedures.* New York: Academic Press.

Kratochwill, T. R. (Ed.) (1981). *Advances in school psychology.* New York: LEA.

Krumboltz, J. D., & Krumboltz, H. B. (1972). *Changing children's behavior.* Englewood Cliffs, New Jersey: Prentice-Hall.

Lahey, B. B., & Kazdin, A. E. (Eds.) (1977, 1978). *Advances in clinical child psychology.* Vols. 1 and 2. New Fork: Plenum.

Lahey, B. B. (1979). *Behavior therapy with hyperactive and learning disabled children.* New York: Oxford University Press.

Loovaas, O. I. (1979). *The autistic child.* New York: Irvington Publishers.

Marholin, D. (Ed.) (1978). *Child behavior therapy.* New York: Gardner Press.

Martin, R. (1975). *Legal challenges to behavior modifications: Trends in schools, corrections, and mental health.*

Mash, E., Hamerlynck, L., & Handy, L. (Eds.) (1976). *Behavior modification and families.* New York: Brunner/Mazel.

Mash, E., & Terdal, L. (Eds.) (1981). *Behavioral assessment of childhood disorders.* New York: Guilford.

Matson, J. L., & Andrasik, F. (Eds.) (1983). *Treatment issues and innovations in mental retardation.* New York: Plenum.

Morris, R. J., & Kratochwill, T. R. (Eds.) (1983a). *The practice of child therapy.* New York: Pergamon.

Morris, R. J., & Kratochwill, T. R. (1983b) *Treating children's fears and phobias: A behavioral approach.* New York: Pergamon.

O'Leary, K. D., & O'Leary, S. G. (1977). *Classroom management* (2d ed.) New York: Pergamon.

Ollendick, T. H., & Zerny, J. A. (1981). *Clinical behavior therapy with children.* New York: Plenum.

Patterson, G. R., & Guillon, M. E. (1968). *Living with children.* Champaign, Illinois: Research Press.

Repp, A. C. (1983). *Teaching the mentally retarded.* Englewood Cliffs, New Jersey: Prentice-Hall.

Ross, A. O. (1976). *Psychological aspects of learning disabilities and reading disorders.* New York: McGraw-Hill.

Ross, A. O. (1981). *Child behavior therapy.* New York: Wiley.

Ross, D., & Ross, S. (1982). *Hyperactivity.* New York: Wiley.

Skinner, B. F. (1953). *Science in human behavior.* New York: Macmillan.

Thompson, T., & Grabowski, J. (1977). *Behavior modification of the mentally retarded.* (2d. ed.) New York: Oxford University Press.

Weiner, J. M. (Ed.) (1977). *Psychopharmacology in childhood and adolescence.* New York: Basic Books.

Wetzel, R. J., & Hoschouer, R. L. (1984). *Residential teaching communities: Program development and staff training for developmentally disabled persons.* Glenview, Illinois: Scott, Foresman and Company.

Yule, W., & Carr, J. (1980). *Behaviour modification for the mentally handicapped.* Baltimore: University Park Press.

JOURNALS

American Journal of Mental Deficiency

Analysis and Intervention in Developmental Disabilities

Applied Research in Mental Retardation

Behavior Assessment

Behavior Disorders

Behavior Modification

Behavior Therapy

Behaviour Research & Therapy

Child Development

Child and Family Behavior Therapy

Education and Training of the Mentally Retarded

Education and Treatment of Children

Exceptional Children

Journal of Abnormal Child Psychology

Journal of Applied Behavior Analysis

Journal of the Association for the Severely Handicapped

Journal of Autism and Developmental Disorders

Journal of Behavior Therapy and Experimental Psychiatry

Journal of Child Clinical Psychology

Journal of Consulting and Clinical Psychology

Journal of Learning Disabilities

Journal of School Psychology

Journal of Special Education

Journal of Speech and Hearing Disorders

Learning Disabilities Quarterly

Mental Retardation

Psychology in the Schools

School Psychology Review

REFERENCES

Achenbach, T. M. (1974). *Developmental psychopathology*. New York: Ronald Press.

Achenbach, T. M. (1982). *Developmental psychopathology* (2d ed.). New York: Ronald Press.

Accreditation Council for Services for Mentally Retarded and Other Developmentally Disabled Persons (1978). *Standard for services for developmentally disabled individuals*. Chicago: Joint Commission on Accreditation of Hospitals.

Addison, R. M., & Homme, L. (1966). The reinforcing event (RE) menu. *NSPI Journal, 5,* 8–9.

Agras, W. W., Kazdin, A. E., & Wilson, G. T. (1979). *Behavior therapy*. San Francisco: W. H. Freeman & Co.

Allen, F. (1942). *Psychotherapy with children*. New York: W. W. Norton.

Association for Advancement of Behavior Therapy. (1977). Ethical issues for human services. *Behavior Therapy, 8,* v–vi.

Axline, V. (1947). *Play therapy*. Boston: Houghton Mifflin.

Ayllon, T., & Azrin, N. H. (1968). *The token economy: A motivational system for therapy and rehabilitation*. New York: Appleton-Century-Crofts.

Azrin, N. H., & Holz, W. C. (1966). Punishment. In W. K. Honig (Ed.), *Operant behavior: Areas of research and application.*

Baer, D. M., Wolf, M., & Risley, T. R. (1968). Some current dimensions of applied behavior analysis. *Journal of Applied Behavior analysis, 1,* 91–97.

Ball, T. S. (1968). Issues and implications of operant conditioning: The reestablishment of social behavior. *Hospital and Community Psychiatry, 19,* 229–30.

Bandura, A. (1969). *Principles of behavior modification.* New York: Holt, Rinehart & Winston.

Bandura, A. (1977a). Self-efficacy: Toward a unifying theory of behavior change. *Psychological Review, 84,* 191–215.

Bandura, A. (1977b). *Social learning theory.* Englewood Cliffs, New Jersey: Prentice-Hall.

Bandura, A., & Walters, R. H. (1963). *Social learning and personality development.* New York: Holt, Rinehart & Winston.

Baumeister, A. A. (1970). The American residential institution: Its history and character. In A. A. Baumeister & E. Butterfield (Eds.), *Residential facilities for the mentally retarded.* Chicago: Aldine.

Baumeister, A. A., & Butterfield, E. C. (Eds.) (1970). *Residential facilities for the mentally retarded.* Chicago: Aldine.

Becker, W. C. (1971). *Parents are teachers.* Champaign, IL: Research Press.

Beers, C. (1908). *A mind that found itself.* New York: Longmans, Green.

Bijou, S., & Baer, D. M. (1978). *Behavior analysis of child development.* Englewood Cliffs, New Jersey: Prentice-Hall.

Bragg, R. A., & Wagner, M. K. (1968). Issues and implications for operant conditioning: Can deprivation be justified? *Hospital and Community Psychiatry, 19,* 229–30.

Braun, S. H. (1975). Ethical isues in behavior modification. *Behavior Therapy, 6,* 51–62.

Bristol, M. M. (1976). Control of physical aggression through school- and home-based reinforcement. In J. D. Krumboltz & C. E. Thoresen (Eds.), *Counselling methods.* New York: Holt, Rinehart & Winston.

Cautela, J. R., & Groden, J. (1978). *Relaxation*. A comprehensive manual for adults, children, and children with special needs. Champaign, Illinois: Research Press.

Cunningham, S. (1984 May). Pennhurst ruling limits federal role. *APA Monitor, 15,* 14.

D'Alonzo, B. J. (Ed.) (1983). *Educating adolescents with learning and behavior problems*. Rockville, Maryland: Aspen.

Dinoff, M., & Rickard, H. C. (1969). Learning that privileges entail responsibilities. In J. D. Krumboltz & C. E. Thoresen (Eds.), *Behavioral counseling*. New York: Holt, Rinehart & Winston.

Drossman, R. (1982). Personal Communication.

Farkas, G. M. (1980). An ontological analysis of behavior therapy. *American Psychologist, 25,* 364–74.

Feretti, R. P., & Cavalier, A. R. (1983). A critical assessment of overcorrection procedures with mentally retarded persons. In J. L. Matson & F. Andrasik (Eds.), *Treatment issues and innovations in mental retardation*. New York: Plenum.

Ferster, C. B. (1957). Withdrawal of positive reinforcement as punishment. *Science, 126,* 509.

Foxx, R. M., & Azrin, N. H. (1972). Restitution: A method of eliminating aggressive-disruptive behavior of retarded and brain-damaged patients. *Behavior Research, and Therapy, 10,* 15–28.

Foxx, R. M., & Martin, E. D. (1975). Treatment of scavenging behavior (coprophagy and pica) by overcorrection. *Behavior Research and Therapy, 13,* 153–62.

Freud, S. (1909). The analysis of a phobia in a five year old boy. *Standard edition of the complete psychological works of Sigmund Freud*. Vol. 10. London: Hogarth Press.

Freud, A. (1981). *Psychoanalytic psychology of normal development*. New York: International Universities Press.

Friedman, P. (1975a). Legal regulation of applied behavior analysis in mental institutions and prisons. *Arizona Law Review, 17,* 39–104.

Friedman, P. (1975b). *The rights of the mentally retarded*. New York: Avon.

Friedman, P. (1977). Human and legal rights of mentally retarded persons. *International Journal of Mental Health, 6,* 50–72.

Goldfried, M. & Davison, G. (1975). *Clinical behavior therapy.* New York: Holt.

Goldfried, M. R. & Merbaum, M. A. (1973). A perspective on self-control. In M. R. Goldfried & M. Merbaum (Eds.), *Behavior change through self-control.* New York: Holt.

Goldiamond, I. (1974). Toward a constructional approach to social problems. *Behaviorism, 2,* 1–84.

Goldstein, A. P. (in press). Relationship-enhancement methods. In F. H. Kanfer & A. P. Goldstein (Eds.), *Helping people change* (3d ed.). New York: Pergamon.

Goldstein, A. P. (1974). *Structured learning therapy: Toward a psychotherapy for the poor.* New York: Academic Press.

Goldstein, A. P. (1980). Relationship-enhancement methods. In F. H. Kanfer & A. P. Goldstein (Eds.), *Helping people change* (2d ed.). New York: Pergamon.

Goldstein, A. P., Apter, S. J., & Harootunian, B. (1984). *School violence.* Englewood Cliffs, New Jersey: Prentice-Hall.

Goldstein, A. P., & Kanfer, F. H. (Eds.) (1979). *Maximizing treatment gains.* New York: Academic Press.

Goldstein, A. P., Sprafkin, R. P., Gershaw, N. J., & Klein, P. (1980). *Skillstreaming the adolescent.* Champaign, Illinois: Research Press.

Graziano, A. M. (1971). *Behavior therapy with children.* Chicago: Aldine-Atherton.

Graziano, A. M., & Mooney, K. C. (1984). *Children and behavior therapy.* New York: Aldine.

Halderman v. Pennhurst. (1977). 446 F. Supp. 1295.

Halderman v. Pennhurst. (1979). 612 F. 2d84.

Hallahan, D. P., Lloyd, J. W., Kauffman, J. M., & Loper, A. B. (1983). Academic problems. In R. J. Morris & T. R. Kratochwill (Eds.), *The practice of child therapy.* New York: Pergamon.

Hammill, D. D., & Bartel, N. R. (1982). *Teaching children with learning and behavior problems.* Boston: Allyn & Bacon.

Harris, S. B. (1975). Teaching language to nonverbal children—with emphasis on problems of generalization. *Psychological Bulletin, 82,* 565–80.

Harris, S. B. (1976). *Teaching speech to the nonverbal child.* Lawrence, Kansas: H. & H. Enterprises.

Haynes, S. N. (1978). *Principles of behavioral assessment.* New York: Gardner Press.

Hersen, M., & Bellack, A. S. (1981). *Behavioral assessment: A practical handbook* (2d ed.). New York: Pergamon.

Hull, C. (1943). *Principles of behavior.* New York: Appleton-Century-Crofts.

Humphrey, J. (1962). Introduction. In G. M. C. Itard, *The wild boy of Aveyron (L'enfant sauvage).* (G. Humphrey & M. Humphrey, Trans.). New York: Appleton-Century-Crofts.

Itard, J. M. C. (1962). *The wild boy of Aveyron (L'enfant sauvage).* (G. Humphrey & M. Humphrey, Trans.). New York: Appleton-Century-Crofts.

Jacobson, E. (1938). *Progressive relaxation.* Chicago: University of Chicago Press.

Jones, M. C. (1924). A laboratory study of fear: The case of Peter. *Journal of Genetic Psychology, 31,* 308–15.

Jones, E. (1961). *The life and work of Sigmund Freud.* New York: Basic Books.

Kanfer, F. H. (1980). Self-management methods. In F. H. Kanfer & A. P. Goldstein (Eds.), *Helping people change* (2d ed.). New York: Pergamon.

Kanfer, F. H., & Phillips, J. S. (1970). *Learning foundations of behavior therapy.* New York: John Wiley & Sons.

Kanfer, F. H., & Saslow, G. (1969). Behavioral diagnosis. In C. M. Franks (Ed.), *Behavior therapy: Appraisal and status.* New York: McGraw-Hill.

Kanner, L. J. (1943). Autistic disturbances of effective contact. *Nervous Child, 2,* 217–50.

Kanner, L. (1948). *Child psychiatry.* Springfield, Illinois: Charles C. Thomas.

Kanner, L. (1964). *A history of the care and study of the mentally retarded.* Springfield, Illinois: Charles C. Thomas.

Karoly, P. & Kanfer, F. H. (Eds). (1982). *Self-management and behavior change: From theory to practice.* New York: Pergamon.

Kauffman, J. M. (1981). *Characteristics of children's behavior disorders.* Columbus, Ohio: Merrill.

Kazdin, A. E. (1977). *The token economy: A review and evaluation.* New York: Plenum.

Kazdin, A. E. (1980). *Behavior modification in applied settings* (Rev. ed.). Homewood, Illinois: Dorsey Press.

Kazdin, A. E. (1981). Behavioral observation. In M. Hersen & A. S. Ballack (Eds), *Behavioral assessment* (2d ed.). New York: Pergamon Press.

Kazdin, A. E., & Frame, C. (1983). Aggressive behavior and conduct disorder. In R. J. Morris & T. R. Kratochwill (Eds.), *The practice of child therapy.* New York: Pergamon Press, Inc.

Kelleher, R. T. (1966). Chaining and conditioned reinforcement. In W. K. Honig (Ed.), *Operant behavior: Areas of research and application.* New York: Appleton-Century-Crofts.

Kendall, P. C., & Hollon, S. D. (1979). *Cognitive-behavioral interventions: Theory, research and procedures.* New York: Academic Press.

Kerr, N., Meyerson, L., & Michael, J. (1965). A procedure for shaping vocalizations in a mute child. In L. Ullmann & L. Krasner (Eds.), *Case studies in behavior modification.* New York: Holt, Rinehart & Winston.

Kimble, G. (1961). *Hilgard and Marquis' conditioning and learning.* New York: Appleton-Century-Crofts.

Kirk, S. A., & Gallagher, J. J. (1979). *Educating exceptional children.* Boston: Houghton Mifflin Co.

Klein, M., Dittman, A., Parloff, M., & Gill, M. (1969). Behavior therapy: Observations and reflections. *Journal of Consulting and Clinical Psychology, 33,* 259–66.

Krapfl, J. E., & Vargas, E. A., (1977). *Behaviorism and ethics.* Kalamazoo, Michigan: Behaviordelia.

Krumboltz, J. D., & Krumboltz, H. D. (1972). *Changing children's behavior.* Englewood Cliffs, New Jersey: Prentice-Hall.

Lambert, N. M., Windmiller, M., Cole, L., & Figureroa, R. A. (1977). Standardization of a public school version of the AAMD adaptive behavior scale. *Mental Retardation, 13,* 3–7.

Lambert, N. M., Windmiller, M., Cole, L., & Figureroa, R. A. (1981). *AAMD adaptive behavior scale: Public school version.* Monterey, California: Publishers Test Service.

Litrownik, A. J. (1982). Special considerations in the self-management training of the developmentally disabled. In P. Karoly & F. H. Kanfer (Eds.), *Self-management and behavior change: From theory to practice.* New York: Pergamon.

Lovaas, I. O., Berberich, J. P., Perloff, B. F., & Schaeffer, B. (1966). Acquisition of imitative speech by schizophrenic children. *Science, 151,* 705–7.

Lucero, R. J., Vail, D. J., & Scherber, J. (1968). Regulating operant-conditioning programs. *Hospital and Community Psychiatry, 19,* 53–54.

MacMillan, D. L. (1982). *Mental retardation in school and society.* Boston: Little, Brown and Company.

Marholin, D. (Ed.). (1978). *Child behavior therapy.* New York: Gardner Press.

Marholin, D., II, Luisell, J. K., & Townsend, N. M. (1980). Overcorrection: An examination of its rationale and treatment effectiveness. In M. Hersen, R. M. Eisler, & P. M. Miller (Eds.), *Progress in behavior modification.* (Vol. 9). New York: Academic Press.

Martin, R. (1975). *Legal challenges to behavior modifications: Trends in schools, corrections, and mental health.* Champaign, Illinois: Research Press.

Mash, E. J., & Terdal, L. G. (Eds.) (1976). *Behavior therapy assessment: Diagnosis, design, and evaluation.* New York: Springer.

Mash, E. J., & Terdal, L. G. (1981a). *Behavioral assessment of childhood disorders.* New York: Guilford.

Mash, E. J., & Terdal, L. G. (1981b). Behavioral assessment of childhood disturbances. In E. J. Mash & L. G. Terdal (Eds.), *Behavior Assessment.* New York: Guilford.

Matson, J. L., & Andrasik, F. (1983). *Treatment issues and innovations in mental retardation.* New York: Plenum.

Matson, J. L., & McCartney, J. R. (1981). *Handbook of mental retardation with the mentally retarded.* New York: Plenum.

Matson, J. L., & Mulick, J. A. (Eds.) (1983). *Handbook of mental retardation.* New York: Pergamon.

May, J. G., Risley, T. R., Twardosz, S., Friedman, P., Bijou, S. W., & Wexler, P. (1975) Guidelines for the use of behavioral procedures in state programs for retarded persons. *M. R. Research, 1,* 1–71.

Meichenbaum, D. E., & Gerest, M. (1980). Cognitive behavior modification: An integration of cognitive and behavioral methods. In F. H. Kanfer & A. P. Goldstein (Eds.), *Helping people change* (2d ed.). New York: Pergamon.

Meyerson, L., Kerr, N., & Michael, J. L. (1967). Behavior modification and rehabilitation: The rehabilitation of special children. In S. W. Bijou & D. M. Baer (Eds.), *Child development: Readings in experimental analysis.* New York: Appleton-Century-Crofts.

Miller, L. K. (1980). *Principles of everyday behavior analysis* (2d ed.). Monterey, California: Brooks/Cole.

Millman, H. L., Schaefer, C. E., & Cohen, J. J. (1980). *Therapies for school behavior problems.* New York: Jossey-Boss.

Miron, N. B. (1968). Issues and implications of operant conditioning: The primary ethical consideration. *Hospital and Community Psychiatry, 19,* 226–28.

Miron, N. B. (1970). A final rejoinder. In R. Ulrich, T. Stachnik, & J. Mabry (Eds.), *Control of human behavior* (Vol. 2). Glenview, Illinois: Scott, Foresman and Company.

Morales v. Turman. (1973). 383 F. Supp. 53.

Morris, R. J. (1976). *Behavior modification with children: A systematic guide.* Cambridge, Massachusetts: Winthrop Publishers.

Morris, R. J. (1978). Treating mentally retarded children. In A. P. Goldstein (Ed.), *Prescriptions for child mental health and education.* New York: Pergamon.

Morris, R. J., Barber, R. S., Hoschouer, R. L., Karrels, K. V., & Bijou S. (1979). A working model for monitoring intervention programs in residential treatment settings: The peer review and ethics committees. *Rehabilitation Psychology, 26,* 155–65.

Morris, R. J., & Brown, D. K. (1983). Legal and ethical issues in behavior modification with mentally retarded persons. In J. L. Matson & F. Andrasik (Eds.), *Treatment issues and innovations in mental retardation.* New York: Plenum.

Morris, R. J., & Kratochwill, T. R. (1983a). Introduction and overview to the practice of child therapy. In R. J. Morris & T. R. Kratochwill (Eds.), *The practice of child therapy.* New York: Pergamon.

Morris, R. J., & Kratochwill, T. R. (1983b). *Treating children's fears and phobias: A behavioral approach.* New York: Pergamon.

Morris, R. J., & Kratochwill, T. R. (Eds.) (1983c). *The practice of child therapy.* New York: Pergamon.

Morris, R. J., & Magrath, K. H. (1983). The therapeutic relationship in behavior therapy. In M. Lambert (Ed.), *The therapeutic relationship in systems of psychotherapy.* Homewood, Illinois: Dorsey Press.

Morris, R. J., & McReynolds, R. A. (in press). Behavior modification with special needs children: A review. In R. J. Morris & B. Blatt (Eds.), *Perspectives in special education: State of the art.* (Vol. 2) Glenview, IL: Scott, Foresman and Company.

Mowrer, O. H. (1939). A stimulus-response analysis of anxiety and its role as a reinforcing agent. *Psychological Review, 46,* 553–65.

Mowrer, O. H. (1960). *Learning theory and behavior.* New York: Wiley.

National Association for Retarded Children. (1975). Guidelines for the use of behavioral procedures in state programs for retarded persons. *M. R. Research, 1,* 1–71.

National Society for Autistic Children. (1975). *White paper on behavior modification with autistic children.* Mimeo.

Neisworth, J. T., & Smith, R. M. (1973). *Modifying retarded behavior.* New York: Houghton Mifflin.

Nelson, R. O., & Hayes, S. C. (1981). In M. Hersen & A. S. Ballack (Eds.), *Behavioral assessment* (2d ed.). New York: Pergamon Press.

New York State Association for Retarded Children v. Rockefeller. (1973). 357 F. Supp. 752.

O'Banion, D. R., & Whaley, D. L. (1981). *Behavior contracting.* New York: Springer Publishing Co.

O'Connor, R. D. (1969). Modification of social withdrawal through symbolic modeling. *Journal of Applied Behavior Analysis, 2,* 15–22.

O'Connor, R. D. (1972). Relative efficacy of modeling, shaping, and the combined procedures for modification of social withdrawal. *Journal of Abnormal Psychology, 79,* 327–34.

Ollendick, T. H. & Cerny, J. A. (1981). *Clinical behavior therapy with children.* New York: Plenum Press.

Ollendick, T. H. & Matson, J. L. (1978). Overcorrection: An overview. *Behavior Therapy, 9,* 830–42.

Pavlov, I. P. (1927). *Conditioned reflexes.* Translated by G. V. Anrep. London: Oxford University Press.

Pavlov, I. P. (1928). *Lectures on conditioned reflexes.* Translated by W. H. Gantt. New York: International Publishers.

Pennsylvania Association for Retarded Children v. Commonwealth of Pennsylvania. (1971). 334 F. Supp. 1257.

Premack, D. (1965). Reinforcement theory. In D. Levine (Ed.), *Nebraska symposium on motivation: 1965.* Lincoln: University of Nebraska Press.

Repp, A. C. (1983). *Teaching the mentally retarded.* Englewood Cliffs, New Jersey: Prentice-Hall.

Reynolds, G. S. (1968). *A primer of operant conditioning.* Glenview, Illinois: Scott, Foresman and Company.

Richards, C. S., & Siegel, L. J. (1978). Behavioral treatment of anxiety states and avoidance behaviors in children. In D. Marholin II (Ed.), *Child behavior therapy.* New York: Gardner Press.

Rimm, D. C., & Masters, J. C. (1979). *Behavior therapy: Techniques and empirical findings* (2d ed.). New York: Academic Press.

Ritter, B. (1968). The group desensitization of children's snake phobias using vicarious and contact desensitization procedures. *Behaviour Research and Therapy, 6,* 1–6.

Rojahn, J., & Schroeder, S. R. (1983). Behavioral assessment. In J. L. Matson & J. A. Mulick (Eds.), *Handbook of mental retardation.* New York: Pergamon.

Roos, P. (1974). Human rights and behavior modification. *Mental Retardation, 12*, 3–6.

Roos, P. (1977). Issues and implications of establishing guidelines for the use of behavior modification. *Journal of Applied Behavior Analysis, 10*, 531–40.

Ross, A. O. (1980). *Psychological disorders of children: A behavioral approach to theory, research and therapy* (2d ed.). New York: McGraw-Hill.

Ross, A. O. (1981). *Child behavior therapy.* New York: Wiley.

Sales, B. D., Powell, D. M., Van Duizend, R., & Associates (1982). *Disabled persons and the law.* New York: Plenum.

Sattler, J. M. (1982). *Assessment of children's intelligence and special abilities* (2d ed.). Boston: Allyn & Bacon.

Schreibman, L., Charlop, M. H., & Britten, K. R. (1983). Childhood autism. In R. J. Morris & T. R. Kratochwill (Eds.), *The practice of child therapy.* New York: Pergamon.

Shapiro, E. (1980). Self-control procedures with the mentally retarded. In M. Hersen, R. Eisler, & P. M. Miller (Eds.), *Progress in behavior modification.* (Vol. 12). New York: Academic Press.

Shapiro, M. H. (1974). Legislating the control of behavior control: Autonomy and the coercive use of organic therapies. *Southern California Law Review, 47*, 237–356.

Shearer, D. (1972). *The portage guide to early education.* Portage, Wisconsin: Cooperative Educational Service Agency No. 12.

Skinner, B. F. (1938). *The behavior of organisms.* New York: Appleton-Century-Crofts.

Skinner, B. F. (1953). *Science and human behavior.* New York: Macmillan.

Smith, D. D. (1981). *Teaching the learning disabled.* Englewood Cliffs, New Jersey: Prentice-Hall.

Smith, D. D., & Snell, M. E. (1978). Classroom management and instructional planning. In M. E. Snell (Ed.), *Systematic instruction of the moderately and severely handicapped.* Columbus, Ohio: Charles E. Merrill.

Snell, M. E. (Ed.) (1978). *Systematic instruction of the moderately and severely handicapped.* Columbus, Ohio: Charles E. Merrill.

Snell, M. E. (Ed.) (1983). *Systematic instruction of the moderately and severely handicapped* (2d ed.). Columbus, Ohio: Charles E. Merrill.

Sparrow, S. S., Balla, D. A., & Cicchetti, D. V. (1984). *The Vineland adaptive behavior scales.* Circles Pines, Minnesota: American Guidance Service.

State of Arizona. Division of Developmental Disabilities and Mental Retardation Services. District II. (1970). *Behavior modification methodology.* Mimeo.

State of Wisconsin. Division of Community Services (1977). *Behavior management guidelines.* Mimeo.

Stuart, R. B. (1978). Protection of the right of informed consent to participate in research. *Behavior Therapy, 9,* 73–82.

Sulzer-Azaroff, B., & Mayer, G. R. (1977). *Applying behavior-analysis procedures with children and youth.* New York: Holt.

Tate, B. G., & Baroff, G. S. (1966). Aversive control of self-injurious behavior in a psychotic boy. *Behaviour Research and Therapy, 4,* 281–87.

Tharp, R. G., & Wetzel, R. J. (1969). *Behavior modification in the natural environment.* New York: Academic Press.

Ullmann, L., & Krasner, L. (1965). *Case studies in behavior modification.* New York: Holt.

Ullmann, L. P., & Krasner, L. (1969). *A psychological approach to abnormal behavior.* Englewood Cliffs, New Jersey: Prentice-Hall.

Ulrich, R., Stachnik, T., & Mabry, J. (Eds.) (1966). *Control of human behavior.* Glenview, Illinois: Scott, Foresman and Company.

Vargas, E. A. (1975). Rights: A behavioristic analysis. *Behaviorism, 3,* 178–90.

Watson, J. B., & Rayner, R. (1920). Conditioned emotional reactions. *Journal of Experimental Psychology, 3,* 1–14.

Watson, L. S. (1973). *Child behavior modification: A manual for teachers, nurses, and parents.* New York: Pergamon.

Wexler, D. (1973). Token and taboo: Behavior modification, token economies, and the law. *California Law Review, 61,* 81–109.

Wexler, D. (1982). Seclusion and restraint: Lessons from law, psychiatry, and psychology. *International Journal of Law and Psychiatry, 5,* 285–94.

Whitman, T. L., Scibak, J. W., & Reid, D. H. (1983). *Behavior modification with the severely and profoundly retarded.* New York: Academic Press.

Wilson, G. T., & Evans, I. M. (1977). The therapist-client relationship in behavior therapy. In A. S. Gurman & A. M. Razin (Eds.), *Effective psychotherapy: A handbook of research.* New York: Pergamon.

Wolpe, J. (1958). *Reciprocal inhibition therapy.* Stanford, California: Stanford University Press.

Wolpe, J., & Lazarus, A. (1966). *Behavior therapy techniques.* New York: Pergamon.

Woodcock, R. W. (1977). *Woodcock-Johnson psycho-educational battery: Technical report.* Boston: Teaching Resources.

Wyatt v. Stickney (1971). 325 F. Supp., 781, 334 F. Supp. 1341; 344 F. Supp, 373, 387 affirmed in part, remanded in part sub nom *Wyatt v. Aderhold.* (1974, 1978). 503 F. 2d 1305; *Wyatt v. Hardin,* M. D. Ala. (1979), *Wyatt v. Ireland,* M.D. Ala. (1979).

INDEX